CASE STUDIES IN DISASTER RESPONSE AND EMERGENCY MANAGEMENT

*Advancing excellence
in public service . . .*

American Society for Public Administration
Book Series on Public Administration & Public Policy

David H. Rosenbloom, Ph.D.
Editor-in-Chief

Mission: Throughout its history, ASPA has sought to be true to its founding principles of promoting scholarship and professionalism within the public service. The ASPA Book Series on Public Administration and Public Policy publishes books that increase national and international interest for public administration and which discuss practical or cutting edge topics in engaging ways of interest to practitioners, policy makers, and those concerned with bringing scholarship to the practice of public administration.

RECENT PUBLICATIONS

Case Studies in Disaster Response and Emergency Management
Nicolas A. Valcik and Paul E. Tracy

Debating Public Administration:
Management Challenges, Choices, and Opportunities
by Robert F. Durant and Jennifer R.S. Durant

Effective Non-Profit Management:
Context, Concepts, and Competencies
by Shamima Ahmed

Environmental Decision-Making in Context: A Toolbox
by Chad J. McGuire

Government Performance and Results: An Evaluation of
GPRA's First Decade
by Jerry Ellig, Maurice McTigue, and Henry Wray

Practical Human Resources for Public Managers:
A Case Study Approach
by Nicolas A. Valcik and Teodoro J. Benavides

CRC Press
Taylor & Francis Group

American Society for Public Administration
Series in Public Administration and Public Policy

Advancing excellence in public service . . .

CASE STUDIES IN DISASTER RESPONSE AND EMERGENCY MANAGEMENT

Nicolas A. Valcik and Paul E. Tracy

CRC Press
Taylor & Francis Group
Boca Raton   London   New York

CRC Press is an imprint of the
Taylor & Francis Group, an **informa** business

CRC Press
Taylor & Francis Group
6000 Broken Sound Parkway NW, Suite 300
Boca Raton, FL 33487-2742

Printed in the United States of America on acid-free paper
Version Date: 20121115

International Standard Book Number: 978-1-4398-8316-7 (Hardback)

Visit the Taylor & Francis Web site at
http://www.taylorandfrancis.com

and the CRC Press Web site at
http://www.crcpress.com

The authors dedicate this book to first responders everywhere. These individuals risk their safety on a daily basis to come to the aid of victims from all kinds of danger and emergency situations. Their efforts are noble, dedicated, and unselfish, and we gratefully acknowledge their professionalism.

Contents

SECTION I NATURAL DISASTERS

SECTION II   MAN-MADE DISASTERS

SECTION III   TERRORISM AND CRIMINAL ACTS

SECTION IV FINAL THOUGHTS

Foreword

Allen Barnes
City Manager of Gonzales, Texas

Early in my career in municipal government the importance of planning for the unexpected was hammered home one warm and bright February afternoon. The natural gas company that serviced our area was required by the Texas Railroad Commission to remove and replace all of the yellow poly pipeline they had laid in the 1970s. Yellow poly was everywhere. Instead of digging and removing the pipe they decided to bore underground in order to be able to pull the replacement pipe into place.

Sitting in my office thinking all was right with the world, I received the call. It was from Martha, who served as our utility clerk and telephone receptionist. "Allen, I just got a strange call from a lady. She said she turned on her gas range and there was water coming out." I knew that Martha knew there was condensation in the gas lines from time to time so I asked, "Did you tell her it might be condensation in the lines?" To which I nearly choked on the response I was given, "Yes sir, but she has about 5 gallons of condensation on the floor and it's still coming out."

The gas company had bored into a water line. The water at 65 psi followed the path of least resistance and infiltrated their 15 psi intermediate gas line. Water quickly began to fill the gas line and enter their distribution system. From the time of the first report, it took the gas company more than 2 hours to find the source of the water. The following 2 weeks, which included the coldest cold snap in years, left a large majority of our small community with no heat. The emergency response on the part of the gas company started out fine but ended up disorganized. After a few days they began digging without regard to other underground utilities and caused problems for the city's understaffed water department by ripping water lines out of the streets. After I pleaded with them to stop their random digging and ultimately threatened one of their vice presidents with, "If you rip out another one of my water lines you and I will have to fix it and I don't know how," they reassessed their approach and took time to plan a strategy that was acceptable to the city. This calamity taught me the necessity of planning for the unexpected.

Having to learn this lesson on the fly showed me that I hadn't served my citizens very well. I learned I should have been ready. From that day forward I said I would never be caught unprepared.

Professors Nick Valcik and Paul Tracy have assembled the case studies in this book to help current and future governmental managers recognize the importance of getting ready for what the next telephone call might bring. The reader takes away an appreciation for the mindset of many of those who worked through each scenario in the book. The reader understands, in most cases, why they did what they did. Good decisions and bad decisions, you get a good understanding for the value to plan for the unexpected. The reader will also be able to assess the actions of governments and their officials after the fact. Written without judgment, this compilation allows readers to put themselves in the place of these officials. Valcik and Tracy show the student and the government official alike that critical proper planning can't stop unexpected events, but that you can be prepared.

You also get an appreciation for the fact that some events cascade beyond all planning. You will see that some events appear to present one set of issues but evolve into situations beyond expectations. The reader sees that all events have a life of their own and every decision made will impact the outcome positively or negatively.

In government service anything can and will happen. Valcik and Tracy have selected a wide variety of case studies to help the reader prepare for that phone call when you least expect it. Now if you will excuse me, I have to catch my phone, it's ringing!

Foreword

Ted Benavides
Executive Scholar in Residence at the University of Texas at Dallas

Seven years ago I had the great pleasure to join the staff of the University of Texas at Dallas (UTD) as part of the Public Affairs program. Shortly after my arrival I had the fortunate opportunity to meet two talented individuals, Nick and Paul, who had a wealth of information to share with me and our other colleagues about dealing with emergency management. With over 35 years of public service experience at the local, state, and federal levels, I have to be involved in a wide variety of emergency management situations. There is no way that a public servant has all the experience and knowledge to deal with all of the emergency management and disasters covered in this textbook. Although public servants are trained to know how to deal every day with public safety emergency situations, understanding the total view of emergency management and disasters is still a challenge to most, as seen during Hurricane Katrina. Using case study analysis helps to build the bridge between technical concepts and the reality of real-life situations.

In reading Nick and Paul's *Case Studies in Disaster Response and Emergency Management*, I have gained a whole new appreciation of the need for a more informed manager. Not only are they academics who know their subject matter from a theoretical point of view, but they are also very familiar with the daily requirements of emergency management professionals in dealing with disasters of all stripes. Nick and Paul have done a superb job in creating a textbook that is both informative and interactive. This book will fill any knowledge gap that you might have in this area of emergency management and disaster preparedness. However, as this book demonstrates, emergency management and disasters occur every day, and they bring new lessons to the profession, and as we are so aware of in today's public service environment staying current with the latest trends is essential.

The case studies and the format used in this textbook will teach us new lessons on how to face and deal with different situations. Nick and Paul outline strategies and ideas on how to cope with extremely difficult situations, communicate with the public, and keep your organization focused on maintaining its edge during emergency situations. It also helps one prepare for any eventualities that may confront public servants when they attempt to protect their constituency from mankind and nature gone awry. The structured format used by my colleagues to analyze each unique situation is intended to ensure that every lesson and new wrinkle in the area of disaster preparedness can be identified and used in whatever emergency management challenges we might be grappling with on the job.

I would like Nick and Paul to be my copilots if I were facing an emergency situation or disaster. This book will be on my office desktop, and I will be referring to it often. I know this book will be dog-eared in very short order. So the next time you are faced with an emergency situation or disaster, I strongly recommend that you either have a hard copy or have this book downloaded to your electronic device of choice.

Preface

One of the profound implications of the terrorist attacks of 9/11 is that considerably greater public policy attention was needed to protect the homeland and provide a focused governmental response to emergency situations that arise due to natural disasters, terrorism, or even criminal activities. The most notable government reaction to 9/11 was the creation of the Department of Homeland Security through the Homeland Security Act of 2002 (Homeland Security, 2011). This new cabinet-level agency was created through the integration of all or part of 22 different federal departments and agencies (Homeland Security, 2011). A comprehensive homeland security and law enforcement agency is supposed to improve communication and intelligence gathering across the different functional areas. Since Hurricane Katrina, Homeland Security has also been in charge of spearheading responses to natural disasters. Whether and how well this new organization handles tasks as wide ranging as domestic law enforcement to the evacuations of citizens during natural disasters remains to be seen.

In most cases, public officials will never face drastic life-or-death situations that require critical decisions. However, when critical decision making is required, public officials need to be aware of situations that occurred previously so that a better and more informed decision-making process can take place. It may seem counterintuitive to refer to historical situations when confronted with modern challenges, but an emergency can shut down electricity and public transportation, thus re-creating situations comparable to previous historical events. The power blackout that occurred in the Northeast in 2003 is an example of how a public official may have to respond to a crisis without modern amenities. Therefore, sometimes it is highly useful for administrators to review past situations and responses in order to formulate a successful plan for contemporary crises. There will always be new challenges, but many emergencies of the past have the potential to occur in the future. Public officials can evaluate the decisions made during these past emergencies and consider how they would have responded in a similar situation.

This case study book is designed to allow public officials to conduct this kind of evaluation on a selection of emergencies that actually occurred. Often there is no right or wrong answer or choice, just choices that will either resolve a problem favorably or cause the situation to actually become worse for the organization. This case study book provides a set of generic questions at different points in the case study to allow students and practitioners to evaluate which decisions were successful and why. The cases are organized by the year that the incident occurred, but the text does not reveal the historical event or its resolution until the end. Some case studies are based more loosely upon a historical event to make the situation more relevant to modern times (e.g., animal magnetism case study) and to give the role assigned a broad decision-making capability for instructional purposes. We understand that more than one choice could improve the situation, but this case study book was developed to assist public officials to understand how to respond to events as well as what issues to think about or take into account.

It may be easy for the reader to criticize the decisions that were made by past public officials. However, the reader must consider the political pressures the administrator was under at the time of the crisis or the limited scope of his or her power in contending with such a situation. Unlike the historic public officials, the reader will not have to make decisions under pressure. The decision-making process for the case studies will give the reader an applied venue to test theoretical emergency management techniques that should work in real-world situations. This book is meant to act as a practical exercise in public administration and emergency management courses and to provide guidance for public officials during emergency management situations.

Acknowledgments

I first thank everyone who has helped me with this project. I thank Dr. Doug Watson, former program director of public affairs at the University of Texas at Dallas, for giving me an opportunity to teach emergency management in the Public Affairs program. In preparation for teaching emergency management, I was inspired to formulate a case study book that would provide students and administrators with real-life disaster situations that could be analyzed. I thank my coauthor, Paul Tracy, for his great work on this book. Paul's insight and revisions have evolved the book into its current form. I also thank my former students Krysten Carrera and Jessica Simpson, who helped review the manuscript, as well as my colleague, Ted Benavides, who provided insight that was very helpful in formulating the book. I thank Hung Vu for providing additional support on gathering research materials and Xu Zhao for providing the authors with information for our case studies that occurred in China. I acknowledge Andrea Stigdon for providing the book with a great cover design and performing the tedious duty of proofing and editing the book. Most of all, I thank my friends, family, and wife, Kristi, for their love and support of all of my endeavors.

Nicolas A. Valcik

I thank Nicolas Valcik, the senior author of the book and the prime mover behind the project right from the beginning. Nick has been tireless in his effort to do the background research on 58 disasters and emergency situations that comprise the case studies in this book.

Paul Tracy

About the Authors

Nicolas A. Valcik currently works as an associate director of strategic planning and analysis for the University of Texas at Dallas and serves as a clinical assistant professor for public affairs for the University of Texas at Dallas. Valcik received a doctorate degree in public affairs from the University of Texas at Dallas in 2005, a master's degree in public affairs from the University of Texas at Dallas in 1996, a bachelor's degree in interdisciplinary studies from the University of Texas at Dallas in 1994, and an associate's degree in political science from Collin County Community College in 1994.

Prior to 1997 Valcik worked for a number of municipalities, across different departments, as well as for Nortel. In 2011 Valcik coauthored with Ted Benavides *Practical Human Resources Management for Public Managers: A Case Study Approach,* published by Taylor & Francis. Prior to 2011 Valcik authored *Regulating the Use of Biological Hazardous Materials in Universities: Complying with the New Federal Guidelines,* which was published by Mellen Press in 2006. Valcik has served as editor for three volumes of *New Directions for Institutional Research* (Volumes 135, 140, and 146), in addition to writing numerous articles and book chapters on institutional research topics and homeland security issues. Valcik specializes in several areas as both a researcher and a practitioner: higher education, information technology, human resources, homeland security, organizational behavior, and emergency management.

Paul E. Tracy holds a PhD in sociology/criminology from the Wharton School at the University of Pennsylvania. He is a criminologist who specializes in the study of crime and delinquency and policy developments in the criminal and juvenile justice systems. He holds a faculty appointment as professor of criminology and criminal justice in the Department of Criminal Justice and Criminology at the University

of Massachusetts at Lowell. He is also the director of graduate studies. His research interests focus
on the measurement and analysis of juvenile delinquency careers, legal and policy issues in juvenile
justice, prediction models of criminal careers, and
drug prohibition policy. He is a recognized expert
in the application of longitudinal research designs
to the study of delinquent and criminal careers.
His study of a large Philadelphia birth cohort of
27,160 people is the largest study of delinquency
and crime ever conducted and is now in its 34th
year. He also conducted the first large-scale delinquency study in Puerto Rico. Dr. Tracy generally
teaches graduate-level courses on methodology and statistical analysis.

Chapter 1

Guidelines and General Information for Public Officials and Administrators

Key Issues to Consider in Emergency or Disaster Response Situations

Case Study Selection and the History of Disaster Response

The case studies in this book were selected for three main reasons. First, some case studies were chosen due to the impact they have had on the development of disaster response and emergency management in modern times. Events such as the Love Canal Disaster in 1970 were used as examples because they had a strong impact on the introduction of new legislation that attempted to prevent such situations from occurring again. Second, other events were selected due to the sheer magnitude of the event, for example, 9/11, Charles Whitman's 1966 attack at the University of Texas at Austin, and the Aum cult attack on the Tokyo subways. Third, other case studies were included due to their unique characteristics or complexity. These events posed unique challenges to the ability of public administrators to resolve the event successfully. Events such as the great white shark attacks of New Jersey in 1916, the Three Mile Island nuclear reactor accident in 1979, and the 1906 San Francisco earthquake pose such challenges.

Throughout the history of disaster response, governments at federal, state, and local levels have attempted to prevent disasters or mitigate their effects by passing ordinances and legislation. Unfortunately, history has a tendency to repeat itself if public administrators are ignorant of the past, or worse, ignore the lessons of history. In such instances, administrators might become lax in upholding building codes or neglect to fully enforce existing legislation. With each disaster case scenario, this monograph will present possible solutions that could be applied or taken into consideration at each stage of the disaster, sometimes differing from what historically occurred. At the end of each section, the text will summarize the case study as follows: (1) failures in the case study, (2) consequences of the failures, (3) implications, and (4) items of note.

Basic Framework and Resources Needed for Disaster Response

Without question, public officials and administrators must always be concerned about emergency situations and the need to be strategically aware of the multitude of response issues that can arise from emergency situations. The public trust requires such diligence because, unfortunately, any community, anywhere, at any time, can be faced with an emergency situation that can negatively impact the community generally and specific public agencies in particular. Emergency situations can arise owing to a number of different sources: (1) a natural disaster such as hurricanes, tornadoes, fires, earthquakes, and floods; (2) accidents involving nuclear power plants, chemical spills, or other industrial incidents; (3) acts of terrorism; and (4) criminal acts, such as arson, snipers, and so on. These emergencies, regardless of source, can pose serious threats to the health and well-being of the citizenry and to community infrastructure. Contending with these situations successfully can mean the difference between life and death, preservation and destruction. As Perrow has stated:

> Disasters from natural sources, from industrial and technological sources, and from deliberate sources such as terrorism have all increased in the United States in recent decades, and no diminution is in sight. Weather disturbances are predicted to increase; low-level industrial accidents continue but threaten to intensify and the threat of cyber attacks on our "critical infrastructure" becomes ever more credible; foreign terrorists have not relaxed and we anxiously await another attack. (Perrow, 2007, p. 1)

While no two emergency situations will be the same, there are crucial lessons that can be learned from the effects of past events and the ways they were handled that can guide public officials and administrators to make sound, effective, and rational decisions that can prevent, or at least mitigate, the deaths, injuries, or damage that can occur. For some situations there will be no perfectly successful strategies that can be implemented. Nonetheless, decision making can be guided by strategic imperatives that can possibly mitigate the harm and destruction that may be inflicted on the community.

Some organizations that are depicted in the case studies in this book were the first to experience a particular emergency situation (e.g., the 9/11 terrorist attacks, which involved the use of hijacked airplanes as weapons). From those past experiences public officials and administrators now know the possibilities that can exist, which may lead them to appreciate the need for having emergency response contingencies in place. The prior experiences of historical events and the way they were handled provide a distinct advantage for the contemporary through experiential hindsight—an advantage that their predecessors did not have when they responded to their emergency events. To this end, therefore, the following topics represent general issues that a public official or agency administrator should consider when responding to an emergency situation.

Basic Framework

Plan of Action

A public official or administrator should always be thinking about how to implement a plan for a positive intervention when a situation arises. As Ricks, Tillett, and Van Meter have stated:

> The only thing certain about planning to protect lives or property from natural or other person-caused emergencies is that there is no location in the world that is absolutely free from danger in one form or another. The varieties of potential dangers can be identified, and measures can be taken to reduce the risk of exposure or strike; however, thorough planning and preparation may prevent the escalation of a dangerous situation into a catastrophe. (Ricks, Tillett, and Van Meter, 1994, p. 329)

For some organizations plans of action will already exist if certain threats are known to be a possibility for a particular community (e.g., a hurricane in a coastal area). Still, the importance of planning for a natural disaster cannot be overstated:

> A natural occurrence can, of course, be more common to one area of the United States than to another.... Modern technology has made most of these natural hazards somewhat predictable. Often it is possible to have several days' warning, and some indication of the probable magnitude of the pending hazard. However, natural hazards can strike without warning, and it is at such times that pre-planning and immediate, adequate reaction capability is of the utmost importance. (Ricks, Tillett, and Van Meter, 1994, p. 66)

When plans of action are formulated by an organization, the plans should take into account several key aspects of the situation.

First, an action plan should be based on a realistic inventory concerning what resources could potentially be available in times of a crisis. When possible (or available), several organizations can use key software tools, such as Geographic Information Systems (GIS), to prepare mitigation plans, or disaster management plans if natural disasters are a possibility (Greene, 2002). By having such plans available, an entity has the potential to prepare effectively for natural disasters that may hit a community. One thing for public officials to keep in mind is that just because a community has resources available to it when the plan is originally formulated does not mean that those resources will be available at a later date. Therefore, it is important to update an action plan on a regular basis if a threat is known to exist and to keep an active inventory on what resources are available.

Second, a plan of action should also include an inventory of the vulnerabilities an organization may have to a certain type of threat. For example, if a community is built in a floodplain there will be several key facilities (i.e., hospitals, schools, etc.) that may be prone to flooding. For mitigation of the possible effects of such emergencies, it would behoove public administrators to use technologies such as GIS if they are available to them.

> As stated by Thomas, Ertugay, and Kemec in referencing Spatial Decision Support Systems (SDSS), the level of coordination and scenario-building aspects necessary for a disaster SDSS may seem somewhat futuristic, but the increasing availability of geographic technologies make it more possible than ever to consider an integrated system that supports disaster management to reduce loss (Tung & Siva, 2001). (Rodriguez, Quarantelli, and Dynes, 2007, p. 86)

Thus, it is important to have an plan of action that addresses what actions the public administrator intends to take if certain facilities are faced with the threat of flooding from a storm. How will the administrator contend with providing medical services to patients if the hospital is under water? What will the administrator do with prisoners if a correctional facility is threatened by floodwaters? The administrator will need to prepare for these types of questions along with answers to resolve the issues favorably. Clearly, there will be several factors in formulating a plan of action, which include the level or degree of authority the administrator has. Relevant questions in this regard are the following:

- What resources are available?
- Who needs to be contacted?
- What is the scope of the intervention?
- What types of threats need to be addressed?
- What are the organization's major vulnerabilities?

Third, an plan of action can be either preplanned or developed as the emergency situation unfolds. A public administrator should be especially prepared, however, to make adjustments to the plan of action as events unfold. The plan should never be static and unmoving since often situations can be unpredictable and change throughout the course of a given event. Thus, emergency events are dynamic and fluid and no administrator should rigidly adhere to a plan merely because it was "the" plan. An effective plan should have a dynamic feature that allows strategic flexibility.

Communication Plan

Emergency preparedness not only requires an plan of action, it also includes another crucially important component—a comprehensive communication plan. Quite simply, without proper communication, an emergency response team runs a serious risk of implementing a plan of action incompletely, ineffectively, or failing to implement it at all. As stated by Sorensen and Sorensen:

> Developing the warning system is both an engineering process and an organizational process. Warning systems are more than technology—involving human communication, management, and decision-making. (Rodriguez, Quarantelli, and Dynes, 2007, p. 184)

Additionally, the communication plan should include aspects to address the situation as it unfolds to gain support and resources to help implement the plan of action. The communication plan often can be used to inform the public of important information and instructions that will be critical to the success of the public administrator's plan of action.

The communication plan should incorporate not only the information that the public administrator needs to transmit and receive, but also the mechanisms by which the information is to be transmitted and received. During some emergency situations it may not be possible to use modern equipment or convenient ways to communicate with other entities. Therefore, the public administrator will need to find other methods to send and receive information as timely and as clearly as possible. For example, if telecommunication networks are inoperable, a public administrator may have to rely on short-wave radio operators or even couriers for communication. When communicating with other officials, the public, or other organizations, public administrators should be clear and concise in how they communicate their intentions. Having good writing and oral communication skills is essential for public administrators and officials when trying to implement an plan of action.

Administrators will need to manage the media effectively. While journalists are seeking information to disperse to the public, administrators can use the opportunity to put a call out for resources that may be needed in a time of crisis. Administrators need to use very different strategies in response to a localized disaster such as the Oklahoma City bombing, compared to the type of response required for something large and regional such as Hurricane Katrina. Both crises will receive media coverage, but a localized disaster response situation will require administrators to be aware of the potential negative impact that the media can play in an ongoing response. For example, if the media discloses clues that can be used in apprehending a killer, it may hinder law enforcement's ability to apprehend or convict the individual responsible for criminal activity. For a larger regional disaster response, media may not be able to access certain parts of impacted areas due to the danger that would be posed to journalists (i.e., flooding, etc.). The large-scale disaster response will require administrators to plan and use the media to benefit their situation in requesting assistance in gaining resources.

Emergency Response Plan

All public organizations should have an emergency response plan to at least provide a framework for how their organization will respond to different forms of crisis. For some organizations emergency response plans should be more specific if the organization can be potentially impacted from known threats (i.e., fire, riots, etc.). An emergency plan of action should identify the resources that are available to the organization as well as where resources can be gathered from external sources in times of crisis. Specifics that should be addressed in emergency response plans could include evacuation plans for populations or logistics for water transportation. These emergency response plans should cover contingency plans in the event that communications fail, electricity fails, medical assistance is unavailable, or additional facilities are needed, to name just a few factors for consideration. Emergency response plans should be widely distributed within the organization and should be easily accessible during times of crisis.

Resources

Public administrators and officials should always be aware that during times of crisis access to key resources will be extremely important in quickly resolving the situation. Resources that public administrators and officials should take into account when creating a plan of action include the following: manpower, food and water, medical supplies and resources, law enforcement, specialized equipment and support, electricity and fuel, transportation, mortuary services, resources for displaced people, emergency facilities, financial resources, and communications.

Manpower

Whether it requires a secretary or an entire battalion of engineers, manpower is almost always required for a disaster response. Keeping in mind that manual, unskilled labor will often be more readily available than specialized manpower, for example, a computer programmer, public agencies will need to determine what skill sets will be needed and can be obtained quickly during times of crisis. When flooding occurs, for example, one of the major tasks required is to fill and stack sandbags to prevent water from flooding into a community. This type of activity generally requires nontechnical volunteers from the community. Other situations, like bracing a failing dam, might require assistance from an organization that specializes in that type of operation, for example, the Army Corps of Engineers. If the community is located in a remote area or an area that lacks sufficient infrastructure, specialized manpower will need to be transported into the disaster region, sometimes across great distances. A public organization that may require outside assistance, particularly for ongoing threats like flooding, tornadoes, or hurricanes, will need to address logistical issues in their plan of action. For specialized manpower, a list of organizations with contact information (name, telephone, email) will need to be disseminated among personnel directly responsible for managing the disaster response. Establish a response agreement with these organizations ahead of time so that these organizations will anticipate contact when an emergency situation arises. If the organization expects the general population to provide assistance during an emergency situation, information regarding where to gather and to whom the people should report must be posted in public notices, in newspapers, and on the agency's website.

Food and Water

Water is the single most important resource that is required for human survival. Water is necessary for medical treatment, sanitation control, and to combat fires. The Federal Emergency Management Agency (FEMA) states the importance of having people store water for a potential crisis:

> You should have at least a three-day supply of water and you should store at least one gallon of water per person per day. A normally active person needs at least one-half gallon of water daily just for drinking. Additionally, in determining adequate quantities, take the following into account: (1) Individual needs vary, depending on age, physical condition, activity, diet, and climate; (2) Children, nursing mothers, and ill people need more water; (3) Very hot temperatures can double the amount of water needed; and (4) A medical emergency might require additional water. (FEMA, 2010)

It is also critical to maintain a supply of ice to keep food and some types of medicine (e.g., insulin) from spoiling. Public officials will need to ensure that an ample supply of water can be obtained quickly, despite damage to the infrastructure or contamination of the local supply, and can be reliably transported to first responders and citizens. Private supplies of water among the citizens coupled with a centralized source provided by public officials can increase the survival odds for the community even if no food is immediately available.

While water may be the most important item to have on hand in times of disasters, food is also a critical resource. If an organization does not have an emergency supply of rations during a significant natural disaster, like a hurricane, many citizens could face starvation or illness from spoiled or contaminated food. In the United States, food has been obtained through military stockpiles of prepackaged rations that do not need to be refrigerated. Other potential sources of food can include local grocery stores and food banks (be sure to establish an agreement with these organizations first). Citizens will need to be informed before a disaster occurs—and reminded after a disaster has occurred—where to gather to obtain food and how food will be distributed. This will help to prevent most citizens from resorting to looting for survival.

Medical Supplies and Resources

Medical supplies and resources will usually be in high demand when a natural disaster occurs. A public agency will need to determine how to obtain trained medical staff, adequate medical supplies, and hospital facilities. Identify public facilities with sufficient capacity and geographic distribution, like schools or community centers, which can be readily converted into makeshift hospitals. Furthermore, plan for the likelihood that patients will need to be transported to locations where proper medical facilities exist in the event local public facilities are destroyed or are inadequate to meet the community's needs. If the disaster is a result of a terrorist attack that uses a biological, chemical, or radiological element, local medical resources might not have the expertise to address the aftermath. As stated by Falkenrath, Newman, and Thayer:

> It is worth noting that the utility of an epidemiological surveillance system in reducing a society's vulnerability to biological weapons attack depends on the medical system's ability to mount an effective medical response without warning. As discussed below, medical response to a biological weapons attack requires an adequate supply of appropriate medicines, trained personnel to deliver them, and a high-readiness mobilization system. While the U.S. medical system has a very high general level of capability, important gaps exist in stocks of key equipment and supplies needed to care for large numbers of biological casualties. (Falkenrath, Newman, and Thayer, 1998, p. 296)

If patients are to be evacuated to areas where better medical facilities are located, then transportation issues will need to be addressed in the plan of action. Public officials will need to review what resources would be available to them in addition to ambulances, such as school buses, city buses, trains, helicopters, and airplanes. When evaluating public facilities that can be converted into medical facilities, several factors should be taken into consideration:

1. Does the facility have adequate space for hospital beds?
2. Is the facility in a safe location (i.e., outside the disaster zone, away from rivers)?
3. Does this facility have an emergency generator?
4. Can this facility accommodate medical equipment (e.g., electrical capacity, ice storage)?
5. Is the facility accessible?
6. Can the facility accommodate medical transportation (e.g., large doors, loading docks, parking lot for helicopters, and buses)?
7. Does the facility have running water and sewer lines?
8. Is the facility air-conditioned?
9. Does the facility have adequate lighting?

These questions, though by no means comprehensive, provide a basic framework to guide public officials in determining what resources may be needed for medical personnel to perform their roles effectively. For obtaining medical supplies and materials, public officials can look to a number of sources that may have those supplies available, such as hospitals, doctors' offices, pharmacies, public schools, and higher education institutions.

Law Enforcement

Law enforcement is essential for protecting citizens from opportunists that may act when society is in a state of disorder. Law enforcement also serves as first responders in emergency or disaster situations and is essential to resolving volatile issues such as a hostage situation. Law enforcement frequently maintain valuable resources such as communication gear, all-terrain vehicles, and security facilities, as well as specialized software such as GIS, which can be used to map public facilities, organize disaster management, and identify evacuation paths (Thomas, Ertugay, and Kemec, 2007). If local police are not adequately trained and supplied to address a substantial disaster situation, a plan of action must include state or county law enforcement. Failing to incorporate adequate security into a disaster response plan can lead to anarchy, as was seen during Hurricane Katrina and its immediate aftermath (Gold, 2005).

Specialized Equipment and Support

Some types of emergency situations require specialized equipment or support services to allow first responders to contain the disaster effectively or provide emergency services to survivors. Technologies such as GIS can often be used to provide invaluable support to decision makers in an event of a disaster. As stated by Roy C. Price, past president of the National Emergency Management Association:

> Geographic Information Systems provide the best method to efficiently support emergency management needs. Emergency crisis events will impact more than people and facilities; they have an impact on the environment, livestock, ocean food stocks, and economic dislocation of communities. GIS provides the means for widely diverse organizational and government agencies to participate in the full range of emergency management activities at all levels of government. (Greene, 2002, p. x)

Excavation equipment, sound detection equipment, heavy lifting machinery, ground penetrating radar, and other types of digging equipment may be required for certain types of natural disasters, such as earthquakes or terrorist attacks (i.e., Oklahoma City bombing). Other disasters can require even more specialized support, such as rescue divers to free trapped survivors from sunken submarines like USS *Squalus* in 1939 or when the *Challenger* space shuttle exploded over the Atlantic Ocean in 1986 (NASA, 2011; Sullivan, 2009). Specialized equipment can often be difficult to obtain and transport. Therefore, it is imperative that public officials determine what is needed quickly to respond to the disaster and then formulate plans to transport those resources to the location where the equipment can have the maximum amount of benefit for first responders. If specialized equipment cannot be obtained quickly enough, then survivors are at risk of dying before a rescue attempt can take place (i.e., Kursk).

Electricity and Fuel

It is important to make sure that there is some source of power, in the form of electricity or fuel, available during a time of crisis. If an entire electrical grid goes offline, then other means should be sought to generate electricity. As stated by Macaulay in regard to critical infrastructure (CI):

> Critical infrastructure (CI) is so important, so fundamental, that most people take it for granted. This is the irony of CI. It has always been there during our lifetime and it has rarely failed us. And when it did fail, it was not for long. It has been designed to be so dependable that we tend to assume it in our equations around the resiliency of our lives, lifestyles, and businesses. CI is a given; it is an assumption. (Macaulay, 2009, p. 1)

Without electricity, many tools and resources that are available to first responders will not function. While vehicles and battery-powered devices may not be affected by the loss of the power grid, lights, televisions, and computers will be rendered inoperable. Any plan of action that relies upon an emergency broadcast through cable television or coordination of personnel via email can fail. Public officials and emergency management coordinators should have a series of backup plans available to restore power or use resources that are not dependent upon centralized power plants. Other sources of electric power can be as common as portable generators or as innovative as wind turbines and solar panels. Public officials should plan to store or obtain a good supply of fuel to power electrical generators, vehicles, and debris-clearing equipment like chainsaws. During times of crisis, fuel may become scarce quickly as citizens take what they need for their own uses. It is ideal for a public organization to store enough fuel for immediate use during a disaster and to have a prearranged means of obtaining more quickly. If an evacuation is needed, a public entity needs to ensure that there is enough fuel so that citizens are not stranded during an evacuation (e.g., Hurricane Rita).

Transportation

During a disaster, a public organization must ensure that there is reliable transportation available to evacuate the citizens, provide ambulance services, transport first responders, and provide mobilized support for equipment and resources. During Hurricane Katrina, insufficient public transportation was provided for the evacuation of citizens who were either too poor or too frail to leave of their own accord, thus leaving many citizens trapped in New Orleans during the hurricane and subsequent flooding (Chen, 2010). School buses that could have been utilized for the evacuation process were not mobilized or safeguarded during the disaster (*Boston Globe*, 2010). As stated by Landy:

> The New Orleans local government failed to make provision for those who were unable to evacuate on their own—those who did not own cars, the disabled, the elderly, and tourists left stranded when the supply of rental cars ran out. School buses were unavailable because they had not been moved to high ground. (Landy, 2008, p. S188)

By having proper use of those transportation resources, more citizens had the potential of being evacuated out of the city to safer locations before the hurricane hit the city.

Mortuary Services

Whether one likes to think about it or not, a public official will have to plan for a proper way to store or dispose of human and animal corpses. A disaster plan of action needs to include a means to recover, store, identify, and dispose of corpses to prevent the spread of infection and disease and contamination of drinking water. Naturally, the first priority is to attend to the living by providing water, food, or medical supplies to survivors; the next priority should be to deal with the dead in a timely and discreet manner. However, a parallel concern is to address the issue of the casualties of the disaster. There are a number of relevant issues. First, facilities must be identified that can serve as collection points either because of the availability of refrigeration or because the location is at a distance from emergency shelters to prevent the spread of disease and psychological trauma among the living. Second, the storing of corpses near bodies of water must be avoided, as this can contaminate emergency sources of food (fish) and water. Third, provision must be made for an adequate supply of body bags—this will facilitate subsequent identification. Fourth, the use of mass graves or cremations must be resisted except in extreme situations. Administrators should also keep in mind that finding survivors is a higher priority than collecting the remains of the deceased (Eberwine, 2005). The World Health Organization suggests looking for empty covered facilities that can serve as a temporary mortuary that can be secured, provide examination tables, and obtain adequate lighting (World Health Organization, 2012).

Resources for Displaced Persons

Public administrators will need to determine where to house evacuees and how long evacuees will be displaced. Does the community have the resources to house evacuees long term? What facilities are available for short-term and long-term housing? What is the source of funds for temporary, or in some cases permanent, relocation of displaced persons? Will another public entity or nonprofit organization be able to assist in housing displaced persons? These are just some of the questions that administrators will need to ask themselves when addressing the needs of displaced persons.

Emergency Facilities

Public officials should develop an emergency plan of action that identifies which facilities could be used during times of a disaster. Some of the questions that should be asked by administrators are the following:

1. What is the size of the facility?
2. What is the capacity of the facility?
3. Does the facility have an emergency generator?
4. Does the facility have running water and sewer lines?
5. Is the facility capable of serving as a harden shelter against tornadoes or hurricanes?
6. Is the facility suitable to use as a command post?
7. Does the facility have modern telecommunications?
8. Does the facility have a loading dock?
9. Is there a kitchen or medical facilities on-site?
10. Is the facility located next to major highways or transportation hubs?

In the past, public administrators often had to convert facilities that were not originally intended for use in a disaster, such as using the Superdome for evacuees during Hurricane Katrina or converting a school's gymnasium into a makeshift morgue during the Texas City disaster of 1947 (Moore Memorial Public Library, 2007). With some threats, such as tornadoes, residents often construct their own shelters in or near their homes. For example, in Tulsa, Oklahoma, an initiative was undertaken by the city of Tulsa and Texas Tech University to demonstrate the feasibility of constructing safe rooms in homes then under construction (Bullock, Haddow, and Haddow, 2009). A public administrator should review all the facilities in the jurisdiction for possible use during a disaster since there will probably not be enough publicly owned facilities, or enough that are properly equipped, to contend with a disaster.

Financial Resources

It is obvious that contending with any type of disaster will be expensive. Moreover, unless a public organization has a history of dealing with a particular disaster (i.e., hurricane), there will not likely be enough money budgeted for disaster management. As the former city manager of Liberty, Texas, Allen Barnes once said, "Save your receipts. We were reimbursed from FEMA quickly because we could show proof of what we spent during Hurricane Rita" (Barnes, 2008). Public officials should always keep in mind how much is spent during disasters and, if possible, show receipts for possible reimbursement. Other entities that have been involved with disasters have had little or no accounting for assets and had much difficulty obtaining reimbursements from FEMA or insurance companies on items lost. For certain communities that live in areas prone to hurricanes, flooding, fires, or tornadoes, a budget line item should be created for a contingency plan. As stated by Bullock, Haddow, and Haddow regarding different sources of monetary relief:

> Resources—As with any hazard mitigation program, resources will dictate much of the success of the program. Multiple sources must be pursued including: Local Funding Source ... Federal and State Government Funds ... Leverage Resources.... (Bullock, Haddow, and Haddow, 2009, p. 205)

Administrators should have a plan in place addresses the rebuilding process after a disaster has occurred. The negative economic impact of a widespread disaster is especially acute from forces of nature, like the 1900 hurricane in Galveston, Texas, which permanently damaged what once was a thriving port economy; or the 2011 Tohoku earthquake in Japan and the subsequent tsunami, which devastated the infrastructure and caused numerous accidents at the region's nuclear plants. An area that has its industrial base ruined, infrastructure damaged or destroyed, and its citizens displaced, will likely be facing a rebuilding initiative that will take years. This rebuilding will require more funds than can be generated from insurance claims and the damaged tax base. In some countries, such funding comes from national, state, province, or local budgets. Public administrators will need to consider what source of funds for rebuilding will be available to them and which portions of the community will be prioritized during rebuilding when formulating their disaster response plans.

Communications

Proper communications is a critical component to the success of any disaster response plan. An administrator should have several contingencies for communicating across the various agencies that will be necessary in a disaster response—both internal and external. Whatever the communication method used, public officials must be very clear and concise in how they will communicate with others. In today's environment cell phones are commonplace tools that many public officials rely upon extensively. However, during a disaster situation, cell phone towers might be damaged, thus rendering cell phones inoperable. Even traditional landlines can be affected in certain emergency situations, particularly if concerned friends and relatives overwhelm the telephone system trying to reach missing people. Therefore, a public official will need to consider other methods for communication that can include, but are not limited to, couriers or short-wave radios.

Intangible Factors That Affect Disaster Response
Coordination with Other Entities

A public official might need to coordinate or get assistance from other federal, state, and local organizations during a disaster. There are many good reasons to coordinate efforts with other government, nonprofit, and private industry organizations. As stated by Bullock, Haddow, and Haddow:

> The most important thing we have learned is that reducing disaster risks and losses is best done at the community level. Outside resources and technical assistance are critical, but effective and sustainable hazard mitigation programs and actions must be designed and implemented at the local level where disasters strike. Without the full support and participation of all stakeholders of a community in this effort it cannot be successful. (Bullock, Haddow, and Haddow, 2009, p. 202)

Other organizations can provide aid in disaster response situations with resources, manpower, specialized training, and logistics. Rather than have multiple organizations carry out a specific task, such as search and rescue, assign the task to agencies that specialize in such work, like the U.S. Coast Guard, which performed such operations well during Hurricane Katrina. The importance of predisaster contracts was noted by Landy during the Pascagoula, Mississippi, response to Hurricane Katrina:

> Describing her refusal to wait for FEMA's permission for response actions that she considered to be of immediate necessity, Pascagoula, Mississippi, city manager Kay Johnson Kell said, "If the ox is in the ditch you got to get him out." … Pascagoula also had the foresight to negotiate a pre-disaster contract, which stipulated what services the contractor was required to provide in the event of a disaster and the prices to be paid for each service. (Landy, 2008, p. S189)

A coordinated effort among many organizations can make disaster response more efficient and effective in several different areas, such as with first responders and logistical supply. As stated by Landy:

> The successes and failures of local government vis-à-vis Katrina display the full gamut of strengths and weaknesses that champions and critics have ascribed to it. One finds petty turf battles, demagoguery, and poor planning, as well as bravery, probity, skillful public management, and far sightedness. (Landy, 2008, p. S188)

Ineffectual coordination can result in overlapping responsibilities among different organizations, which can lead to bickering and wasted efforts, or ineffective control, which can lead to gaps in capabilities and responses. However, administrators also need to be aware that too much preparation can lead to apathy among employees and the populous. Administrators will need to find a balance between preparedness and oversaturation to potential disaster response situations.

Authority

Public officials should have an understanding of the scope of their authority over a disaster response situation, including the limitations of their power over different agencies, organizations, and geographic boundaries. As stated by Ricks, Tillett, and Van Meter:

> An emergency response leadership team, developed from existing high-level supervisors or managers, should coordinate the response decisions and activities for the organization during the emergency. These people should be selected from the regular company leadership so they have the necessary sense of loyalty and responsibility to protect the interests of the organization. Written authority should exist to organize certain personnel into a special force during an emergency. (Ricks, Tillett, and Van Meter, 1994, p. 330)

Power is derived from how others perceive an administrator as well as the leverage an administrator may actually have over other individuals' well-being (i.e., safety, career, salary). If an administrator is perceived by others to be incompetent or his or her decision-making process is suspect, there is a very good chance that his or her power will be greatly diminished. In short, an administrator should demonstrate good leadership qualities to retain or expand his or her authority as needed.

In some states and local municipalities, the top elected official is in charge of the disaster response effort and will oversee the supervision of municipal personnel. However, the elected official might not have the proper training to fulfill this role effectively. This is when trained administrators should attempt to provide as much professional guidance and support to those elected officials as possible.

Larger cities and state agencies might have personnel or even an entire department dedicated to responding to a crisis, whereas smaller organizations may assign the crisis response to individuals who already have other job responsibilities, which could potentially reduce their effectiveness. Typically, municipalities assign disaster response to fire, police, emergency management, or local homeland security offices. The organizational structure of the agencies that respond to disasters can vary widely, depending upon the size of the organization, organizational culture, and knowledge, skills, and abilities of the organization's personnel.

Scope of Operation

Administrators should be cognizant of the scope of a potential operation and the boundaries of their authority in a given circumstance. Failure to recognize the appropriate set of duties and responsibilities during an emergency situation can overextend organizational capabilities and exceed the organization's mandate. Furthermore, if an administrator assumes additional roles and responsibilities, he or she will be in danger of being assigned those roles and responsibilities permanently without the benefit of more resources. Public administrators should be generally aware of the capabilities of their organization's personnel and the resources available to them. Failure to maintain an inventory of capabilities can lead to failure during a time of crises and the risk of being viewed as ineffectual, which happened to FEMA during Hurricane Katrina.

Political Disposition

Public agencies have to contend with political pressures, both internal and external, particularly from other public organizations, the public, and elected officials. These entities hold public administrators accountable for their actions and decision-making processes. When decisions are being formulated, public administrators should always keep in mind that there can potentially be negative consequences to risky or incomplete decision-making processes that can significantly impact their organization. At times a public administrator may make a decision based on the political boundaries from elected officials or the public. In essence, the public administrator is making a bounded rational decision. While the decision may not be the most effective or the preferred action by the administrator, it may be the best decision that can be made under the political realities faced by his or her organization. Administrators at the local, state, or federal level should be careful to avoid entanglement with other levels of administrators, which can potentially lead to disaster. The roles of federal, state, and local administrators should be clearly defined by an emergency plan of action, which should allow for cooperation and resources to be utilized effectively.

Time

During a disaster or emergency, a public administrator should keep the variable of time in mind when considering a plan of action or response. Does the response or plan that the administrator has formulated have time to work within a given set of parameters? If a terrorist destroys a public building and produces a great deal of rubble, does the public administrator have enough time to mobilize digging equipment or heavy lifting equipment to assist first responders? If time is a significant factor (as it almost always is in any emergency situation), how does the public administrator get resources to the first responders more quickly to save survivors? In some situations, however, it may be more prudent to allow for more time than usual. An example of this would be a hostage situation in which the situation is contained but law enforcement needs as much time as possible to apprehend the aggressors peacefully and free the hostages safely.

Threat Level/Threat Assessment

A public organization should take an inventory of what threats could be posed to its community to prepare effective emergency response plans. These threats may include such situations as a nearby nuclear plant accidentally releasing radioactive material, like with Three Mile Island, or a chemical plant nearby that releases toxic chemicals into the environment, which happened in Bhopal, India (Perrow, 1999). Other organizations will have to plan for recurring natural disasters, such as winter storms, earthquakes, floods, hurricanes, tornadoes, fires, and tsunamis. Some public organizations will have to assess threats differently since their mission is to respond to disasters across a wide geographical area, such as the U.S. Coast Guard's search and rescue operations.

NATURAL
DISASTERS

1

Chapter 2

Case Studies: Disasters from Natural Forces—Fires

Richmond Theater Fire, Virginia, 1811

Stage 1 of the Disaster

You are the city fire marshal of Richmond, Virginia. On December 20 you learn that a benefit performance is to be held on December 26 at the old theater hall (*Richmond Then and Now*, 2007). The hall is very rickety and you believe that only small audiences, if any, should be allowed inside the building to watch a performance (Watson, 1812).

1. *What is your plan of action?* As the city fire marshal it would be important to first determine if the theater should even be allowed to operate for public events due to the condition of the structure. If the structure is safe for public events to be held in the auditorium, then a strict room capacity limit should be posted for the auditorium and an evacuation plan should be formulated for fire and medical services should an incident occur.
2. *With whom in city government do you communicate your concerns?* The city fire marshal should communicate these concerns to all of the department heads in the municipality. Should an emergency occur, it will be necessary to utilize an array of city services to ensure the well-being of the patrons and citizens that are attending the performance.

3. *How will you enforce the rules and regulations your department has formulated for the theater to operate?* If the theater owners do not comply with the regulations that have been set forth, it is the responsibility of the city fire marshal to shut down the performance hall for noncompliance of municipal guidelines.

Stage 2 of the Disaster

On December 23, you received word that a very well-known actor will be performing at the benefit performance. The theater has already sold 300 tickets and the building will need to be heated adequately since the weather is extremely cold outside (Watson, 1812).

1. *What is your plan of action?* At this point the city fire marshal should remind the theater operators of the maximum occupancy level for the performance hall. If there is additional demand beyond the safe capacity, the theater could then consider running multiple performances. Since heating will be used in a wooden structure, suitable firefighting apparatus should be on hand to contend with a potential fire. Additionally, escape routes should be well marked and free of clutter in the aisles and hallways.
2. *With whom in city government do you communicate your concerns?* The city manager should be made aware of any concerns as well as the police chief and the director of planning and zoning. In addition, it would probably be a good idea to discuss the issue with the local medical community in case an incident did occur.
3. *How will you enforce the rules and regulations your department has formulated for the theater to operate?* At any point, city officials have the authority and responsibility to close the theater for noncompliance of the rules. Failure to close the theater without the proper safety guidelines will cause the municipality and its administration to be liable for any incident that occurs. This can result in criminal prosecution or civil lawsuits, to not only the theater operators but also the municipality's administrators.

Stage 3 of the Disaster

On the day of the scheduled performance, December 26, you learn that 600 people have bought tickets to the benefit performance and will be attending (*Richmond Then and Now*, 2007).

1. *What is your plan of action?* The city fire marshal should at this point coordinate with other city officials and ensure that no more than 300 people are allowed to enter the performance hall. If the theater owners are so inclined, they can have a second showing the next evening. Otherwise, the performance hall needs to be closed.

2. *What is your communication plan?* You need to calmly communicate your concerns to the patrons that are attempting to gain entrance to the theater as the surplus attendees are prevented from entering the performance hall when the safe occupancy level has been reached. You should tell the patrons who were not allowed entrance that they can contact the theater owners in regard to either gaining entrance to a second showing or receiving refunds for their tickets. Additionally, you should provide written notice to the theater owners that they are in violation of safety codes and that fines could be levied against them if they do not comply with safety guidelines that were previously set forth.

3. *What resources do you have in place for an emergency response?* If, despite your concerns, other city officials allow 600 people into the performance hall (which is actually what happened in this case study), then you will need to have sufficient firefighting equipment on hand, medical and firefighting personnel to attend to any emergency, and a contingent of police officers for crowd control. In addition, there should be cooperative agreements in place with other municipalities for medical assistance and firefighting resources if needed.

Stage 4 of the Disaster

Two ceiling lamps flicker and then sparks fall onto the wooden stage area (*Richmond Then and Now*, 2007). Considering the age of the performance hall and the condition of the overall building, this should be a major cause for concern.

1. *What is your plan of action?* You should evacuate the theater immediately and try to get as many people out of the building as safely as possible. The second action item that should be undertaken is to get firefighters into position quickly to extinguish the fire as soon as possible.

2. *What is your communication plan?* Officials need to use loudspeakers to not only evacuate the crowd, but also to give the city employees the correct instructions since the environment will be noisy and hard for first responders to hear. The police chief will need to be kept apprised of the situation since those resources will be needed in evacuating the theater. The city administrators will need to be kept in close contact with since they may be needed to gain additional resources from other municipalities.

3. *What resources do you have in place for an emergency response?* With proper preparation, city officials have put firefighters and medical personnel in place to contend with a fire hazard. There will be several people hurt or possibly killed if the occupancy level is exceeded, so medical personnel will be critical when contending with victims that have suffered from smoke inhalation, among other ailments.

Stage 5 of the Disaster

After approximately 10 minutes, the entire building is engulfed in flames. People are screaming and jumping out of box seating areas to the stage, the roof has now caught on fire, and the flames are spreading throughout the entire theater (Watson, 1812).

1. *What is your plan of action?* If a delay has occurred in evacuating patrons (as was the situation in this case study), city officials can anticipate a high death toll among the 600 patrons plus the additional staff that was working the performance hall. Any patrons that have not yet been evacuated should be evacuated immediately. Firefighters should attempt to extinguish the flames, and any police in the area need to begin crowd control procedures to ensure that bystanders will not be injured by the fire or any debris. At this time medical personnel should be rushed to the scene to begin triaging patients that have been injured and taking those that are critically injured to the hospital immediately. People that have minor injuries should be treated on the scene if medical supplies and personnel are available.
2. *What is your communication plan?* As city fire marshal you need to begin to coordinate with other departmental directors and make sure that your first responders are operating in concert to alleviate the crisis. First responders should also begin to take counts of how many people may be trapped inside to determine what is the best procedure to rescue those persons.
3. *What should your primary focus be for the emergency?* The focus of the first responders should be to ensure all patrons have been rescued that can be saved and treating injured persons with medical treatment. Any bodies that are in the open sight need to be removed and stored for identification purposes.

Stage 6 of the Disaster

You notice that the governor of the state has just run back into the building to save his son (Watson, 1812). Others are scrambling around in an attempt to get to safety. You also know at this point that there have been some people killed in the fire.

1. *What is your plan of action?* The governor went into the structure at his own risk. You cannot risk your personnel to save him at this point since you have evacuated all of the persons that are known to still be alive that were in the theater. The focus should be on getting the fire put out, treating the injured, and then evacuating the injured to a proper medical facility.
2. *What is your communication plan?* As city fire marshal, you should begin to find out exactly how many people are unaccounted for and inquire with the families that are available to talk to if they are missing anyone. This will be the start of a list of people that are unaccounted for, and there may

be a slim hope of finding them alive in the rubble. If no one is found alive, then the list will serve to help identify the bodies that are removed from the performance hall. You may need to contact other neighboring cities for additional medical personnel and resources if the resources in your own city are overextended.

3. *What resources do you not have on hand that will be required later?* With many people being killed or injured in the fire, you will most likely be short of medicine, medical personnel, medical facilities, and first responders. In addition, you may require excavation equipment, body bags, and dogs to assist in removal of bodies or the slim possibility of finding a victim alive in the rubble.

Key Issues Raised from the Case Study

Building and fire codes are necessary to prevent catastrophes from occurring. There are quite a few what-if situations concerning any number of building or fire codes that should have been in place (and then been enforced), thus potentially avoiding the tragedy in the first place.

This case study in particular shows why building codes are so important. The theater was overcrowded and beyond the design capacity of the structure. In addition, the manner by which the building was constructed led to the fire being extremely destructive. This allowed the fire to spread quickly and engulf many victims in the flames. There was also no provision to protect the governor and his family. At most venues, very important persons (VIPs) have additional safeguards that provide them more protection and a quicker evacuation route from the venue. What is not clear from the case study information is how many resources for fire-fighting were close by the venue to put the fire out.

Items of Note

The fire resulted in 72 fatalities (*Richmond Then and Now*, 2007). In addition, the state of Virginia lost a political leader when the governor was killed in the fire attempting to rescue his son. This represents the first case study regarding contending with a fire. Throughout the book one will see the patterns of failure being repeated, with the same deficiencies being present even in modern times.

Great Chicago Fire, 1871

Stage 1 of the Disaster

You are the mayor of Chicago. Your city has recently been experiencing a very long drought and the city's firefighters were busy the day before fighting blazes that had cropped up around the city. It is October 8, around 10:00 p.m. (Debartolo, 1998) and you are just about to go to sleep when one of your firefighters appears at your house with a very weary look on his face. The firefighter explains to you that there is a fire that is spreading rapidly (due primarily to strong winds and the susceptibility of buildings that are largely constructed of wood) and the fire is causing serious problems for the firefighters (Chicago: City of the Century, 2003). You have the additional problem of your citizenry not being too worried about the spreading fires.

1. *What is your plan of action?* If you have a plan of action regarding fires in the city, now is the time to employ any preplanning that exists. If no plan exists, you need to start by gathering as much information as possible and identifying possible available resources. Chicago, at the time, is a very large municipality and communication avenues are pretty primitive, so you need to establish some type of central command post that can be employed to send and receive information in a timely manner.

2. *What is your communication plan?* You need to start by communicating with the first responders that are available and call up any volunteers that may be needed since many of your firefighters are already engaged in fighting blazes elsewhere. In addition, you need to start alerting residents to the danger of the fire that is sweeping through the city and prepare to evacuate residents in areas that are known to be at risk from the fire.

3. *How do you intend to contain the situation?* Once the area of the fire has been identified, several different initiatives can be tried to contain the fire. If water is available, it can be hosed on wooden structures in an attempt to prevent the flames from spreading. If water is not available, some wooden structures could be knocked down as a fire break in an effort to prevent the flames from spreading to another area of the city. If there is no wood to burn, there is no fuel for the fire to continue and spread.

4. *Where are you going to direct your resources?* Once it has been established where the fire is and how the fire is spreading, any available firefighters can be directed to tackle first those blocks that are already on fire. Volunteers can be used to alert residents and help any evacuation process that would be required if the fire starts to spread to other neighborhoods. Medical personnel and medical assets also need to be mobilized for any incoming casualties.

Stage 2 of the Disaster

The fire has just jumped the river that divides your city and is currently burning on both sides of the river as well as engulfing several boats. Your citizens still do not appear to be too concerned about their well-being (Sheahan and Upton, 1871). The next action you take will be crucial in protecting your citizenry.

1. *What is your plan of action?* This disaster will tax the resources of the city since the fire is now out of control on both sides of the river, several ships are on fire, and others are endangered. Any ships that are undamaged should be moved immediately out of harm's way. You need to start having your volunteers go door to door to get citizens to evacuate out of areas that are in the path of the fire. Since you have a river available, you may be able to route some of the water from the river into areas of your city to give you additional fire breaks as well as cut down the number of areas to which the fire can spread.

2. *Where are you going to direct your resources?* With the fire on both sides of the river, it would probably be a calculated move to get some engineers and construction workers to channel water from the river to both sides of the city to limit the blaze.

Stage 3 of the Disaster

You have made calls to neighboring cities but your calls are not heeded by any of them (Sheahan, 1871). Since receiving assistance from other entities does not appear to be forthcoming, what will you do with the resources that you currently have under your control?

1. *What is your plan of action?* Your displaced persons will need shelter, food, and water, so you will need to start mobilizing resources to gather assets that can provide those essentials to your citizens. At this point in the disaster you realize that you are on your own since no neighboring communities seem to be forthcoming with help. Therefore, you will have to maximize the resources that are available to you.

2. *What is your communication plan?* It would be a wise idea to continue to contact other cities and state government officials to acquire additional resources. With the fire spreading, you need to continue to gather intelligence on how many resources are available and how much of your city is on fire. Without having adequate intelligence, it is hard to dole out resources appropriately to contend with the blaze.

3. *At this point your containment of the fire has failed, what do you do next?* You need to attempt to evacuate the people in certain sectors that positively cannot be saved. In addition, you need to start thinking about a strategic plan concerning which parts of the city can be saved so that you can funnel more resources to those areas.

Stage 4 of the Disaster

Your city's water supply has just been cut off (Sheahan, 1871). Remember that water is just as critical for human survival as it is for fighting the fire. What should your next set of decisions and actions be to protect the citizenry?

1. *What is your plan of action?* This would be a good point in the disaster to put your engineers and construction workers to work on rerouting the water lines so that your displaced persons have water to drink and your firefighters have water to put on the blaze. Without water you have very little hope in saving much of your city.

2. *How do you keep the morale of your firefighters high in a desperate situation?* Your fire chief should be attempting to keep morale up among his personnel. If the fire chief is not taking a leadership role, find someone in the fire department that is competent and willing to take charge. With no leadership, the fire department will become disillusioned and morale will begin to fail. In addition, attempt to funnel in any volunteers that can be found to help alleviate the manpower shortage in the fire department.

Stage 5 of the Disaster

Your firefighters are now out of water and have given up; you have a mass of citizens that are panicking and running across the bridge, jumping in the lake, and diving into the river (Sheahan, 1871). How do you regain control of the situation and what should you to do to evacuate the remaining endangered citizens successfully?

1. *How do you stop your citizens from panicking?* Any first responders that are available should be sent to alleviate the pressure of a potential riot breaking out along the waterfront. Any ships that have not been damaged could be summoned to ferry displaced persons away from the city to safety. For the rest of the residents, you need to develop a means of safe passage for them out of the city.

2. *What is your communication plan?* The biggest communication need at this point is to show the public that you are a leader and you are in charge. Try to keep the public as calm as possible and assure them that help is coming and that a safe passage will be opened for those that are not evacuated by way of the river.

3. *What resources should you mobilize at this point in the crisis?* Any police that are available should be mobilized to assist in evacuation of citizens. Additionally, land transportation and any ships that are seaworthy should be mobilized to evacuate the citizens from the burning city.

Stage 6 of the Disaster

A general from the U.S. military appears on the scene and offers to coordinate relief efforts between the military and the staff of your municipality (Sheahan, 1871). You decide that as mayor a declaration of martial law should be issued (Sheahan, 1871). What are the advantages and disadvantages to having an arrangement between the civilian government and the military? This issue will come up later with the San Francisco earthquake in 1906.

1. *What is your new plan of action?* If assistance becomes available that appears to offer resources that could help the situation, take advantage of the resource. The military has resources that can help get food and shelter to displaced citizens as well as getting citizens evacuated to safety. In addition, the military can provide a stabilizing presence that will instill some confidence in your citizens as well as provide support in manpower to your police and fire departments.

2. *What are your most pressing issues?* It is important to determine what additional resources are needed. You should begin to repair infrastructure to your city, which will allow citizens whose homes are still intact to return home.

Stage 7 of the Disaster

The fire has now died down due to a light rain that is falling and the wind has subsided as well. Your city now has 34 blocks reduced to absolute rubble (roughly a third of the city) (Long, 2008). The fire has claimed over 300 lives (Jeter, 1997). The areas destroyed include your downtown areas, business district, upscale residences, and several harbor areas (Sheahan, 1871). You now have an additional problem on your hand—90,000 of your 300,000 residents are homeless (Jeter, 1997). As the chief administrator, what should your first priorities be in the aftermath of the disaster?

1. *What is your new plan of action?* A high priority is to build temporary shelter and develop the logistics to provide food, water, and medicine to your displaced persons. The repairing of infrastructure should be completed by engineers and construction workers, and then the salvaging and clearing of ships from the river area so that supplies can arrive to support your citizens.

2. *What are your most pressing issues?* Shelter, water, food, and medical resources for your displaced persons represent resources that could be provided by surrounding cities and organizations. Someone should be proactively contacting top-level administrators of nonprofit groups, local officials, and state officials in an effort to get more resources sent to the city to provide relief to the citizens.

Key Issues Raised from the Case Study

The case study illustrates a situation that is still relevant today—having proper building codes that can prevent a fire from spreading. Building codes are crucial in the prevention of fires, especially for densely populated areas. Chicago's buildings were mostly constructed of wood and packed close together. In combination, this allowed the fire to spread rapidly and reduced the city of Chicago to rubble. The lesson of having a redundant infrastructure should not be forgotten. If one loses water, power, communication, or transportation, then one faces a situation resembling an emergency in 1775 rather than an emergency in modern times. The city of Chicago had no redundant water supplies or means to obtain additional water. Maintaining agreements with external agencies is critical in times of crisis for fighting fires, providing security, providing medical assistance, evacuating citizens, or repairing damaged or destroyed infrastructure. The city of Chicago did not appear to have any agreements with neighboring communities or organizations for assistance in times of need. Without these agreements, the city of Chicago could not depend on any additional manpower to supplement its exhausted firefighters. In addition, the emergency warning communication plan appeared to be nonexistent. Therefore, citizens were not evacuated in a timely fashion once the fire was raging uncontrollably.

An entire industrial city was essentially burned to the ground due to multiple failures in building codes, having no previous agreements with external organizations, and no redundancies in infrastructure. Three hundred people were killed as a result of not having a proper evacuation plan or emergency warning plan in place.

Items of Note

The fire spurred the redevelopment of Chicago into a vibrant and modern city. The myth that a cow kicked over a lamp to start the fire is untrue. The best hypothesis is that the fire started in a small building (Sheahan, 1871).

Peshtigo Fire, Wisconsin, 1871

Stage 1 of the Disaster

You are the county commissioner in a state that is in the Midwestern region of the United States. It is October 8 and you can see smoke off in the distance from your office building (*Washington Post*, 1997).

1. *What is your plan of action?* As a county commissioner, you need to gather information on (1) the exact location of the fire, (2) the direction/path the fire is heading, and (3) how many people have already been hurt. Next you need to see what type of resources you can assemble to fight the fire.
2. *What is your communication plan?* After you find out where the fire is heading, you need to alert the communities that are in the path of the fire to evacuate and mobilize their resources to fight the fire. You also need to begin communicating with your first responders and medical personnel to mobilize and address the issues that have already occurred. At this point in time it is important to contact surrounding organizations and start gaining support and resources to fight a fire that can potentially be widespread.
3. *What resources do you need to acquire or mobilize?* In addition to firefighters, medical resources, and other first responders, you will need a central command post established to manage your communications, and you will need

to establish a logistical chain for food, water, evacuation of residents, and medical supplies since those resources may be needed at any given point. Any volunteers that can be rounded up to assist firefighters, first responders, or medical personnel should now be mobilized.

Stage 2 of the Disaster

A source has now informed you that the forest surrounding the area is completely ablaze and that the fire is spreading at lightning speeds due to the high winds that are in the area (United Press International, 1996). You are very concerned since the area is very dry and the resources you have at your disposal are not very mobile (United Press International, 1996). In addition to those problems you have the problem of your county being located in a very rural and remote area (Hipke, 2007b).

1. *What is your plan of action?* Since you are in a rural area, it will be important to spread as much water as possible to the already affected areas to hamper the fires from spreading to additional forests. This will be difficult since you have no infrastructure, aircraft, or chemicals to assist in containing the fire. This means that firefighters will have to be deployed and create fire breaks, which is a labor-intensive process. You might want to pre-position your firefighters at locations that look likely to catch on fire in an effort to control the spread of the fire.
2. *What is your communication plan?* Since the area is rural, you will need to have first responders evacuate residents in the countryside that have no form of communication. Some towns and cities may be very small, and thus it is important to have a courier contact those population centers as soon as possible. Electronic communication is possible in some communities but not others. In communities that do not have electronic communications, it will be important to have a courier contact those communities directly.
3. *What resources do you need to acquire?* As the county commissioner, you need more firefighters and first responders to fight a spreading fire. Logistics is also a growing concern in the aspect of getting firefighters moved to the correct locations and evacuation of rural communities. Medical assets are also a premium, as well as temporary shelters for those residents that had to evacuate.

Stage 3 of the Disaster

You are now receiving reports that towns in your region have been completely decimated (Hipke, 2007a). Many reports are now starting to come in that casualties are high across different parts of the region (Associated Press, 1988). You are concerned that your resources are limited and that the fires are widespread and regional. Several reports are now indicating that the firestorm is so intense that houses and other massive objects are being swept up in an almost tornado-like fashion (United Press International, 1996). How do you communicate over such a wide, primarily rural area?

1. *What is your plan of action?* The fire is now out of control and you have residents that are flowing into areas that have not been impacted by the fire—yet. To get residents to a safe zone it is important to evacuate those citizens to other cities that are well away from the fire and that have more resources to assist you. Your first step should be to make arrangements with those other local governments and evacuate as many residents as possible via railroad to those locations. This is a temporary situation, but at least it will give you time to assemble more resources to tend to those citizens that you cannot evacuate immediately. Additionally, you need to send out more scouts to see if any additional communities need to be evacuated due to the fire. Any persons that are injured and able to be moved to major cities with proper medical facilities should be evacuated first.
2. *What is your communication plan?* As county commissioner you need to communicate with local counties that surround your county to coordinate firefighting efforts as well as gain resources. In addition, it is important to gain resources from major cities that have electronic capabilities and railroad lines that connect to your area to try and get resources shipped in for firefighting, medical assets, food, water, and temporary shelter.

Stage 4 of the Disaster

The fire eventually dies out and the death toll and destruction become all too apparent. As an administrator what should your first priorities be in the aftermath of the disaster? What would you do to be proactive in preparing for the next fire that could occur in the future?

1. *What is your plan of action?* If you have evacuated your residents, it is important to build temporary shelters and stockpile any supplies that will be needed before residents return to the area. There will be quite a bit of rebuilding that will need to be undertaken before your citizens' lives return to any type of normalcy.
2. *What is your communication plan?* You need to communicate with any citizens that have been displaced that it will be safe to come back after a certain date. Additionally, you will need to communicate with other surrounding areas in an attempt to get resources you will need to rebuild the communities in the county. Families will need to be contacted in an attempt to identify those victims that have perished in the fire so that the dead can be buried.

Key Issues Raised from the Case Study

Fires that occur in open plains areas can be difficult to contain if resources cannot be brought to bear down on the initial epicenter where the fire started. After a fire begins, it can go in any direction, which could destroy vegetation or even consume large populated areas. The costs resulting from the damage of such fires can be tremendous to a community in terms of human suffering, dollars, natural resources, and wildlife. In this case study, there was no apparent plan of action to contend with the large-scale forest fire that swept through the area. Unfortunately, there was no available water supply to tap into to fight the fires. There were very few resources that could be utilized or deployed to combat such a fire in the era when the disaster occurred. Unlike modern times, there were no aircraft, firefighting chemicals, or other infrastructure that could be used to bring in water or other resources quickly.

Items of Note

An estimated 1,670 people (Associated Press, 1988) were killed and an area equal in size to the state of Rhode Island was scorched (Greer, 1986). This is the deadliest fire in U.S. history, and it actually caused more damage and deaths than the Great Chicago Fire that occurred that same day (*Washington Post*, 1997).

Big Blowup, Washington, Idaho, and Montana, 1910

Stage 1 of the Disaster

You are the governor of a Northwestern state. On August 19, you are notified that a forest fire has started and the winds are causing the fire to spread quickly through your state (Petersen, 2005). You are told by your staff that that there is not enough equipment available in the area where the fires are located to handle or contain the spread of the fire (Petersen, 2005).

1. *What is your plan of action?* The first step is to determine what resources the state has and what resources exist at local levels that can be used against a forest fire. Next, the governor should see what manpower is available to fight a forest fire. In many cases the Army Reserve or National Guard can be called in to fight forest fires. Additionally, the governor should begin to make plans to safeguard communities that are near the forest fire where a big loss of property and life could occur. These areas should be targeted to receive resources first. Second, the governor should also take into account how to get these resources to the areas of need quickly by freeing up as many transportation routes as possible so that resources will have dedicated transportation corridors.

2. *What is your communication plan?* The governor should keep in contact with all local officials who are in the vicinity of the fire as well as those officials that have resources that can be deployed to the firefighting zone.

Stage 2 of the Disaster

You are having difficulty getting resources to the fire location because the roads are not adequate and the terrain is rocky (Petersen, 2005). Also, the fire has now spread to two more states in addition to yours, and the winds are causing the fires to spread rapidly due to dry grasses and timber (Petersen, 2005).

1. *What is your plan of action?* As a governor, you now need to consider evacuation of areas that are in the path of the fire since you cannot get resources to certain areas quickly enough. You should develop a plan to fight the fires closest to population centers where you can get firefighting resources on the scene quickly.
2. *Where will you get your much needed resources that are currently not available?* The governor now needs to find out what resources are in neighboring states as well as any resources available at the local and federal levels to battle against the spreading fire.
3. *What is your communication plan?* The governor should contact the governors in the other two states where the fires are spreading as well as local and federal officials that can possibly provide resources to fight the fire. The local officials should be contacted about possible evacuation of their communities if the fires sweep toward these locations.

Stage 3 of the Disaster

You and the other two governors now have 10,000 people (by paying an hourly wage to volunteers) battling the blazes across the three states (Petersen, 2005). In addition, the U.S. Army has now been thrown into the fray to battle the forest fires (Petersen, 2005).

1. *What is your plan of action?* The key aspect of fighting the fire effectively is to make sure the resources get to where they are supposed to be positioned most effectively. Having 10,000 people fighting fires is only effective if the resources are being used efficiently. The governor should review how all of the efforts are being coordinated and see how any improvements in transportation can be made to make it faster to get resources where they need to be positioned.
2. *What is your communication plan?* The governor should make every effort to ensure that local, state, and federal resources that are battling the fires are coordinated and in synch with one another's efforts. Local leaders need to be

reassured that resources will be forthcoming to provide their communities with temporary shelters, medical assistance, and food and water.

3. *How will you protect your first responders?* One method that can increase the safety of first responders is to gather more personnel and attempt to get state-of-the-art firefighting equipment to fight the fires as well as perform search and rescue operations. The governor should also attempt to improve logistics to the first responders by ensuring that the first responders have plenty of supplies for operations (e.g., water).

Key Issues Raised by the Case Study

The problems in this case study were the lack of infrastructure, poor coordination with different firefighting units, and a lack of resources to fight the fire effectively. A couple of preventative measures that may have assisted the firefighters in controlling the blaze would have been to thin out the trees in densely wooded areas as well as clear dead and dry debris from fallen trees so that if a fire did begin, it would have less fuel to burn. This is a practice that is employed often in modern times. In addition, stockpiling firefighting resources and pre-positioning certain assets can also improve the chances of responding more quickly and effectively to a fire.

Items of Note

The fire burned 3 million acres of forest and killed at least 86 people (Petersen, 2005). This incident is possibly the largest forest fire in American history, if not world history, and had no determined cause (Petersen, 2005).

Hartford Circus Fire, Connecticut, 1944

Stage 1 of the Disaster

You are the fire chief for a large metropolitan city on the east coast of the United States. The Ringling Brothers and Barnum & Bailey Circus has come to your city to do a series of performances. The circus has a traditional big top and 8,000 of your residents (the majority are women and children) have gone to see the show. The big top itself is canvas and has been waterproofed with a combination of paraffin wax and gasoline (Willow Bend Press, 2007).

1. *What is your emergency action plan?* You do not have the authority to ban canvas that has been waterproofed in this manner. The city council has this authority. You will need to construct an evacuation plan for the residents in case a fire occurs in the big top. In addition, you will need to plan and

pre-position firefighting equipment in the vicinity of the circus so that you can respond quickly if a fire does occur. You also need to inform city officials about the danger of having such a structure for public events since the tent is highly flammable. The organizers of the circus should be made to comply with fire codes that require all exits to be marked and cleared of obstructions.

2. *What emergency resources do you have on hand in case of an emergency?* As the fire chief, you will need to have firefighting vehicles and ambulances on standby in case an emergency does occur. In addition, medical supplies and fire extinguishers should be on hand and available at the circus.

Stage 2 of the Disaster

As the show begins, a fire has started on the canvas of the big top tent, which sends thousands running for their lives as the fire quickly engulfs the structure (Willow Bend Press, 2007). As the evacuation progresses, you realize that the crowd is evac-uating *toward* the fire (Brown, 2008). Furthermore, you notice that several of the exits are blocked by animals that are in cages (Willow Bend Press, 2007).

1. *How will you adapt to the crowd running toward the wrong exit?* You need to have your firefighters become more involved by actively directing the crowds toward the correct exits and moving the animal cages to free up more exits. This should reduce the number of individuals that could be trapped by the tent that is now collapsing. In addition, the fire trucks should be deployed to spray water on the fire as well as on the rest of the tent to prevent the flames from spreading.

2. *What are you going to do about the blocked exits?* The exits must be cleared, so the fire chief will either need to deploy vehicles to clear the cages or have the circus organizers use other resources—for example, elephant power—to move the cages that can be utilized.

Stage 3 of the Disaster

The big top's tent poles and canvas have now totally collapsed (Brown, 2008). You also have hundreds of people that are injured and in need of treatment (Brown, 2008). As an administrator you should think about what resources should be obtained quickly and how those resources will be deployed to the disaster.

1. *What is your plan of action?* You will need to begin search and rescue opera-tions as well as ensure that the fire has been totally extinguished. You will also now have to triage the wounded so that the most critically injured can receive medical care first.

2. *What resources do you need on-site?* You will need as many first responders and medical personnel on-site as possible, as well as medical supplies and water. In addition, you will need to begin to recover the bodies of those that have

been killed in the fire and have those bodies taken to the local mortuary for identification. You will then need to begin accounting for everyone that was at the circus so that no one is unaccounted for after the accident has occurred.

Key Issues Raised from the Case Study

This case study should be used to illustrate why city codes for large venues are so important. Without proper ordinances or code enforcement, tragedy can arise if improper materials are used for such an event. One of the biggest failures in this scenario was the city of Hartford allowing the circus to use a tent made of flammable materials. This one factor alone caused the fire to spread much more quickly and reduced the ability of the circus patrons to be evacuated safely. Additionally, a clear plan should be drawn up with the circus managers and the firefighters before approval is given for such an event that will allow for an orderly evacuation of patrons during a disaster situation. There were no clear lanes of evacuation for the patrons since one pathway was blocked by animal cages. In addition, instructions to the patrons to proceed to the end of the tent that was not on fire were not communicated effectively.

Items of Note

In about 10 minutes, this fire resulted in 168 people perishing in the flames (Willow Bend Press, 2007). A pyromaniac later admitted to setting the fire that consumed the circus tent (Brown, 2008).

Nightclub Fire, Rhode Island, 2003

Stage 1 of the Disaster

You are the city manager for a suburban municipality. There is a new business that is petitioning for an occupancy change for a 1930s restaurant that is being remodeled into a nightclub. This new business will be hosting musical acts and is asking for a substantial increase in occupancy beyond that of the original restaurant.

1. *What issues would confront a city manager?* The city manager should be very concerned that a renovation must conform with current building and fire codes as well as the regulations of the Americans with Disabilities Act, all of which the 70-year-old structure may lack.
2. *How will you communicate these concerns to the local businesses and to your employees that are supposed to enforce building code guidelines?* The city manager needs to gain the support of the mayor, city council, and other municipal departments to make sure that all elected officials and relevant

departments recognize the need to enforce current building and fire codes with new businesses. The economic development director should also be made aware of all zoning codes and ordinances that new businesses may face in terms of costs if such businesses are recruited to the city. The economic development director should attempt to find the right building for the right business in terms of having the correct facility for them to move into without having to spring for additional renovation costs.

Stage 2 of the Disaster

On February 20, you receive a call at home that the new business has burned down to the ground during an evening rock concert that included a pyrotechnic show (Arsenault, 2003). After the fire, it is discovered that the nightclub did not have a fire sprinkler system installed, as it should have, when the occupancy level was changed, and that the foam used for insulation of the sound was flammable. The fire inspectors of your municipality did not cite the business for failing to install a sprinkler system when the business was remodeled to a nightclub (University of Texas at Austin, 2006). The governor of your state has just banned pyrotechnics at venues under 300 people (Madigan, 2003), and the nightclub owners have been indicted as well as the band's tour manager, who set off the pyrotechnics (Karl Kuenning RFL, 2005).

1. *How do you proceed with existing nightclubs from a safety aspect?* Existing nightclubs should be reinspected to see if they are in accordance to current fire code and Americans with Disabilities Act regulations. If businesses are not compliant, they should be given a grace period to come into compliance with the existing guidelines. If the businesses do not come into compliance within the time period, then the city should begin to fine the businesses or condemn the buildings (i.e., close the businesses down).
2. *What should the city manager do about employees that did not cite the infractions of the nightclub prior to the fire?* A city manager has a wide range of actions available that can be taken against employees that were negligent in the performance of their duties. The city manager can write up employees, suspend employees with pay, suspend employees without pay, or even terminate them from their position. In this situation the city manager will need to review what city employees knew about the new business and what steps were taken (if any) to ensure that the new business was compliant with city guidelines.

Key Issues Raised from the Case Study

By not enforcing existing ordinances, the city administrators have created a significant liability and safety concern for the residents and visitors to businesses in the city.

If the fire sprinkler system had been installed, and materials used in the nightclub had not been flammable, the loss of life could have potentially been much lower.

The building codes that the city had previously set forth were not followed by the nightclub owners, nor were they enforced by the city code enforcement office. The failures were due to both lack of city administrative oversight on renovation projects (i.e., lack of proper inspections) and lack of supervision of administrative departments (i.e., were inspections of the business followed up by inspectors?).

Items of Note

This incident is the fourth deadliest nightclub fire in the United States. The fire left 100 people dead and over 200 people injured (Parker, 2007). Three individuals were charged with crimes by the criminal justice system (Fortili, 2003).

Black Saturday Brushfires, Australia, 2009

Stage 1 of the Disaster

You are in charge of all emergency personnel for the Australian state of Victoria. For the past few years, the environment in your area has seen very little rain and has seen a considerable amount of heat, which has dried out the vegetation throughout all of the countryside (The Day the Sky Turned Black, 2012). As in most countries, there are many areas that would be considered rural, with some fairly big cities such as Melbourne that are densely populated.

1. *Are there actions that you should take given the dry conditions in your state?* Given that the conditions are extremely dry, a good precaution would be to have interagency agreements that could bring in first responders to fight fires if any fires begin to start in the rural areas. Having the proper equipment to combat large-scale fires is important since the conditions would appear to be optimal for a fire to spread quickly owing to the extent of dry vegetation available to keep the fire fueled. There should also be a series of Geographic Information Systems maps that should be constructed that would indicate how to fight fires if they started in the rural areas, as well as showing possible evacuation routes from different cities and towns if fires were to occur in those areas.

2. *What resources do you need if a potential fire were to break out in the country-side?* If available, firefighter vehicles and planes could provide a good means to put out any fire quickly, if the fire is sighted soon enough before it begins to spread throughout the surrounding countryside. Water and chemicals that are used to fight fires can be stockpiled and pre-positioned in areas where fires could potentially cause harm to larger populations of residents.

3. *What should you do for a communication plan at this point in time?* You should communicate with the citizens of the state of Victoria with a recommendation not to burn any type of waste, be extremely careful if they go camping by making sure that all campfires are extinguished, and that cigars and cigarettes can be deadly if improperly disposed of in dry vegetation. Additionally, there could be a very forceful campaign to prevent any type of arson from occurring by reminding the populous that stiff criminal charges can be filed if one is caught perpetrating arson.

Stage 2 of the Disaster

On Saturday February 7, 2009, you receive word that over 100 fires have been sighted (The Day the Sky Turned Black, 2012). With winds gusting over 60 miles per hour and temperatures that are over 100°, you know that the fire will spread quickly if action is not taken immediately (Siddaway and Petelina, 2009).

1. *What is your plan of action?* At this point you should gather all resources available given the number of fires, and that you have to protect not only the land that has not caught fire yet, but also and primarily the citizens. Therefore, you will need to mobilize your first responders to combat fires around populated centers first, and then go after the fires that are primarily in rural areas as a secondary priority.

2. *What resources do you need to mobilize?* Any person that is a firefighter or first responder needs to be mobilized immediately, along with any type of vehicle that can support those efforts. Any firefighting plane that can be obtained to combat the fires should be utilized as soon as possible. You should also begin to think about what types of resources will be needed to help evacuate and temporarily shelter displaced residents if the fires begin to threaten populated areas of the state.

3. *What is your communication plan?* Any residents that live in the path of the fires will need to be told to evacuate. Agencies at the local and central government levels need to be contacted to request assistance with additional manpower, vehicles, logistics, or medical resources. You should be very diligent about communicating with your first responders to make sure that firefighting efforts are fully coordinated.

Stage 3 of the Disaster

You have now learned that there are 400 separate fires, accompanied by strong winds that are over 70 miles per hour, and they are not only occurring but changing direction, causing all of the fires to increase dramatically in size and ferocity (Siddaway and Petelina, 2009; The Day the Sky Turned Black, 2012). In addition, you now have five towns that have been obliterated in addition to the 173 people that have been killed, over 5,000 people have been injured, and 2,029 homes have been destroyed (Australian Broadcast Corporation, 2012).

1. *What is your plan of action?* The aftermath of the disaster still poses many problems for your management skills. The bodies of the dead will need to be recovered and identified. The displaced individuals will need to be assisted, which will create quite a logistical challenge with 2,029 homes destroyed, and people that will need housing, food, water, medicine, sanitation infrastructure, and medicine. The next challenge that will be posed to public administrators is how to rebuild the communities in the state and where the money will come from.

2. *What resources do you need to mobilize?* Medical resources will be in high demand in the short term until the majority of injured are treated. Temporary housing and communities to host those temporary shelters will need to be found quickly and then stockpiled with supplies to support those individuals.

3. *What is your communication plan?* You need to communicate with the local and central governments about what has been done to date, what needs to be done, and what resources you need to support all of the displaced persons. The displaced persons will need to be contacted to let them know that they are being provided for and what the plans are to get them in a more permanent state of housing.

Key Issues Raised from the Case Study

There were definitely signs that a wildfire could occur in the area before the fires broke out in Victoria given the drought conditions and dry vegetation. Areas that are prone to brushfires will need to take certain precautions and stock up provisions that will be needed to fight a massive fire. Accordingly, it would be wise for administrators to make cooperative agreements with other governmental agencies that could provide resources in times of crisis.

Items of Note

A number of government policies have been reviewed in light of the brushfires and are currently being revisited on how best to respond to brushfires in the future (Hill, 2012).

Chapter 3

Chapter 3

Case Studies: Disasters from Natural Causes—Hurricanes

Newfoundland Hurricane, 1775

Stage 1 of the Disaster

You are a colonial governor of North Carolina.* On September 9 you are notified that a very large hurricane is heading toward your colony's coastline (Cox, 1997). You anticipate that there will be only limited capability for communication and personnel may have to carry messages to various locations.

1. *What is your plan of action?* The first thing to take into account is whether your office has an emergency plan. If an emergency plan is available, then your office should make sure that any resources required by the plan are in place for the impending emergency. You also need to ensure that everyone in your office has the emergency plan available. If no emergency plan is available, then your office should develop a plan (if there is time) and distribute it throughout your staff.

2. *What is your communication plan?* Since the hurricane might disrupt any communication lines you are accustomed to using, you will need to find alternative methods to communicate to the other organizations across the colony

---

* Even though this is the Newfoundland hurricane, the hurricane in fact hit North Carolina and Virginia colonies, which are now states.

and to your first responders. There is the additional, important necessity of communicating to the public that the hurricane is coming and that all low-lying areas of the colony should be evacuated, as well as ships that are in port areas should be moved to other areas that will be out of harm's way. If couriers are the only method available to you, then you will have to ensure that enough couriers are sent to all parts of your colony with the same unified message. Consistency in the message to the first responders and the public is extremely important.

3. *How will you contend with your limited ability to communicate with the community?* To contend with the issue of having limited communications, one method is to establish more coordination through local governments and have them each send a representative to a series of command centers that can be set up in a distributed pattern to allow for communication to occur more quickly. The distributed communication centers would receive messages from the central communication center.

4. *How will you distribute your resources to contend with the hurricane?* On a colony-wide level resources will be spread rather thin throughout the countryside. However, it would be more important to put more resources in the lower-elevation areas that are densely populated, where more damage, deaths, and injuries could occur.

5. *What will you use for energy in place of electricity?** Depending if you have the assets and resources to have an alternate power source, wind and hydropower would seem to be the most likely resources that could generate some power. In a modern crisis, batteries and gasoline for portable generators would be ideal for producing power.

Stage 2 of the Disaster

You are now told that the storm has wreaked untold havoc and is heading north to a neighboring colony. You know that several ships have been sunk or damaged and you have over 150 people that have been killed (Stone, 2006).

1. *What is your plan of action?* This is obviously a powerful storm that is closing in on other population centers. It is important for you to gather as much information as possible about where the hurricane has caused damage so you can redistribute your resources to those areas in need. It will take time to shift your resources around the state since you have no power and no communications that are very quick or effective.

---

* This disaster occurred before modern-day power plants existed, but there were methods to generate power (i.e., horses, windmills, and water wheels in mills). If power is nonexistent in a centralized infrastructure, the administrator will need to come up with an alternative manner to generate power.

2. *What is your communication plan?* A key item that needs to be communicated is that the hurricane is moving toward a neighboring colony. That neighboring colony's government should be warned, so a courier should be sent to communicate that the hurricane is on the path for their area. In addition, you need to communicate to your first responders where the hurricane has struck once you get more information.

3. *How will you contend with your limited ability to communicate with the community?* Since you have limited ability to communicate with your population, you will need to have a stable of couriers as well as a distributed network of command centers that you can not only send messages to, but also receive information on the current hurricane damage and needs of communities for resources.

4. *How will you distribute your resources to contend with the hurricane?* Now that people have been injured and killed, you will need more medical personnel and coroners to recover the bodies to prevent disease and infection from being incurred on your population. The last thing you need now is a pandemic of bacterial or virus infections to afflict the rest of your community that was not directly impacted by the hurricane.

5. *How will you coordinate your rescue efforts with your neighboring colony to the north?* There may be some common resources that could be used by both colonies for rescue and recovery operations. Certain skilled laborers may be available in one colony and not the other that can be sent to the neighboring colony that needs specialized services. The neighboring colony in return may be in a position to send resources to your colony.

Stage 3 of the Disaster

You are now receiving word that multiple dams have either been broken or are flooding due to the winds and high volume of water that is coming in from the hurricane (U.S. Department of Commerce, National Oceanic and Atmospheric Administration, 2012; Ruffman, 1996). In addition, you are now receiving damage reports that your cornfields have been laid to waste (U.S. Department of Commerce, National Oceanic and Atmospheric Administration, 2012).

1. *What is your plan of action?* With the dams breaking you will need to shore up those structures and stop any additional flooding. In addition, you will need to send out inspectors to investigate the status of other dams that have not broken and repair the dams if the situation warrants emergency repair work.

2. *What is your communication plan?* Using your communication network, you will need to summon all workers that can possibly work on dam and breakwater structures to perform repair work, as well as inspect other structures. In addition, you will now need to communicate to the populations around dams that could break that evacuations should occur for residents in those areas.

3. *How will you distribute your resources to contend with the hurricane?* Your organization has two additional problems to contend with: (1) finding food for your citizens and (2) finding engineers and construction workers for the dam projects. If the dams are not repaired or inspected properly, you could even have more agriculture destroyed, more citizens displaced, and possibly more citizens killed if the dams do not hold.

4. *What priority should you place on rescue efforts?* Rescue operations should be the first priority. However, the dam inspection and construction projects, as well as finding food for your citizens, should be placed as high-priority problems that need to be resolved. Since the rescue process involves first responders, the other two issues should not detract personnel from working on resolutions to those issues.

5. *What will you do about the food supply being destroyed?* This situation calls for sending out feelers to surrounding states to see if stockpiles of food may be purchased or donated from other colonial governments. If that approach fails, see how many canned and preserved foods can be gathered up and sent to population centers that will be affected by the food shortage.

Stage 4 of the Disaster

The storm has now subsided. You are receiving reports that a number of people have been displaced and need both food and shelter (Stone, 2006). In addition to that news you are told that the storm has left over 4,000 people dead all along the coastline (BBC Weather, 2007). You send out riders on horseback to use as couriers for communicating with your various emergency crisis units in the field, and you attempt to gain the confidence of your citizenry that stability will eventually occur.

1. *What is your plan of action?* A major priority at this point in the disaster is to make sure that there is enough temporary housing for all of your displaced citizens. One option is to appeal to neighboring communities to take in displaced persons until housing can be provided. You have neighboring colonies that can also be called upon to assist with the recovery of the state after the hurricane. Medical personnel and morticians will be needed to take care of the injured and collect the dead to prevent infection and disease from spreading. There will still be some ongoing rescue efforts, but at this point in time your resources should shift to more of a recovery nature. Calling up any military aid would be reasonable at this time to show the citizens that the government is in control of the situation, and this action would also add additional manpower that would be employed with the recovery effort. The issue of setting up logistics for food, water, and medicine coming from neighboring states would also need to be established to relieve your citizens' plight.

2. *What is your communication plan?* You do not have motorized transport and communication has to occur through couriers that travel either by foot or on

horseback. It is very important to keep the messages simple and to the point. The more complex a message is, the more likely the message will be distorted. At this point in the disaster, it would be wise as a leader to make visits to areas where the hurricane has hit and provide confidence to your citizens as well as gain firsthand knowledge of the actual situation.

3. *What will you do about the food supply being destroyed?* Refrigeration did not exist during this emergency. However, even in modern times there is a possibility that electricity could be cut off and refrigeration of food would not be possible. In this situation it is important to get as much cured or preserved food as possible. Having preserved food allows for stockpiles of food to be stored and transported more effectively. Since you have to consider that wagons are the best transportation you will have at this point, the food will have to be able to be hauled over long distances in all sorts of climates and still be edible upon delivery.

4. *How will you deal with the population that is displaced?* There is no perfect answer to this question. The results will often be based on what resources are available to construct housing (e.g., wood, carpenters, etc.). Another remedy might be to put up a large amount of tents until more permanent housing can be constructed, but one has to keep in mind that the climate might prove to be too harsh for certain populations, particularly the very old or very young, to tolerate for a great length of time.

Key Issues Raised from the Case Study

The case study illustrates the challenges of dealing with shelter, supplies, and evacuation issues in the absence of modern resources. The issue of infrastructure (i.e., dams) failing during the storm is the same problem that occurred in more recent storms (i.e., Hurricane Katrina). With no power or modern communications the colonists had to overcome the communication issues by using couriers on foot or on horseback to relay messages. In modern times the infrastructure may exist for more modern communication, but that does not always guarantee it will be working properly during times of crisis. Administrators need to have an alternate plan that will consist of more rudimentary forms of communicating in case modern telecommunications infrastructure fails.

Without having the ability to shore up infrastructure, such as dams, the hurricane actually caused more damage than would have occurred naturally. When structures such as dams fail, it can lead to a large amount of flooding that will not only kill or injure people, but also cause damage to other infrastructure, such as bridges, houses, and businesses. Administrators need to be cognizant of the dangers of dams bursting during a hurricane or earthquake and should regularly inspect and upgrade that infrastructure accordingly. The damage caused by burst dams can be so severe that the British developed a specialized dam-busting weapon during World War II to flood the industrial heartland of Germany (Rainey, 2011).

In addition to the human life lost, ships were sunk, infrastructure was damaged, and the agricultural industry was left in ruins. In the time of when this crisis occurred, modern communication, transportation, and construction materials did not exist, which in many parts of the world may still be the case if a natural disaster occurs. Administrators in underdeveloped parts of the world should take heed of these issues and attempt to reinforce infrastructure as much as possible to weather a natural disaster.

Items of Note

This was the eighth deadliest hurricane of all time (Stone, 2006).

Galveston Hurricane, Texas, 1900

Stage 1 of the Disaster

You are the city manager of a large coastal city of 42,000 inhabitants (Cline, 2000). You are concerned about the possibility of hurricanes hitting your city and causing widespread death and destruction. You have just witnessed the city of Indianola get hit twice by hurricanes and ultimately abandoned by the residents due to the damage that was inflicted upon their community (Texas State Historical Association, 2001). You have some residents that favor building a sea wall to limit the potential damage by a hurricane, but their pleas fall on deaf ears (Cline, 2000).

1. *What is your plan of action?* The city manager needs to galvanize support for the construction of a seawall. To gain this support, the city manager needs to win over the mayor and the city council to bolster the necessary political support that will be needed to build a seawall. Additionally, the city manager should have his staff develop an emergency plan of action for the city with a particular focus on hurricanes. A related effort should concentrate on developing evacuation plans as well as identifying vulnerable at-risk facilities that will need attention by first responders in case of a hurricane. A communication system should be put in place so that residents can be warned if they need to evacuate the city. A storm warning tower system could be installed that would allow for signal flags to be raised if a hurricane or storm approached the coast. The use of different color flags would denote the seriousness of the storm. While this system appears obsolete today, the storm towers were very useful before the age of modern telecommunications. A telegraph would also be another device that would be useful to indicate that a storm is coming toward the community in the event that a storm had been spotted by another entity before the storm's arrival.

2. *What resources should you have in place in case a hurricane hits your city?* The city manager should ensure that his city has a stockpile of food, water, and medicine on hand in case of an emergency. In addition, the city manager will need first responders identified with particular tasks (e.g., utility line shutdown, search and rescue, etc.). A telephone or telegraph communication system is ideal, but the city manager should have a backup system of couriers in place in case the primary system fails.

Stage 2 of the Disaster

The residents and city council believe that there is no need to worry about hurricanes since there has never been a storm that has inflicted significant damage. Your citizens believe that they are safe and do not see any need to have a plan of action for such an occurrence (Cline, 2000). However on September 4, you receive word that a tropical storm is possibly heading toward your city (NOAA Celebrates, 2007).

1. *What steps do you need to take in order to prepare for a hurricane that may hit your city?* The city manager should begin to evacuate the city by train, boat, and wagons since the evacuation process will take a long time. In addition, the city manager should begin to reinforce identified facilities from the impending hurricane and make sure that all supplies have been gathered for the population that may not be able to escape the city before the hurricane hits.
2. *How will you implement your plan in the face of resistance of the citizens and the city government?* The city manager has power over the municipal staff and should exercise his influence to collect any resources that are under the city's jurisdiction. The city manager should inform residents that choose to stay when the hurricane hits, they will be on their own since first responders will not be dispatched to situations that have been deemed extremely hazardous.

Stage 3 of the Disaster

A National Weather Service bulletin has now been issued stating that the hurricane will hit your city on September 7 (NOAA Celebrates, 2007). Your citizens show little interest in evacuating since the weather is currently extremely mild (Galveston Newspapers, 2007). On September 8 at 9:45 a.m., the train tracks to the mainland are washed out and passengers on that particular train have to transfer to another relief train to finish evacuating to safety. Another train that left later is stranded by the rising water, with 95 people on board. The hurricane is now hitting your city and over half of your city streets are underwater (Cline, 2000). You are completely cut off from the mainland with no communication or bridges to get evacuees off the island or bring resources to the island. As an administrator you have some serious obstacles to overcome to protect the citizens of your city.

1. *What resources do you need?* The city manager will need the resources required to rescue the 95 people that are stranded on the train. Additionally, the city manager will need to see if enough shelter is available to residents for protection from the hurricane.
2. *What is your plan of action?* At this point, the city manager can do very little except wait until the storm is over. The city manager, in good conscience, cannot commit first responders to perilous conditions while the storm is raging.
3. *What will you do about the 95 people that are stranded on board the train?* If the city manager has personnel that are willing to make a rescue attempt, and the means are available to successfully get to the stranded train, then the city manager may decide to send first responders to rescue the passengers. Otherwise, those 95 people may perish.

Stage 4 of the Disaster

You have now learned that 10 people on the train have made it successfully to a nearby lighthouse, and that 200 other residents are there as well. Eighty-five of the people on the train died when the train was flooded (Frank, 2003). You have also learned that over 3,600 buildings and homes have been destroyed (Weather Channel Interactive, 2007) and that 8,000 to 12,000 people have been killed (Texas State Historical Association, 2002). A large city on the mainland has been providing assistance for your city, and the governor of your state is sending resources to assist your municipality in your time of need (Lester, 2006).

1. *What resources do you need the municipality and governor to send?* The city manager will need first responders, food, water, medicine, repair workers for infrastructure, and medical personnel. In addition, the city manager will need personnel for body recovery and burial. With so many buildings and homes destroyed there will be a high need for temporary housing as well.
2. *How will you communicate with your community and other governmental agencies?* If the telephone system is working, then that can be a primary way to communicate to the outside communities and government agencies. Otherwise, the telegraph system is a possibility, as well as courier on horseback.
3. *What is your plan of action now that the hurricane has passed?* The city manager's priority will be to carry out search and rescue operations. The second priority will be to find shelter for those residents that are now homeless and to provide the survivors the necessary resources for sustainability.
4. *What aspects will you need to focus on to address new and developing situations?* Municipalities that are regularly threatened by a particular type of natural disaster need to have agreements with local communities to provide mutual support in times of crisis. These types of agreements allow cities to support one another with resources such as food, water, personnel, and medical care.

Key Issues Raised from the Case Study

The need to have an evacuation plan is crucial to prevent the loss of life. This case study precluded the ability of city administrators to have an accurate advanced warning of an impending hurricane that is now possible in modern times. A seawall may limit potential damage, but ultimately a city should be evacuated when a hurricane is approaching in the vicinity of an inhabited community. The 1900 Galveston, Texas, hurricane is still listed as the deadliest hurricane to ever hit the United States. It killed between 8,000 and 12,000 people and destroyed much of the city (Cline, 2000).

Items of Note

Galveston was the main city for commerce for the area in the Gulf of Mexico until the hurricane. After the hurricane, much of commerce capability was developed around the city of Houston instead of Galveston.

Hurricane Katrina, 2005

Stage 1 of the Disaster

You are the governor of Louisiana. On August 23, you are advised that a hurricane could be heading toward a major seaport city in your state (Preparation for Hurricanes, 2007). While the city has been hit by hurricanes before, this hurricane has been predicted to hit with Category 3 force (Solar Navigator, 2007). The storm is currently near Florida. On August 26, the U.S. Coast Guard starts to position forces and activates 400 reservists in anticipation of the coming hurricane. You have requested the federal government to declare a state of emergency so that you can obtain resources if they are needed (USCG Stormwatch, 2007).

1. *What is your plan of action?* For the seaport city, the governor should work closely with the mayor to ensure that an adequate evacuation plan exists. In addition, there needs to be adequate transportation resources to evacuate residents that do not own their own vehicles or are unable to drive (e.g., hospital patients, nursing home residents, etc.). The governor should also make sure that the National Guard is on alert and ready to be deployed to any area that is struck by the hurricane to evacuate residents or provide support to communities in the form of constructing water barriers (e.g., sandbags). All shipping to the port city should be suspended, and ships in the port city should be ordered to leave the city before the hurricane hits.
2. *What is your communication plan?* The governor should stay in communication with local community officials as well as federal agencies that can provide assistance if the hurricane hits the area. Additionally, the governor

should remain in contact with his or her department heads that are in charge of emergency management, law enforcement, and infrastructure.

Stage 2 of the Disaster

While 80% of the citizens of your port city have been evacuated, you still have 20% that have not been evacuated for one reason or another (Brown, 2005). You have requested emergency assistance from the Federal Emergency Management Agency (FEMA) (*New York Times*, 2005). You have not heard back from them as of yet. Your state is supposed to begin a three-phase evacuation of the population from the affected areas. The largest coastal city's population should be evacuated 30 hours before the storm hits the coastline (Louisiana Homeland Security and Emergency Preparedness, 2007). However, you are now receiving news that many private hospices, medical facilities, and retirement communities in your largest city cannot evacuate their residents because the private transportation firm will not comply with transportation plans (*Times Picayune*, 2005b). In addition you receive word that fuel is in short supply, rental cars are scarce, and public transportation is largely shut down and unavailable (Office of Public Affairs, 2005).

1. *What action do you take?* As governor you need to contact the local officials at the port city to see why the evacuation has not been completed. The shortfalls that exist for the evacuation that was supposed to be carried out must be remedied by sufficient resources dedicated to affect the complete evacuation of the city. The levee system needs to have state engineers and public transportation workers assigned to shore up the levee system, if nothing else, to delay the collapse of the levees until all of the residents have been evacuated. If the residents have not been evacuated due to a lack of transportation, have units of the National Guard allocated to evacuate the city via truck or helicopters.

2. *What resources do you need?* The governor needs manpower in the form of engineers, construction teams, and transportation drivers, as well as the vehicles and heavy equipment necessary to carry out such mandates.

3. *What is your communication plan?* The governor needs to stay in close communication with the local officials as well as the National Guard, department of highway transportation, and other state agency department heads that are in charge of first responders. The governor should also call in assistance from FEMA and the U.S. Coast Guard to provide support to residents that have been forced to flee or need to be evacuated due to the hurricane and the flooding.

Stage 3 of the Disaster

On August 28, the mayor of the largest port city orders a mandatory evacuation for residents and the hurricane is upgraded to Category 5 status (Solar Navigator, 2007).

The mayor has designated a local sports arena that holds 26,000 people as a refuge center. However, this refuge center does not have any water or food in storage (*Times Picayune*, 2005a). On the same day, the Canadian National Railway, the Amtrak system, and the Waterford nuclear power plant have all been completely shut down (Angelfire, 2005).

1. *What is your plan of action?* Since local officials have been unable or unwilling to evacuate the city, the governor should step in and order the National Guard to evacuate the residents that have not been transported out of the city. In addition, state emergency personnel should make it a priority to provide food, water, medical supplies, and security to the designated shelter since FEMA has not responded to calls for assistance as of yet.
2. *What is your communication plan?* The governor should make a direct appeal to the public to evacuate the city for any citizens that have the means to escape the hurricane. In addition, the governor needs to contact surrounding communities to see if they can provide transportation, food, water, and medical supplies to the port city. The governor should keep attempting to contact FEMA and keep requesting assistance.
3. *Your infrastructure is beginning to be shut down; how will you evacuate citizens and provide need areas with electricity?* The governor needs to try to obtain any portable generators for areas where residents are currently located to provide some form of electricity. The state highway department should be ordered, if it is at all possible, to ensure that major highways stay open and operable for evacuation purposes.

Stage 4 of the Disaster

On August 29, New Orleans, the largest city in your state, is hit by the hurricane (Think Progress, 2007). As a result, 53 major levees have failed and over 80% of that city is now underwater (MSNBC, 2005). You are receiving reports of citizens being isolated in their homes as a result of the flooding, and electricity has been cut to several hundred thousand residents throughout your state (U.S. Department of Energy, 2005). Injury and death are now confirmed and Lake Pontchartrain is flooding due to the rainfall, impacting multiple suburban communities that are near your port city. The flooding from the lake has also damaged or destroyed several bridges that connect those communities to your main port city. Toxic chemicals are now in much of the water supply due to inundations at wastewater facilities. Supplying potable water to citizens could be a serious concern (Angelfire, 2005).

1. *What is your new plan of action?* The governor needs to request that the Coast Guard provide assistance with search and rescue operations since they have the assets (i.e., helicopters and manpower) to make rescue operations. In addition, the EPA needs to be contacted about the hazardous materials that

are now leaking into the city. A priority also needs to be given to getting the levee system back in operation and having pumps that can extract the water repaired in order to decrease the flooding throughout the city.

2. *What resources do you need to acquire?* The governor needs transportation and search and rescue teams to evacuate any residents that are currently trapped by the flooding. In addition, construction crews and engineers will need to be assigned to work on the levee system to stop any more flooding from occurring. If there is any bridging equipment that is available, those resources need to be employed to provide an evacuation route out of the city.

Stage 5 of the Disaster

The hurricane begins to sweep past your state on August 30 (U.S. Department of the Interior, 2007b). However, you have a new set of challenges when the citizens of your largest port city begin looting and creating mayhem and violence. There have been several snipers taking shots at local law enforcement, and you have now mobilized the National Guard with orders to stop any criminal acts. Containing the violence becomes more difficult because many police and firefighters abandoned their responsibilities and fled the city (Thevenot, 2005). In addition, the citizens in the port city have not been provided any aid by FEMA in the way of food, water, or shelter. You have several nonprofit organizations, such as the American Red Cross, that want to provide supplies and support, but the area is too dangerous to allow support workers to gain access due to the ongoing criminal acts. The U.S. Coast Guard did manage to successfully rescue over 33,500 citizens among the 60,000 that were stranded (U.S. Government Accountability Office, 2006).

1. *How will you contend with the violence and criminal acts that are occurring in the port city?* The governor should mobilize the state police, and if possible, ask other communities for law enforcement assistance to provide security for the nonprofit organizations' relief efforts. The National Guard should be tasked to stop violence at the designated shelters and have orders to stop snipers as well as looting.

2. *How will you get resources successfully to the citizens that are still stranded?* The governor will have to rely on entities that have helicopters that can get food and water to people stranded on their properties. Other methods might be to use small boats to transport items to stranded residents.

Stage 6 of the Disaster

As a result of the hurricane and its aftermath, 1,836 people were killed and $86 billion (2007 estimate) worth of damage was inflicted upon the region (U.S. Department of Health and Human Services, 2007). The director of FEMA resigned, the mayor of the main port city was viewed ineffective in contending with the crisis, and your administration is viewed with suspicion (Associated Press, 2005a).

1. *What is your next plan of action?* A primary focus of the governor at this point is to provide temporary shelter to residents that have fled the area. In addition, the governor will need to put more resources into fixing the levee systems along with their corresponding pumps that are needed for any additional storms that may approach the port city in the near future. Finally, the governor should review how residents will get back to the port city and where they will be housed when they come back if their property was destroyed.

2. *What is your communication plan?* The governor should communicate a plan for recovery to the public and coordinate efforts with FEMA and the American Red Cross to get supplies to displaced persons. Residents that are currently in other cities should be told to stay where they are at if possible until temporary housing becomes available.

Key Issues Raised from the Case Study

Large government agencies that are involved with disaster response need to be prepared, not only for a potential disaster, but also to work effectively with other state and federal agencies in times of crisis. If efforts are not coordinated effectively, a breakdown in delivery of services may result, which will lead to potential problems in search and rescue operations and the evacuation of large populations. In addition, the failure of the different levels of government to work together effectively at the city, state, and federal organizational levels led to the crisis being far worse than what would have been expected from a hurricane landing at New Orleans. Issues such as the lack of transportation, infrastructure being shut down, and having the proper amount of food and water on hand at designated shelters are only three of the many factors that were made worse by the dysfunctional interoperational aspects by the different levels of government in action. Local government must be prepared to make use of the resources that are available to them if state or federal aid fails to materialize. Municipalities should make cooperative arrangements with other surrounding municipalities that can potentially provide aid to an entity in times of crisis.

There were a number of failures in this case study, which included the failure to evacuate the citizens of New Orleans, the failure to provide a mechanism for citizens that had no transportation to evacuate, the failure of multiple levees around the New Orleans area, and the failure of the federal government to render immediate and effective aid to stranded citizens of New Orleans. Additionally, there were a number of failures in logistics as well as in controlling criminal activity effectively during the crisis. A number of citizens were killed or injured, and there was significant property damage that required a considerable amount of resources to repair or rebuild. The citizens of New Orleans have relocated (many permanently) to other cities, which effectively reduced the population of New Orleans in the short term. Criticism and investigations were launched into a number of government agencies that were involved with Hurricane Katrina, which revealed shortcomings in operational procedures, logistical controls, and operational planning, as well as having no effective leadership in emergency management during a crisis.

Items of Note

Reports of widespread violence in the Superdome turned out to be exaggerated. In fact, violence was much lower than what the media reported (Thevenot, 2005).

Hurricane Rita, 2005

Stage 1 of the Disaster

You are the director of a federal agency that is tasked with overseeing rescue and relief aid to areas that are affected by natural disasters. On September 20, the National Hurricane Center determines a hurricane has formed and is heading for the United States (National Weather Service, 2007).

1. *What is your plan of action?* The director should begin to take an inventory of what supplies are on hand to contend with such an emergency, such as food, water, and medical supplies. In addition, the director should also begin to formulate a plan concerning how those supplies will be delivered quickly and, if it is possible, how to position some of those resources in depots close to where the hurricane may strike the coast.
2. *What resources will you need to acquire?* The director will need manpower to move the supplies and vehicles to carry the supplies to key locations. In addition, the director will need temporary shelters for personnel as well as mobile generators and refrigeration units to store food and medicine that may be needed in case of an emergency.
3. *What governmental agencies will you need to interact with?* Interacting with state and local officials that are in the possible strike area of the hurricane is critical to determine what resources may be needed by those communities. In addition, the director will need to communicate with other federal department heads to coordinate efforts on getting supplies where they will be needed the most.

Stage 2 of the Disaster

On September 21, the governor of one state activated 1,200 National Guardsmen, 1,100 state guardsmen, and state game wardens to contend with the impending crisis. In addition, the governor of that state reversed the flow of traffic, making the interstate highways one direction—only out of the major port city of that state for evacuation purposes (Hays, 2005). You are receiving some good news that patients from certain major hospitals and some shut-ins have already been transferred to cities out of reach of the hurricane (Easton, 2005). However, you are now aware that traffic has been gridlocked for one state in particular and that evacuation is not occurring as fast as you would like. In addition, much of the nation's oil refinery production centers are vulnerable (Townsend, 2005).

1. *What is your plan to get evacuations moving smoothly?* The director should attempt to provide fueling points for vehicles that are along the evacuation route as well as food and water to the drivers. The director should contact the state emergency response coordinator and see if there are any alternative ways that traffic can be rerouted or phased into certain highways to temporarily alleviate the traffic jams.
2. *How will you safeguard the refineries?* The director should work closely with the EPA for resources to safeguard the refineries. If at all possible, as much oil and chemicals as possible should be removed prior to the hurricane strikes to avoid chemical and hazardous material situations.
3. *What is your communication plan?* The director should stay in close contact with other federal agency directors as well as state and local government officials in order to coordinate effective disaster response relief efforts.

Stage 3 of the Disaster

On September 24 the hurricane makes landfall between two neighboring states (Hurricane Headquarters, 2007). As the hurricane hits the coastline, three communities in one state are completely obliterated, with another six communities suffering heavy damage (Struck and Milbank, 2005). Two million people are now without electricity (Diamond, 2005), and the estimate for property damage stands at $10 billion (National Weather Service, 2007). The death toll has reached an estimated 82 people that have been killed by either direct causes of the storm or indirect causes (Knabb, Brown, and Rhome, 2006).

1. *What will you do to rectify the situation for the power loss to 2 million people?* The director should attempt to see if mobile generators are available to be deployed to communities where power has been knocked out by the storm. The director should also attempt to get fuel to those plants that have not been resupplied so that they can be back up and running fairly quickly.
2. *What is your plan to get aid to the communities that have been struck by the hurricane?* The director needs to be very proactive in getting logistics moving toward cities that have no food, water, or medical supplies. The cities that have been hit the hardest will get relief aid as soon as roadways are available that can be used to transport goods to those areas. For areas that are isolated, helicopters will be needed to transport goods to those communities.

3. *What is your communication plan for interacting with other agencies and non-profit organizations?* The director will need to stay in contact to ensure that all communities are being served and assisted by FEMA, another federal agency, a state agency, or a nonprofit organization. If the director does not maintain communication with the other organizations, there is a danger that relief will not be distributed properly to the affected communities, with some areas receiving too much aid while others receive nothing at all.

4. *What is your plan to help citizens relocate back to their homes?* There will need to be temporary housing provided for residents whose homes have been destroyed or damaged. Temporary housing could range from portable housing (e.g., trailer homes) to hotels and the like.

Key Issues Raised from the Case Study

Evacuations on a massive scale not only require the necessary infrastructure to handle a heavy traffic load, but must also take into account the support structure necessary for increased vehicular use (e.g., gasoline). If evacuations are conducted in stages, it is necessary to ensure that those stages are rigidly adhered to in order to avoid a massive infusion of vehicles all using the same roads at the exact same time.

The traffic gridlock caused by evacuees is a focal point in this particular case study. Millions of people used the same interstate highways at the same time, forcing traffic to a crawl. People who voluntarily left the city were in their cars for hours and had not moved very far at all when the formal evacuation order was given. At least one former city manager in Liberty, Texas, discussed how he and his staff were handing out cups of water to motorists that had been stuck in traffic for hours. The logistical planning was incomplete and resulted in lack of water, food, and gas for motorists that were attempting to get clear of the Houston metropolitan area where Hurricane Rita had the potential to make landfall.

Items of Note

Hurricane Rita resulted in $8 billion of damage to Texas alone, which also resulted in thousands of people being unable to return home for weeks due to infrastructure damage (Struck and Milbank, 2005). At least 90 tornadoes were associated with Hurricane Rita and produced the most tornadoes ever recorded in Jackson, Mississippi, in a single event to date (2012) (Knabb, Brown, and Rhome, 2006).

Chapter 4

Case Studies: Disasters from Natural Forces—Floods

Johnstown Flood, Pennsylvania, 1889

Stage 1 of the Disaster

You are the mayor of a town of 30,000 people. Your town mainly consists of blue-collar steel workers that are of German descent. Unfortunately, your town has been built on a floodplain where two rivers meet and the riverbanks have been narrowed to give the town more land to construct residential housing and other buildings. This leads to some minor flooding from time to time. In addition, the South Fork Dam located upstream needs maintenance badly, but is not being maintained by the local hunting and fishing lodge that is responsible for its upkeep (U.S. Department of the Interior, 2007a).

1. *What is your plan of action?* As the leader of the community, you should encourage precautionary measures on the issue of flooding because it is a recurring problem and can be a potentially bigger problem in the future. The mayor should undertake a study that will review the planning and zoning ordinances of the town and direct the town council to take action on restricting certain development along the river. An emergency plan of action and evacuation plan should be developed for the citizens of the town as well as identifying resources that may be needed in case of an emergency.

Additionally, the South Fork Dam should get the proper maintenance and evaluation to ensure that the town is fully protected from any type of catastrophic dam failure.

2. *What is your communication plan?* The mayor's communication plan should include the town council members and make them aware of the potentially dangerous situations that can occur if certain issues are not dealt with appropriately. Additionally, the mayor should begin to develop support for better planning and building ordinances with the town's staff as well as the housing developers. The mayor should be in contact with the party responsible for maintenance of the South Fork Dam as well as the town's first responders. The community at large should be made aware of any emergency or evacuation plans that currently exist. Resources need to be put in place to ensure that the mayor can communicate with the town residents in times of crisis.

3. *What resources do you need to acquire for the problems that have occurred or that could occur?* One of the bigger problems that the mayor will face is getting the resources to fix the South Fork Dam. The general population currently does not feel any sense of urgency in making repairs or even maintaining the dam.

4. *What government entities do you need to interface with to accomplish your plan of action?* As stated earlier, the mayor needs to interface successfully with the town council. Communications with the town council are imperative for getting the resources needed to repair the dam, as well as for passing any type of building or zoning ordinances concerning the development that is continuing along the river. The mayor will also need to communicate with the town's top administrator to get staff support for developing an emergency or evacuation plan.

Stage 2 of the Disaster

On May 31, at 4:07 p.m., the South Fork Dam collapses after a heavy rain fall. The collapse sends 20 tons of water that is 60 feet high hurtling toward your town at 40 miles per hour (U.S. Department of the Interior, 2007a).

1. *What is your plan of action?* You must communicate to your staff that the town needs to have all available first responders evacuate the town, starting with the residences nearest to the river. Other than attempt to evacuate the town, there is very little you can do at this point since the flood is quickly coming toward the town. Your time to act and your options to take different approaches to blunt the impact of the flood are extremely limited at this juncture. Evacuating the town is the best plan of action to take with the factors that are at work in this disaster.

2. *What is your communication plan?* The mayor needs to enact an evacuation of the town. To do this, the mayor must get word to the residents by any means possible that they should evacuate to higher ground. You have no modern communications, so you will need to rely on couriers on foot with

megaphones or individuals on horseback that can relay the message to the town quickly.

3. *What resources do you need for the impending crisis?* The mayor will need all forms of communication, from foot couriers to horseback couriers, available to both relay information to citizens of the town and coordinate first responders in an effort to evacuate the town. If using a telegraph system is an option, the mayor should attempt to contact other communities to get food, medical resources, and first responders. Otherwise, the mayor will need to send out horseback riders to communicate with other outside entities.

Stage 3 of the Disaster

In 10 minutes, thousands of people are swept away or trapped underneath pier works at a stone bridge downstream. At least 80 people are killed by fires that started on the debris that was trapped in the structure of the bridge. Thousands more people are alive but drifting on debris or are trapped in the attics of their houses (U.S. Department of the Interior, 2007a).

1. *What are your priorities for the current crisis?* The mayor should direct the first responders to conduct search and rescue operations to pull residents out of the water as soon as possible. The next phase of search and rescue operations should be to locate people that are trapped in their attics and pull them to safety. As mayor, you should begin to contact surrounding municipalities to get first responder assistance for search and rescue operations.

2. *What plan of action do you have in place?* At this point in the emergency, there is no effective plan that exists. Therefore, the mayor needs to devise a plan to create an effective search and rescue strategy that will include putting out the fire on the pier as well as begin to rescue people that are trapped in their attics. Equipment such as axes and other wood chopping implements will be needed to open up escape avenues for the citizens that are currently trapped in their homes.

3. *How are you able to communicate to the population and other government agencies?* Communication is nonexistent, and there is no way for the mayor to contact outside government agencies unless they have a working telegraph capability. Communication may be possible with horseback couriers to other outside municipalities.

Stage 4 of the Disaster

The dead and wounded are piling up at an alarming rate. The city has been completely demolished, and you now have to worry about getting food and medicine to affected citizens (U.S. Department of the Interior, 2007a). As an administrator, you face a daunting task of taking care of your citizens. What will be your priorities in the aftermath of the disaster?

1. *How will you proceed to alleviate hunger and illness in the community?* Food and water will have to be imported from outside the town in order to sustain the surviving population. Medicine and medical personnel will have to be imported into the area from surrounding areas, or injured and sick individuals will need to be transported to medical facilities outside the town.

2. *What resources should you obtain?* The mayor will need to get shelter, food, water, medical supplies, and medical personnel to assist with the survivors. In addition, the mayor will need to assign personnel to recover bodies and arrange burial so that disease and illnesses do not become an issue among the survivors.

3. *What plan of action do you have for displaced residents?* The mayor should have temporary shelters built as soon as possible. For those that can go to another municipality to stay with family or friends, transportation should be provided to move those individuals so that they will have a place to stay. Any resident housing that can be repaired quickly should be given first priority so that the need for temporary shelters will be decreased. Additionally, the mayor will need to make sure that the victims will have financial assistance so that they can be provided relief and be able to rebuild their lives. Financial assistance will probably have to be sought from external entities at the state or federal level of government.

Key Issues Raised from the Case Study

The disaster was caused by the privately owned South Fork Dam that was not maintained properly. The dam's maintenance was crucial for preventing harm to the town since the town's residences and businesses were all constructed along a valley that would funnel water down toward the town with a great amount of force. Ordinary buildings and even commercial buildings would have difficulty withstanding such an onslaught of water pressure hitting the structures. A flood of this magnitude would have washed away even the most modern of structures. The speed of the water would also limit the amount of time that the citizens would have to evacuate the area safely.

Enforcement and monitoring are required even on private property if infrastructure is located on it that will impact the safety of the local population. Additionally, building properties on the riverbanks where floods are prone to occur should be avoided. This case study demonstrates why planning and zoning efforts are so critical to municipalities. With proper planning and zoning, the homes and businesses could have been located away from the floodplain areas around the waterways.

Items of Note

The Johnstown flood killed over 2,209 people and left many citizens homeless (Johnstown Flood Museum, 2012). The blame for the dam's failure was placed largely on the hunting and fishing lodge that was responsible for the condition of the South Fork Dam (U.S. Department of the Interior, 2007a).

Great Lakes Storm, 1913

Stage 1 of the Disaster

You are a city manager of a large Midwestern industrial town and port city. On November 7, you are surprised to find that the temperature is rapidly dropping, winds are increasing, and rain has started to fall. The winds are now gusting up to 40 miles per hour, causing trees and communication lines to be toppled over (Ohio Historical Society, 2006). In addition, you now have an increase in freezing rain and wet snow that is beginning to build up, making transportation hazardous (Ohio Historical Society, 2006).

1. *What is your plan of action?* As city manager you should locate all of your available resources and personnel for cold weather emergencies. In addition, you should contact the local media to advise citizens to take precautionary measures against inclement, cold weather, such as wrapping water pipes, ensuring that resources are at hand to properly keep their house heated, and having plenty of provisions for food and water.

2. *What resources do you feel that you need at this point?* Since the bad weather can paralyze communications and transportation, you need to be sure to have the proper resources on hand to clear the roads as well as repair any telecommunication lines. Additionally, shelters should be made ready to receive homeless persons that will need a place to stay during the cold snap. Medical facilities and personnel should be placed on full alert for potential patients.

Stage 2 of the Disaster

You are receiving reports that ships in the channel are sinking, and you now have a food shortage, since all the dairy and food supplies are stuck on railroad cars that are inaccessible (Ohio Historical Society, 2006).

1. *What is your plan of action?* The city manager should direct any maritime rescue units to perform search and rescue operations for ships that are sinking in the channel. A high priority should be given to both getting the communication lines repaired and clearing the roads so that food and water shipments can be made to people that are unable to get supplies. Consider using any type of transportation that does not need roads to make food and water deliveries to residents.

2. *What is your communication plan?* The city manager should send out communication to all ships that are in the channel to dock until the storm has passed. In addition, the city manager should attempt to communicate with surrounding areas to see what resources are available to help with infrastructure repair as well as attempt to gain more resources from other local municipalities and state and federal entities.

3. *How will you contend with the ships in the harbor that are beginning to sink?* The city manager should begin to recruit any engineers or salvage experts that can be found to assist with repairing ships that are currently sinking. In addition, if harbor tugboats are available, those ships can be used to tow any distressed vessel to port until repairs can be made.

Stage 3 of the Disaster

The winds have now picked up and are gusting to over 74 miles per hour (Dallaire, 2004). The latest report from the harbor is not good. You have learned that 235 sailors have now died and 12 ships have sunk (Ohio Historical Society, 2006). The good news is that farmers are delivering dairy and food supplies with sleds drawn by horses (Ohio Historical Society, 2006). You have asked the Boy Scouts to clear fire hydrants of snow in case fires break out. Fire is a concern because several buildings have collapsed and the roads are impassable (Ohio Historical Society, 2006).

1. *What resources do you need at this point?* The city manager should seek out medical supplies and medical personnel as well as morticians to contend with the rising death toll. Clearing the roads is becoming very critical, not only for food and water deliveries, but also to allow first responders to respond to fires that could break out and allow passage for ambulances that need to get to patients. You will need to redouble your efforts on getting assistance to the harbors for the ships that are in danger of sinking and evacuating crews that are freezing and starving to death.
2. *What other organizations should you seek assistance from at this point?* The city manager should focus on recovery once the storm passes. There may need to be temporary shelters constructed as well as more provisions being transported into your city. To do this, the city manager should reach out to organizations such as the American Red Cross, as well as federal and state agencies that can assist the community in times of need.
3. *What areas should you focus on for assistance to the citizens and ships after the storm has occurred?* The city manager will need to focus on water, food, medical, and housing needs for the citizens. For the sailors, the city manager will need to provide assistance getting those individuals food and water as well as assistance in getting their ships repaired or salvaged in order to clear the harbor.

Key Issues Raised from the Case Study

The Great Lakes storm was one of the largest storms to ever hit the Great Lakes. With hurricane-force winds, it caused 250 fatalities and $5 million in damage (McLeod, 2011). The case study illustrates the need to prepare for isolation in the event of a major winter storm. Stockpiles of food, medical supplies, and fuel should be kept on hand in case transportation links are cut for any length of time. Additionally, it is important to establish an effective communication link with all entities in and around the area so that preventative measures can effectively be taken. The single biggest failure in this case study was not maintaining a stockpile of supplies for such an event. The second biggest failure was not ordering the ships out of the area before the full force of the storm was felt, nor evacuating the sailors from the damaged ships. However, the modes of communication available in 1913 may have prevented effective notification to the ships that were out of port.

Items of Note

Twelve ships were lost and five remain unaccounted for to this day (Dallaire, 2004).

Banqiao Dam Flood, China, 1975
Stage 1 of the Disaster

You are an emergency management coordinator in charge of safety and disaster management for the Henan Province in China. The Banqiao Dam and many other dams were constructed beginning in the 1950s under a government program (Watkins, 2012). In your province, the area is considered rural, with many small towns that are densely populated compared to cities in Europe or the United States (Zhao, 2012). In many towns along the river system, telephones are the exception to the rule, with most towns having no modern means of communication (Zhao, 2012). On the Banqiao Dam in particular, your government has received assistance from the Soviet Union to help reinforce and modify the dam to make it stronger than what was originally designed (Watkins, 2012). You are confident that the dam is sufficient since the modifications have taken place and the dam has been developed for a 1,000-year flood (Watkins, 2012). It is now August and you have just seen the forecast, which is projecting a typhoon that is coming toward Henan Province.

1. *What is your plan of action?* The emergency management coordinator should begin to get estimates on how much water the storm could potentially produce to see if the dams could contain that much water. Additionally, since you do not have a reliable or a limited modern communication system, you will need to establish some type of reliable and fast communication system.
2. *What is your communication plan?* With the possibility of a typhoon coming toward your province, you should communicate with the towns along the river that there is a storm coming and that each town should have an evacuation plan available and publicly posted so the community will know what to do if evacuation is necessary. In addition, you should have a system

of runners or couriers on standby in case there are problems with the dam's capacity, which would allow water to overflow or ultimately break the dam. Having time to evacuate is critical for a town's survival if something does go wrong with the dam. Furthermore, you need to establish close contact with personnel at the dam, local and central government figures, and personnel that monitor weather conditions.

3. *What resources should you begin to mobilize?* With only a limited modern telecommunication system available, you will need to recruit and train couriers who can deliver notices to evacuate to the towns and villages that will be impacted if a flood does occur. You will also need to assist towns with evacuation plans for their communities, which can increase the survival rate of their citizens.

Stage 2 of the Disaster

The rain is falling more than was originally forecasted, and instead of a 1,000-year flood, which the dam was designed to contain, the rainfall is for a 2,000-year flood, which is far above what the dam was constructed to withhold (Watkins, 2012). In addition, you have learned that telegraph lines (which are the only forms of communication to the dam) have been severed (Watkins, 2012). There has been a request to the dam to open the floodgates for a controlled release of water, but this as of yet has not occurred, since the communication lines have been cut. You have the additional problem of the timing of the storm since many people are at home asleep and there is no electronic communication system in existence to notify these residents that danger is imminent. This can potentially increase how many residents are killed if they cannot be notified they need to evacuate quickly.

1. *What is your plan of action?* You need to immediately get your couriers and other open lines of communication to the towns that will be impacted by a flood so that there will be time to wake up the population areas and have them evacuate to safety. Since you have not heard back from the dam about controlled water releases, you must conclude that there is no effective communication with the dam personnel that could potentially alert the populous.

2. *What is your communication plan?* The communication plan should be to alert the communities and attempt to establish communication with the dam itself by any means possible. You may need to assign a courier to make contact with the dam if there does not appear to be an open and reliable line of communication. Officials of both the local communities and the central governments should be contacted at this time to notify them that you are giving the towns along the river notice to evacuate for safety. This would be a good point in time to notify the governments that you will need additional resources to evacuate the populous, and that there may be a need to send telecommunications engineers to the dam to reestablish communications.

3. *What resources should you begin to mobilize?* The couriers should be mobilized, and any type of telecommunication engineers to get limited communications back up and active are essential to the emergency management plan. In addition, vehicles that can evacuate the population should be highly sought, as well as getting medical resources notified and mobilized for potential patients.

Stage 3 of the Disaster

You have now been notified that the Banqiao Dam has failed. You have also learned that the Shimantan Dam has failed, which is upstream of the Banqiao Dam, and has caused water to come rushing toward the Banqiao Dam (Watkins, 2012). These events have now been climaxed with 62 dams that have failed, causing 6 billion m³ of water to be released in total, which has caused a massive wave 6.2 miles wide and 23 feet high rushing down the river at 31 miles per hour (Xinhua, 2005; Mufson, 1997; Watkins, 2012).

1. *What is your plan of action?* You must find a way to evacuate all of the towns along all of the rivers as quickly as possible through whatever means possible. Any available helicopters for search and rescue will be needed since the flood is so powerful and widespread.
2. *What is your communication plan?* At this point you must communicate the evacuation order to all towns that could be impacted. In addition, you should contact all medical resources to mobilize them since those resources will now be needed. The government should be contacted to request any assistance in the form of search and rescue personnel and equipment. Structural engineers should be contacted to see if anything can be potentially done to block remaining water from escaping dams that have already failed by adding additional barriers to the damaged areas.
3. *What resources should you begin to mobilize?* All search and rescue personnel and equipment should now be mobilized as well as medical resources and engineering support. You should begin to take an inventory of all facilities that can house medical resources as well as housing displaced residents. With such a large population, you will also need to find resources for food, water, sanitation, and medicine for those individuals.

Stage 4 of the Disaster

You have now learned that communications were completely inadequate or had failed completely. You have received word that signal flares were not seen, telegraphs were never sent or completed in transmission, and several couriers were lost in the rush of water. In addition, other dams have failed or have been bombed by the military to reverse the water flow, communication lines are nonexistent, electricity has been lost over wide parts of the region, transportation lines have been completely severed, and you have over a million people who are isolated by floodwaters (Watkins, 2012; Navarro, 2008). After several days it has now been reported that over 200,000 are dead from the flood, with several communities wiped from the face of the earth (Navarro, 2008; Watkins, 2012).

1. *What is your plan of action?* You will need to get the million or so people out of the isolated area or get some type of transportation line open to them so that food and other supplies can be sent to them before famine occurs. The infrastructure will need to be fixed quickly so that supplies, people, and engineers can begin to repair the dams and evacuate anyone in need from the area. Another issue that will now have to be dealt with is collecting and storing the corpses so that drinking water and other areas are not contaminated. This will require facilities that are undamaged to be designated as a repository so that bodies can be stored and eventually identified.

2. *What is your communication plan?* Until the communication infrastructure is operable, you will need to rely on couriers to send and receive any type of messages. Therefore, a priority should be placed on getting engineers working to restore the telecommunication lines and switching. This will also require getting the power restored since telecommunications is reliant on electricity in order to function.

3. *What resources should you begin to mobilize?* Until transportation infrastructure such as roads and railroads is repaired, you will have to rely on aircraft or boats to deliver supplies and perform search and rescue operations. Medical resources will be needed not only to treat the wounded, but also to treat individuals for disease that could have come into contact with contaminated drinking water. Safe drinking water must be made available to all of the displaced persons, support personnel, and individuals that are cut off and isolated by floodwaters.

Key Issues Raised from the Case Study

This case study presents an emergency manager with a communications nightmare. The communication that exists is rudimentary, and the mode of communication (telegraphs) is limited to those communities that have access to such devices. China in 1975 is very different from China in 2012. China in 1975 would be considered a developing nation since the majority of the population in rural areas did not have access to telephones or any type of electronic communications that were available to residents in cities. The situation today in many developing countries is much the same, and emergency managers in this type of situation will need to develop redundant and robust strategies for communicating with their governmental agencies as well as the population that will be impacted. Conditions seen in this case study in the forms of communication mirror the communication gaps that existed in the Newfoundland hurricane in 1775. In addition, government officials appeared to be overconfident in the dams that were constructed, which proved to be fatal since there were no apparent emergency management plans in place if a flood were to occur. Emergency managers should always prepare for the worst-case scenario and be prepared to execute their plans to prevent or at least diminish the tragedy that can befall a community.

Items of Note

Eleven million residents were affected by the flood, and the reconstruction of the Banqiao Dam was not completed until 1993 (Watkins, 2012; Mufson, 1997). Additionally, more residents were killed by epidemics and famine than by the flood itself (Navarro, 2008).

Chapter 5

Case Studies: Disasters from Natural Forces—Tornadoes

Natchez Tornado, Mississippi, 1840

Stage 1 of the Disaster

You are a county commissioner for a port city in the southern region of the United States. On May 7, you are inspecting a county road when you notice a big funnel-shaped cloud over the horizon (Tornado Project, 2007).

1. *What is your plan of action?* Your first plan of action should be to warn everyone in your area to take cover since a tornado is visible and coming in the direction of your community. Second, you should activate your emergency plan for tornadoes if one exists. Third, you should put all county and local personnel on alert as well as start identifying the locations of resources that you may need at a later time.
2. *What is your communication plan?* Your communication plan should consist of sending out alerts to your community to take cover and to notify all first responders as well as county and local officials that a tornado has been seen and is coming in the direction of your community.
3. *What resources should you begin to mobilize?* In this early stage of the disaster, you should mobilize personnel to get word to the community that a tornado is on the way and that the citizens should take shelter immediately.

Medical resources and personnel should be identified and put on standby for any possible casualties that may result from a tornado.

Stage 2 of the Disaster

The town of Natchez has been hit forcefully by a Force 5 tornado (Tornado Project, 2007). Buildings and residential dwellings were completely flattened. As one of the chief administrators, how will you attempt to protect the citizenry of the town?

1. *What is your plan of action?* First, you should get an accurate assessment of what parts of Natchez were damaged or destroyed so you can send your first responders to where help is needed the most. The second step that needs to be taken is to mobilize your first responders. There will be several people that need to be pulled from debris and rubble. Third, your medical personnel and facilities need to be activated and ready to receive casualties, because with that much damage, there will be injuries among your citizens.

2. *What is your communication plan?* You need better intelligence on the situation, so you need to set up a command post where messages can be received and sent to the surrounding areas. Also, if it is possible, you should notify other counties or localities in the area that a tornado could potentially be heading in their direction.

3. *What resources should you try to attain for your county?* If possible, you should try to accumulate additional resources in the form of more first responders, medical assets, and engineers to help shore up structures that are in danger of collapsing or to assist with rescue efforts of persons that are trapped underneath rubble and debris.

Stage 3 of the Disaster

The town of Natchez has had approximately 48 people killed at this point. The tornado is beginning to move down the river and is beginning to sink a number of ships that are tied up along the river (Tornado Project, 2007b). The winds are so strong that the ships and their crews are literally being flipped up in the air, and then the crews end up drowning in the river (Nelson, 2004).

1. *What is your action plan?* If at all possible, you should attempt to evacuate all persons that are on board the ships. Additionally, you need to try to get as many people as possible to shelter that are in the path of the tornado. The tornado still has force behind its winds and is still quite capable of killing or injuring people.

2. *What is your communication plan?* The main concern right now should be to communicate with persons that are in the path of the tornado to alert them that a tornado is coming and that they should evacuate the area.

Stage 4 of the Disaster

The tornado has killed an additional 269 people along the river, along with the destruction of several ships in the river (Tornado Project, 2007). Your hospitals are overflowing with wounded as the count of injured persons now stands at 109 (Tornado Project, 2007). The demand for medical care is overwhelming your current resources. In addition, you have no electricity and you have no penicillin nor any other antibiotics for your wounded.* How will you contend with the lack of medical resources?

1. *What is your plan of action?* Since your medical facilities are over capacity, it will be necessary to try to convert existing structures that can be used as temporary hospitals for the wounded. Your first responders will need to go to the river and see if there is anyone that can be saved from the ships that have been sunk or damaged.
2. *What is your communication plan?* Your communication plan at this point should be to coordinate with other localities to get additional resources as fast as possible in the form of medical assets and more first responders. In addition, you want to make sure that families are contacted and the dead start to be identified.
3. *What resources should you mobilize?* Any engineers and construction workers should be mobilized to begin work on restoring infrastructure and ensuring that displaced persons have shelter. Logistics in the form of water and food should also be attained as soon as possible. Since the river is the lifeline of your city, you will also want to make sure that it is cleared of obstructions and that ships that have been sunk or damaged are not blocking the river channel.
4. *What should your next focus be for your plan of action?* Your focus should be rebuilding, burying your dead, and making sure your displaced persons have food, shelter, and water. The river and roads leading to Natchez need to be open since that is the only way you can get additional resources.

Key Issues Raised from the Case Study

Whether or not the ships' crews could have been evacuated from the area effectively is unknown. What is known is that more people died along the river than from where the tornado struck in the actual town (Nelson, 2004). From the information gathered on the case study, there is no indication that any tornado shelters existed where residents could have taken shelter. In 1840 there was no Doppler radar or weather forecasting that could have produced an early warning for the citizens or sailors, which would have allowed them to take refuge before the tornado struck. For underdeveloped areas these remain issues that administrators may face.

---

* Modern medicines such as penicillin did not exist until at least 1910 (asphenamine). There is always a possibility that during times of crisis modern medicine will not be available, so a contingency plan should be created to deal with such an event.

Currently, science cannot predict where and when tornadoes will touch down. Until science can predict such occurrences accurately, administrators will always need to have a plan to have their citizens take shelter on the possibility that a tornado can inflict damage on a projected pathway.

In the case of Natchez, there was no effective way to communicate with the residents on the river where the tornado chose as a pathway for destruction (Nelson, 2004). The takeaway for all administrators should be the importance of communication for residents during a disaster response situation. Without proper notification, effective evacuation is impossible.

Items of Note

The single tornado that hit Natchez is still listed as the second deadliest in U.S. history (Tornado Project, 2007).

Goliad Tornado, Texas, 1902

Stage 1 of the Disaster

You are the city administrator of a very small town. Services and resources are limited and you have a restricted budget for municipal facilities. On May 18, you are notified that a tornado has just touched down at 3:35 p.m. on the bank of the San Antonio River (Victoria Internet Providers, 2007).

1. *What is your communication plan?* The city administrator should attempt to get communication out to the residents telling them to take shelter immediately. In addition, all first responders should be put on alert as well as informing the city council that a potential disaster could be eminent.
2. *What is your plan of action?* The city administrator should take an inventory of all of the resources that the city currently has at its disposal for an emergency. The city administrator should also contact other cities to see if resources can be obtained, as well as seek permission to transport any casualties to their medical facilities since your city has very little in the way of proper hospital care.
3. *What resources will you attempt to get?* The city administrator should mobilize first responders and medical personnel as quickly as possible for the damage that will potentially occur. In addition, the city administrator should find as many areas that can shelter residents as possible.

Stage 2 of the Disaster

As the tornado moves through your city, a number of houses and businesses are flattened. You observe the African-American Methodist Church being destroyed by the tornado (Victoria Internet Providers, 2007). The tornado has now passed through your city, leaving death and destruction in its path. How will you contend with the devastation that was wrought?

1. *What is your plan of action?* Since the city has no hospital, the city administrator will need to designate a facility to serve this purpose. The city administrator needs to direct search and rescue personnel to find anyone that may be trapped under the rubble or injured. The next step is to triage the injured persons at the designated hospital, have medical personnel take care of the worst injured persons first and then, if possible, transport those that are in stable condition to surrounding communities' medical facilities.

2. *What resources will you attempt to get?* Shelter, medical supplies, food, and water will be the top items to gather for a city that has been hit by a natural disaster on this scale. There are many wounded, so personnel that can treat injuries will be critical. Additionally, at some point getting communications reestablished with the surrounding communities as well as effective transportation will be essential.

3. *What cooperation will you seek and from whom will you seek help?* Since you do not have proper facilities, you turn the Goliad County Courthouse into a temporary hospital and morgue (Victoria Internet Providers, 2007). Any infrastructure that has been damaged will need to be repaired, and to do so Goliad will need communities to donate supplies and workers to assist with those repairs. Additionally, you will need to find medical assistance and first responders from surrounding communities.

Key Issues Raised from the Case Study

This tornado resulted in 114 people killed (50 were killed in the Methodist Church alone), 230 people injured, and an estimated $50,000 worth of damage (in 1902 dollars) (Victoria Internet Providers, 2007). Small cities and towns such as Goliad have limited resources available to them. Therefore, it is more important for those types of organizations to have agreements and arrangements with surrounding organizations to provide support in times of crisis.

Goliad did not appear to have a plan (or a hardened shelter) to provide safety to its residents against tornadoes. Construction around the early 1900s largely consisted of wooden structures that would not have withstood tornadoes. In Texas, tornadoes are common and cities in tornado zones should have an emergency action plan to contend with sheltering residents, obtaining resources (i.e., medical, first responders, etc.) from other entities, as well as having an effective communication plan. The officials in Goliad did make adjustments to the lack of facilities and used the courthouse, for example, as a stopgap solution to a deficiency that the city had with facilities in a time of crisis.

Items of Note

The 1902 Goliad tornado was one of the most deadly tornadoes in Texas and ranks 10th on the deadliest tornadoes in the United States (Dan, 2003).

Tri-State Tornado, 1925

Stage 1 of the Disaster

You are the director of FEMA. The date is March 18 and three states are experiencing significant storm activity.

1. *What is your current plan of action?* One of the first actions that the director needs to take is to make contact with the governors of the three states where storm activity is taking place and determine if there are any plans to contend with natural disasters. In addition, the director should assess where federal resources are located for emergency management purposes and put certain personnel on notice that they may be deployed to a disaster area. The director should also make sure that he or she has sufficient communication pathways established to receive incoming reports on weather and needs that may arise from the three different states.

2. *What agencies should you contact for coordinated assistance?* The director should coordinate with all federal agencies that can provide any type of assistance or resources in case of an emergency (e.g., Department of War,* Department of the Interior, etc.). At the state level, it is important for the director to keep in constant contact with the governor's office in each state about the situation as well as what resources each state can assemble in times of crisis.

Stage 2 of the Disaster

You are now receiving reports that there are several tornadoes that are occurring across three states. A town named Murphysboro has been completely obliterated by a tornado (Ishman, 2001).

1. *What resources do you need to mobilize?* As director you need to see how many medical and recovery teams you can assemble from federal agencies. In addition, the director can put a call out to other state and local agencies that may be able to send additional resources to Murphysboro. Food, water, shelters, medical supplies, and excavation equipment will need to be sent to Murphysboro as soon as possible.

---

* The Department of War would become the Department of Defense in 1947.

2. *What is your communication plan?* The director needs to stay in constant contact with on-site supervisors to notify them of the situation as it develops so that more resources can be deployed if necessary. Additionally, the director should maintain contact with other federal agencies as well as state officials to ensure that the efforts are coordinated and effective.

Stage 3 of the Disaster

You now have received reports that approximately 250 people have died in Murphysboro, another 500 are wounded, and fires have broken out across the city causing property damage (Ishman, 2001).

1. *What resources do you need to mobilize at this point?* Search and rescue teams will become even more critical to survivors who may be trapped underneath the rubble of destroyed buildings. Priority should be given to deploy search and rescue teams and obtain medical supplies. Any type of firefighting apparatus that can be assembled and deployed to Murphysboro should also be given a high priority so that more buildings are not destroyed and those surviving buildings can provide shelter for anyone that may be displaced. Besides food and water, there also needs to be some thought given to requesting security forces to the area to prevent criminal activity from occurring.
2. *What should be your next plan of action?* Once the search and rescue phase of the operation is completed, the recovery of bodies will be the next step, as well as constructing any type of temporary housing that may be required. If the wounded can be moved to other hospitals in the area, they should be transported to alleviate the burden on local medical facilities.

Key Issues Raised from the Case Study

There were 695 people killed and 2,027 people injured by the tornadoes as well as the resulting destruction to Murphysboro, which itself had 234 citizens killed (National Weather Service, Paducah, Kentucky, Forecast Office, 2010). Over 15,000 homes were destroyed, which impacted 3 different states, 13 counties, and over 19 communities (National Weather Service, Paducah, Kentucky, Forecast Office, 2010).

Forces of nature such as tornadoes are unavoidable. Precautionary measures are the only measures that can be taken, which may or may not be successful in certain types of situations. For example, in tornado-prone areas, local government has the ability to construct shelters for residents in times of a tornado. However, this type of action will be completely dependent upon whether the municipality has the resources to construct such shelters. Government agencies with limited resources should forge agreements and alliances with other surrounding organizations that can be called upon to provide support in times of crisis.

Items of Note

The tri-state tornado was spread out over three states: Indiana, Illinois, and Missouri (Ishman, 2001).

Chapter 6

Case Studies: Disasters from Natural Forces—Earthquakes and Volcanoes

San Francisco Earthquake, 1906

Stage 1 of the Disaster

You are the assistant city manager for a large metropolitan port city. You are in bed when suddenly you are thrown onto the floor. Items are falling off shelves, pictures falling off the walls, the floor and bed are trembling, and the sounds are otherworldly. The day is Wednesday and the time is 5:12 a.m. (USGS, 2006). You have just experienced the first shock wave of a massive earthquake. Twenty seconds later you are violently shaken by a second series of tremors, which leads you to believe that the world is coming to an end. You realize that you must get to city hall to take action steps.

1. *What is your first action step as the assistant city manager?* The first step of any public official is to determine exactly what has occurred to your organization. In this case, an earthquake has hit your city and you first need to determine how much damage has been done and which locations have been impacted by the earthquake. As with any situation that requires leadership, the responsible public official needs to be in contact with his or her subordinates in order to gather information and relay orders to contend with the situation.

In this scenario, city hall would be the most likely municipal complex to set up a command post to gather intelligence on the situation and coordinate first responder efforts. However, there may be occasions in which the responsible city official cannot get to the command post for one reason or another and where communications are not functional. For these reasons, it is valuable for the organization to set up a chain of command in case the primary responsible organization official is unable to lead the entity through the crisis.

2. *What public organizations are at your disposal to contend with an apparent earthquake?* As a responsible public administrator, it is always important to know not only what types of first responder assets are available, but also how to contact and implement those resources if necessary. During a time of crisis, the public administrator in charge of a situation will need to be able to designate certain types of resources to contend for a variety of situations that could occur. In this case study, an earthquake has just occurred and the assistant city manager will need to mobilize the fire department, police department, medical services, and public works department.

   For first responder purposes, it would seem apparent to mobilize the fire department, police department, and medical services to contend with injuries and engage in recovery operations. But why would one need to mobilize the public works department? First, the public works department usually has access to heavy equipment that can be used for recovery operations for injured persons that may be trapped under rubble and debris. Second, the public works department may be required to repair (or in some cases shut off) natural gas lines, water lines, sewer lines, and electrical infrastructure components. As will be seen later in the case study, this particular municipality will have severe issues with damaged infrastructure. A public organization should plan a rally point and multiple ways to contact its workers in case of a power outage or a communications blackout.

3. *How will you prioritize your limited resources?* In any organization there will be limited resources. Therefore, as a public administrator you will need to prioritize how those resources will be allocated. For example, if the fire department is primarily tasked to find and rescue survivors from a collapsed bridge, then those resources will not be fighting fires that could have resulted from the earthquake. A public official will have difficult choices in the decision-making process, but life is more valuable than property, which makes the decision to allocate the resources toward the bridge survivors somewhat easier. However, if the fires were also resulting in injuries and death, the decision-making process could be far more complicated for the public administrator. So the basic question becomes how to rank your priorities (e.g., lives over property) to maximize your resources more effectively.

4. *What will be your means of communication to other public organizations and the citizenry of your municipality?* At this particular point in the case study there is no indication that you have electronic capabilities, power,

or any other type of modern convenience. So as a public administrator, what do you have available to you at this point? The answer is that you have access to municipal employees, and you could potentially have access to civil service organizations. This pool of available human capital can operate as communication relays to various parts of the citizenry and other parts of your organization that need to relay orders and receive intelligence on the situation. While this method is not a modern approach, it can work in large municipalities with dense populations when no other means of communication is available.

Stage 2 of the Disaster

You arrive at city hall and realize that the earthquake has leveled most of the buildings in the city and thousands of citizens are trapped beneath rubble. You now realize that there are two other major problems plaguing your city administration. The first is the Salinas River, which had been diverted by the earthquake and is now flooding different parts of your city (U.S. News Rank, 2012). The second consists of a number of fires that have broken out across your city (*New York Times*, 1906).

1. *How will you now allocate your resources?* As discussed earlier, a decision on how resources will be allocated is critical. You only have so many employees in the fire department, police department, medical services, and public works department. Some of your citizens will die from their injuries if they are not found in time, and others could potentially be killed by flooding from the Salinas River or from the fires that have broken out across the city. If possible, volunteers could be used to help find survivors in the rubble. This will free up some of your first responders to fight fires and perform rescue operations in the flooded parts of the city. A smaller group of firefighters that are trained for recovery operations could work in coordination with your public works department—since they have the access to heavy digging equipment—to free survivors that are trapped in the rubble. In the meantime, the police could patrol the various areas that were impacted by the earthquakes, both to stop criminal activity and to search for injured citizens.

2. *What is the priority of emergency services that need to be provided?* The priority should be to find the survivors in the rubble since many of these victims will require hospitalization due to blood loss, concussions, or internal injuries. Time is critical to saving lives, and therefore getting injured parties to the hospital is paramount. Second, the fires will need to be controlled to protect citizens, and as many existing structures as possible will be need to provide shelter for the citizens that have lost their housing and have no other place to go. In addition, you will need to be able to provide water and sanitation for your citizens, which requires your fire department and public works department to keep as much infrastructure intact as possible.

3. *What additional resources may you seek to contend with the new emerging problems?* At this point, the lead public administrator should contact the federal authorities, state authorities, and other local administrators to get more resources into the area. It is very common for municipalities to have a mutual arrangement service agreements with other municipalities made prior to any disaster. Unfortunately for this municipality, there were no prior agreements in place, so the city administrators must request additional resources after the earthquake has caused the damage.

Stage 3 of the Disaster

You now realize that the fires are taking a great toll on your city, you have several natural gas lines that are broken, and you have a rash of fires from a combination of campfires and arson that are spreading quickly. One other problem is that most of your water mains are broken due to the earthquake, making fighting fires extremely difficult (*New York Times*, 1906).

1. *How will you deal with the shortage of water?* Keep in mind that you may not have any modern firefighting equipment available to you. Furthermore, what little electrical output is available from your damaged infrastructure must be reserved for your public works personnel, who will need machinery like welders and cranes to repair water lines and other strategic areas of the city's infrastructure. Therefore, plan for the possibility that no water will be available through the city's water mains, and you must rely upon fire pumper equipment to transport water to the trouble spots. These fire pumpers will have to be refilled from a large pool of water, such as a reservoir, river, or bay. Filling fire pumpers in this manner will take more time and energy for your personnel to fight the fire, but it may be the only means available in this type of situation. The other modern-day alternative is to use chemicals to fight the fires, which can now be done with aircraft. In addition, the public officials will now need to devote resources to catch arsonists that are starting fires around the city.
2. *What priority will you give to fixing the city's infrastructure (i.e., water mains and natural gas lines)?* Natural gas lines can explode, so it is imperative that those lines be completely shut down since fires are raging across the municipality. Electrical power will be necessary to restore in order for the water lines to be repaired so that the fires can be fought more effectively. In addition, the electrical lines could cause additional death, injury, and property damage, so it would be critical to fix these lines next. The third lines of infrastructure to fix would be water lines, which could then be used in the firefighting effort, as well as dispense water to citizens, which is crucial to survival. The last lines to be repaired would be the sewer lines since sanitation can be dealt with on a temporary basis by digging latrines or using portable outhouses.

Stage 4 of the Disaster

At this point, everything you have tried has failed to contain the fire. Your mayor has now issued an order to shoot looters on sight. This results in over 500 people being killed. The military attempted to create fire breaks by using black powder, dynamite, and artillery barrages. This action douses the fire but results in more buildings being destroyed (PR Newswire US, 2006).

1. *How do you interface with the military?* The arrival of the military introduces a political aspect that did not exist when the situation began. The municipal officials need to agree with the military on who is in charge and how the military's resources can be best deployed to contain the situation. At this point, the situation is bordering on anarchy and the military has taken over command and control of the decision-making process. In the case study, many of the looters that were shot were, in fact, ordinary citizens attempting to gather their own belongings after their residences were destroyed. The case study provides an insight to where due process for looters is not necessarily being employed by the police or the military. How does a municipal official attempt to regain control over the situation? While bringing in the military had some advantages, there were also significant disadvantages. Military personnel are in general not trained as policemen, which can introduce problems when contending with civilians in an emergency management situation.

2. *What steps need to be taken to ensure that law and order is being enforced judicially and correctly?* City officials will need to ensure that military personnel that are deployed in this type of situation understand that civilians do have a right to due process and that shooting looters should be a last resort, not a first one. In addition, the municipal officials in the particular case could have redeployed their police officers to accompany the military on patrols to where their judgment and training could potentially alleviate soldiers shooting alleged looters.

3. *What type of communication plan should you have in place?* At this point communication is very fragmented. The municipal officials will need to devise a new communication plan to communicate with the resources that are deployed to work on the different issues at hand, as well as the citizenry to state where food, shelter, and medical assistance can be found.

4. *Do you agree with the mayor's order to shoot looters on sight?* If the resources are on hand to send active patrols with troops and police through the city to show a presence, then the order should not have been given. In a large emergency management situation such as the case study earthquake there are multiple situations that are ongoing (e.g., search and rescue, repairing of infrastructure, people recovering their possessions, etc.). Declaring martial law would have also had drawbacks since there are so many people without

housing or any place to go. There needs to be a plan to arrest suspected looters and have them taken to a temporary holding pen for detention and processing.

Stage 5 of the Disaster

The full impact is now starting to set in with you and the rest of your municipal staff. Not only has the majority of your city been destroyed by earthquake or fire (80%), but you now have 225,000 to 300,000 people (USGS, 2006) that have been displaced, $6.5 billion in damage (2006 estimated damage) (Evans, 2007), and over 3,000 people that have been killed (Berkley Seismological Lab, 2007).

1. *Now that the initial emergency has passed, what are your priorities for resources?* The immediate problem you face is an ongoing search and rescue operation for survivors as well as ensuring food, water, shelter, and medical assistance are provided to those citizens that need them. Secondary concerns should be to call in additional resources from other organizations, get an effective communication system up and running, and complete repairs to your infrastructure.

2. *How will you shelter that many people temporarily?* There are several methods to house people temporarily. One method is to construct temporary housing such as tents. Another method is to have those citizens removed to other municipalities where temporary shelters could be staged (e.g., arenas, schools, etc.). Another alternative is to have mobile trailers set up for temporary housing until better accommodations can be located.

3. *What is your recovery plan?* First and foremost, a logistical plan has to be in place or formulated to get food, water, medical supplies, and housing to those who are in need. Next, there will need to be a plan in place to inspect the infrastructure to ensure that the repairs that were made were more than a temporary stopgap measure. Infrastructure such as critical roads, bridges, and sewer lines can now be focused on for your recovery plan. Removing debris and rubble will also need to be addressed since new resident housing and potentially other damaged facilities will need to be constructed or repaired in order to move your temporary residents to more permanent structures. Last, there is a need to formulate a plan for future earthquakes to mitigate the damage and loss of life that could potentially occur. Ensure that supplies are positioned and stockpiled to facilitate quick distribution to municipalities and citizens in the event of a large emergency management situation.

4. *What other emergency may result from not recovering the dead quickly?* For sanitation reasons, corpses should be recovered to prevent the spread of disease through the remaining citizenry. This issue could further compound any strains on your medical resources that city officials are using to treat the injured.

Key Issues Raised from the Case Study

There is a great danger in letting the military act as a police force. While the military has discipline, soldiers are not trained in law enforcement, which can lead to additional problems. The military should be used as a police force as a last resort to restoring law and order. This case study also demonstrates the importance of repairing damaged infrastructure to assist not only in combating the disaster (i.e., fire) but also in preventing more problems from occurring (i.e., broken natural gas lines). In this case study, failure to repair the infrastructure quickly resulted in 80% of the city burning down. Whether or not the resources existed to repair such infrastructure is unknown, but what is known is that the earthquake damaged both water mains and natural gas lines, which caused more damage to occur. The failure to cap off natural gas lines quickly and repair the water mains in essence allowed the fires to spread unabated throughout the city. In addition, there were individuals who were not looting, but attempting to retrieve their own possessions from the rubble who were shot by the military (U.S. Department of the Interior, National Parks Service, 2010).

Items of Note

In addition to the monetary damage that resulted, many landmark buildings (e.g., the Palace Hotel) and scientific research laboratories were lost (Cooper, 2011; *New York Times*, 1906). Many residents and business owners burned down their structures through arson since insurance would not cover damage or destruction through earthquakes (Virtual Museum of the City of San Francisco, 2012).

Aleutian Island Earthquake, 1946

Stage 1 of the Disaster

You are the governor of Hawaii, an island territory in the United States.* On the morning of April 1, you have been alerted to an earthquake that has occurred in the Pacific Ocean (Joint Australian Tsunami Warning Center, 2008).

1. *What are the concerns you should have at this point?* The main concern for any island or coastal area is that a tsunami could result from an earthquake, which could devastate any population or infrastructure in a low-lying coastal region. An additional concern would be the evacuation of populations located in certain regions that may be impacted by a tsunami.
2. *What resources should you start to mobilize?* First responders should be activated as well as mobilizing any type of transportation that could be used

---

* Hawaii and Alaska were territories of the United States until they became states in 1959.

to assist in the evacuation of citizens in the areas that a tsunami could hit. National Guard units should be activated and temporary shelters should be made ready to receive citizens that have to be evacuated.

3. *What is your communication plan?* The citizens of your state need to be alerted to the possibility of a tsunami hitting the coastal areas of the state. The citizens need to be prepared to evacuate on short notice to temporary shelters that will be set up to receive anyone who has to evacuate.

Stage 2 of the Disaster

You have new information that a state on the western coast of the United States has just been hit with a tsunami that caused the destruction of a reinforced concrete Coast Guard lighthouse and the deaths of all of its occupants (Joint Australian Tsunami Warning Center, 2008). Five hours after the tsunami hit the western coast, the tsunami slammed into one of your islands, completely wrecked the beaches, and killed over 159 residents (Joint Australian Tsunami Warning Center, 2008).

1. *What is your plan of action?* The governor should have search and rescue teams deployed to search for any survivors that may still be in the area where the tsunami hit. Medical teams and resources should be mobilized to take care of the victims of the tsunami in addition to ensuring that displaced residents have shelter as well as provisions.

2. *What is your communication plan?* The governor needs to communicate with local government officials to ensure that assistance is arriving quickly and effectively to those communities in need of assistance. In addition, victims' families or next of kin need to be notified of citizens that have been killed or hospitalized.

3. *What resources do you need to mobilize?* Teams need to be mobilized for body recovery and removal of rubble. The rebuilding of infrastructure, homes, and businesses will need to commence after the initial recovery operations are completed.

Key Issues Raised from the Case Study

Once a warning has been sounded, government officials need to immediately communicate with low-lying communities in coastal areas to evacuate or have an evacuation plan ready. In addition, search and rescue resources need to be earmarked as soon as possible to respond to any population that could not evacuate the area successfully due to lack of transportation or infrastructure. In this case study the failure to successfully evacuate towns and cities in areas led to a loss of life where the tsunami impacted the coastline. Communication and effective planning are critical to successful disaster response to a crisis.

Items of Note

The Aleutian Island earthquake caused $26 million (1946 dollars) worth of damage to Hawaii and Alaska. The Aleutian Island earthquake led to the creation of the Pacific Tsunami Warning Center in Hawaii (Joint Australian Tsunami Warning Center, 2008).

Great Chilean Earthquake, 1960

Stage 1 of the Disaster

You are a director of a federal agency in the United States. On May 22 a 9.5-magnitude earthquake has just been reported off of the coast of Chile (USGS, 2008).

1. *What is your communication plan?* First, the state governments that have coastal areas in the Pacific Ocean should be notified of the earthquake and the potential tsunami that could impact their regions. Second, all of the people around low-lying coastal areas in the Pacific Ocean side of the United States should be warned of a possible tsunami, and those residents should be advised to evacuate areas that are vulnerable to floods from the coastline. Third, you should contact other federal agency department heads that could provide support in case a tsunami does in fact hit any area of the United States.

2. *What is your plan of action?* The first item of business is to determine what areas of the United States could be impacted by a tsunami. Second, you will need to pre-position any resources that may be useful in providing relief to areas that are impacted by a tsunami or have logistical transport that can reach areas quickly with assets if they are needed.

Stage 2 of the Disaster

Hawaii and the states along the Pacific Ocean are now reporting that a tsunami has hit their coastlines (Duke, 1960).

1. *What resources should you mobilize?* Any type of cargo plane that can reach the affected areas should be mobilized to transport food, water, and shelter as well as first responders that may be needed. In addition, any ships that can be sent to the region to assist with medical supplies or facilities should be sent to areas that have been heavily impacted by the tsunami. U.S. Navy vessels can be deployed to areas to supply a large amount of hospital resources and search and rescue assets to coastal cities.

2. *What organizations should you contact for assistance?* Usually there are several departments that can be contacted to give assistance at the federal level.

Departmental agencies such as the Department of Defense and Environmental Protection Agency have certain resources that will be critical to your success in contending with the emergency situation.

3. *What is your communication plan at this point in the emergency?* As a federal administrator, not only is it important to stay in touch with other federal agency department heads, but it is also important to keep in tight communication with state and local governments to relay information to and from those organizations. If communication is flowing freely, then resources can be directed to more devastated areas as information comes to your office.

Stage 3 of the Disaster

You have now learned that Hawaii has suffered 62 people killed and over $75 million worth of property damage from the tsunami (USGS, 2008).

1. *What is your plan of action?* Since Hawaii has been hit the hardest of all of the states, you want to make sure that adequate resources can get to the islands via aircraft to take care of any medical emergencies or shortage in basic essential supplies. In addition, you will want to send more first responders to Hawaii to perform search and rescue operations.

2. *What other organizations should you have involved with the recovery effort?* Quite a few nonprofit organizations can be utilized at this point to provide relief to citizens in addition to governmental entities. Organizations such as the American Red Cross perform many humanitarian operations across the country every year in times of natural disaster.

Key Issues Raised from the Case Study

An earthquake of that magnitude can have a devastating effect on a wide area. From South America to Hawaii, devastation was wrought upon a number of populated areas that resulted in people being killed, injured, and left homeless. An administrator must be prepared for this type of disaster if his or her organization potentially can be impacted by such an occurrence. To this effect, building codes must be more rigorous, supplies must be kept on hand for such an emergency, and resources to perform search and rescue operations must be maintained and ready to go at a moment's notice. Communication infrastructure as well as planning for tsunamis must be redundant and robust to anticipate any number of situations where one system or plan will fail, which will allow for another system or plan to take its place. It is difficult, if not impossible, to reinforce structures around the entire island to withstand a tsunami. Therefore, the only other action is to evacuate areas that could potentially be in danger of flooding to a higher elevation.

Items of Note

The great Chilean earthquake produced casualties all over the Pacific Ocean. In Chile alone, 1,655 people were killed, 3,000 were injured, and 2 million were left homeless (USGS, 2008). This earthquake was the most powerful to date, rating a 9.5 on the moment magnitude scale (MMS), and the tsunamis resulting from that earthquake not only affected Hawaii and Chile, but also impacted Japan, New Zealand, Australia, and Alaska (Pararas-Carayannis, 2011).

Good Friday Earthquake, 1964

Stage 1 of the Disaster

You are a state governor. At 6:15 p.m. on March 27—the Christian holiday of Good Friday (USGS Newsroom, 2004)—you are enjoying an evening at home with your relatives when you are notified by state officials that a port city in your state has been hit with a tremendous shock wave that appears to be caused by an earthquake.

1. *What is your first response to the situation?* The governor should be very concerned about a tidal wave hitting the coastal areas near highly populated areas. Since the earthquake hit near a port city, this city should be notified that a tidal wave could impact its area. If evacuation plans exist, they should be carried out in areas that have large populations in the shock wave area.

2. *What is your communication plan?* The communication plan should entail keeping in close contact with the state agencies under your jurisdiction, as well as local officials that are near the coastline. First responders that are state employees should be put on alert that they may be deployed to a possible tsunami disaster area within a certain time frame.

Stage 2 of the Disaster

You have received more information. The earthquake has measured 9.2 (USGS Newsroom, 2004) on the seismograph and lasted 4 minutes (USGS Newsroom, 2004). The earthquake hit at 5:36 p.m. during rush-hour traffic. In addition to the earthquakes, many tsunamis have hit the coastline, causing death and destruction, and rock slides have been reported to be causing damage around the state.

1. *As governor, what are your priorities?* If evacuation plans exist they need to be implemented immediately. For those communities that do not have evacuation plans, the state should intercede in helping residents get to safety. For areas that have been impacted by tsunamis and rock slides, state employees

and National Guard troops need to be involved in search and rescue operations for survivors. Any injured citizens need to be taken to medical facilities as quickly as possible.

2. *What resources do you need to mobilize to contend with the crisis?* The governor will need as many first responders as possible for search and rescue operations as well as medical resources to handle the influx of injured citizens. Transportation needs to be a resource that is mobilized quickly either through state agencies or the National Guard.

3. *What other issues may in fact be an additional problem to the actual natural disasters?* The governor needs to be aware that infrastructure such as water, electrical, and sewer systems could all be damaged, which impacts first responders being able to respond to emergencies as well as citizens being able to survive. The infrastructure repairs will need to be carried out fairly quick to enable first responders to douse fires with water, for example.

Stage 3 of the Disaster

As night begins to fall, you have learned that two towns, Girdwood (Timberline Drive Bed & Breakfast, 2007) and Portage (Wicker, 1982), were completely destroyed and both sites are now underwater due to the tsunamis. Two other coastal states are now reporting that over 16 people have been killed as a result of the tsunamis (USGS, 2007). Other Native American villages have been completely razed by the tsunamis (Associated Press State and Local Wire, 2006), and Clear Air Force Station, responsible for ballistic missile detection, was offline for a short time. Fires are now being reported in various areas due to burning oil floating in the water (Rozell, 2009). The prime minister of Canada has now contacted your office to inform you that Canada has also suffered damage. More information is now coming into your command center. Some parts of your state have actually been liquefied by the earthquake; you have nine confirmed dead from the earthquake itself, 106 confirmed dead (USGS, 2007) from the tsunamis, and in 2007 U.S. dollars over $1.8 billion in damage has been inflicted upon your state (USGS Newsroom, 2007).

1. *What is the governor's next plan of action?* Now that the initial crisis is over the governor will need to focus on search and rescue of locations that may be in very remote areas as well as repairing infrastructure. Temporary housing will need to be erected and bodies will need to be recovered to prevent any type of health issues from arising.

2. *Will any of the information cause you to readjust your allocation of resources?* The resources will need to be deployed into the hardest-hit areas. Additionally, if resources that are not around the coastal areas of the state are not being utilized, they should be temporarily shifted to assist in reconstruction efforts or sent to help Canada if resources are desperately needed.

Key Issues Raised from the Case Study

It is difficult to manage a crisis across a large coastal area such as Alaska when terrain and weather can vary considerably. Therefore, communication and logistical support are essential for successfully evacuating a population out of coastal areas. To manage a disaster response effectively, an administrator must plan for all types of contingency situations. In this case study, the ground actually liquefied, which would have required any type of evacuation by primarily helicopters. In places such as Alaska where the terrain and weather are very difficult for vehicles to operate, plans will need to incorporate the use of specialized personnel and equipment that can be used in disaster responses. A type of vehicle that may prove to be useful would be a hovercraft, which can go over any terrain for search and rescue operations.

Items of Note

People were killed in not only Alaska but also the West Coast of the United States. In addition to damage in Alaska, Canada also sustained property damage during the earthquake, which was felt as far away as Texas and Louisiana (U.S. Department of the Interior, 2011). The Good Friday Earthquake is also known as the Great Alaskan Earthquake.

Mount St. Helens, Washington, 1980

Stage 1 of the Disaster

You are a county commissioner in a mountainous region of the country. It is the end of March and you are tending to your routine duties when a volcanologist appears in your office. The volcanologist tells you that the volcano appears to be active: two earthquakes have already caused the north side of the mountain to cave in, and steam is starting to vent from the mountain (USGS, 2012). You have a logging industry, tourist industry, and residents that are in the area of the mountain (USDA Forest Service, 2007).

1. *What is the threat to human life?* With a volcano, the amount of damage can often be determined by what type of volcano one is contending with in relation to the type of activity that can occur. There are three main types of volcanoes. The first type is a shield volcano, which is usually defined by long, shallow sloping sides that form toward the top of the volcano. A shield volcano typically has a lava flow but typically does not create a large amount of debris spread out over a wide area. Shield volcanoes are found in Hawaii and are typically nonexplosive when an eruption occurs (USGS, 2009). The second type of volcano is a cinder volcano, which is constructed of pyroclastic debris.

These volcanoes typically spew large amounts of ash and lava during eruptions. The third type of volcano is a composite volcano. Some of the most devastating volcanoes in history have been composite ones (USGS, 2009). Eruptions from composite volcanoes include pyroclastic debris and ash violently ejected over a large area accompanied by a great deal of lava flowing down the volcano's slopes. The volcano that you are currently facing in this case study is a composite volcano that can inflict damage, injury, and death over a very wide area.

2. *What is your plan of action?* At this point it would be a good idea to alert citizens as well as state and local employees that the volcano is active. Citizens should be advised to keep emergency supplies on hand and be prepared to evacuate on short notice. Identify resources that potentially will be needed for search and rescue operations, traffic control, medical personnel, forest firefighters, and public utility workers. In addition, equipment and resources such as helicopters, fire water bombers, trucks, medical supplies, food, water, gas masks, portable generators, and portable respirators should be located and tagged for mobilization in the event of an eruption. An evacuation plan for the population living near the volcano should be drafted quickly. An administrator should also be keenly aware of any potential political bottlenecks that may result in resources being withheld by other federal, state, or local agencies. These political bottlenecks will need to be addressed and resolved with agreements being made with the agencies in question and in place before any disaster occurs.

3. *What is your communication plan?* As county commissioner, it is your responsibility to ensure that communications are fully functional to enable people to prepare for a possible evacuation and to gather survival supplies in the event residents are trapped and unable to evacuate. The logging industry should be highly encouraged to restrict its operations away from the volcano for safety reasons. County and local employees must be alerted and informed of the volcano's activity and advised where resources will be available for evacuations, search and rescue operations, fighting forest fires, and repairing infrastructure. In addition, county and local first responders will need the most current maps, contacts lists, and a set of duties that are to be carried out in case of an emergency.

4. *What resources will you allocate to the emergency?* As stated earlier, medical supplies, food, water, respiration equipment (e.g., gas masks, portable respirators), helicopters, construction equipment, firefighting equipment, planes, and trucks will need to be designated if the volcano erupts. Additionally, facilities will need to be set aside for disaster relief purposes and headquarters will need to be designated to coordinate efforts and communication with all first responders at the federal, state, county, and local levels. Roadways need to be selected as evacuation routes, and all efforts should be made to ensure those roadways can be made safe and clear for

the large volume of traffic that will vacate the area. Agreements should also be made with neighboring communities and counties to provide assistance. If time allows, first response personnel can conduct drills to hone their skills.

Stage 2 of the Disaster

It is now the end of April and the mountain is beginning to bulge (USGS, 2010). You have one resident in particular that refuses to leave his home, even after you have communicated to him that the situation is extremely dangerous for him to remain on the mountain (Associated Press, 1980).

1. *What is the threat to human life?* In this case study, the volcano is indeed very active and is an imminent threat to human life, particularly to those who refuse to evacuate. Since composite volcanoes spew large amounts of ash and debris into the atmosphere, there is a high probability of people suffocating and being buried by hot ash, similar to what had occurred at Pompeii in 79 A.D. Individuals can also be killed or injured by flying debris. Snow on the mountain can become torrents of fine mud, which can flood nearby towns.

2. *What is your plan of action?* The plan of action for evacuating certain areas of the county needs to be put into effect immediately before the volcano erupts. Individuals that refuse to evacuate after repeated warnings must be left to fend for themselves because dozens of state, county, and local employees would be put at great risk to rescue a small number of holdouts. Resources should be prioritized to contend with the impending eruption and to assist the thousands who heeded the evacuation warnings.

3. *What is your communication plan?* Evacuation orders should be given to your citizens and contact should be made with other communities in preparation to receive assistance. Both FEMA and the American Red Cross should be notified at this point that a volcanic eruption can potentially occur very soon and that assistance will be needed to house and feed evacuees.

4. *What resources will you allocate to the emergency?* Shelters should be opened and emergency personnel dispersed to assist displaced citizens that have been forced to evacuate. Traffic control personnel will need to be positioned to maintain an orderly flow of evacuees. Vehicles must be sent to evacuate residents that have no other means of transportation. Helicopters must be on standby to locate and evacuate those who might get trapped. Firefighters and public works personnel should be placed on alert. At this point, it is necessary to open the designated headquarters. Communication gear should be tested to ensure it is in good working condition. First responders must be issued gas masks, water, food, and first aid kits.

Stage 3 of the Disaster

On Sunday, May 18, you hear an explosion and see a black, rolling cloud that blots out the sun (USDA Forest Service, 2007). You realize that a massive volcanic explosion has just occurred. You will later learn that vegetation and buildings for 230 square miles have been laid waste (USDA Forest Service, 2007). You feel very fortunate that the logging industry did not have anybody working on the mountain that day (Tilling, 1990).

1. *What is your plan of action?* This is the point at which public administrators need to identify what areas residents are most at risk to provide evacuation and what areas need to receive search and rescue operations immediately. Once residents have been successfully evacuated and search and rescue operations have been completed, government officials will need to see what needs to be rebuilt or reforested after the crisis has ended.
2. *What is your communication plan?* The public will need to be informed about the events that will be ongoing for several days. Scientists will need to be contacted to determine if the volcano will cause any more danger to the population and how to nurse the environment back to the condition it was in prior to the volcano erupting. Additionally, administrators will need to contact other entities at the federal, state, and local levels to receive additional aid in the form of temporary housing, food, water, search and rescue personnel, and medical resources.

Key Issues Raised from the Case Study

The administrators were very fortunate that there were no logging industry workers in the area when Mount St. Helens erupted. If there were workers in the area the death toll could have been much higher. The issue of the resident who would not leave his home was a choice that he made on his own accord. The resident had received repeated warnings to leave the area. If people are warned adequately, then those residents are taking a risk on remaining in a potentially dangerous environment and should not expect any assistance from government entities while the disaster is occurring. This would put first responders in additional jeopardy for residents who were already previously warned to leave the area.

The government officials in this case study could not predict when the volcano was going to erupt. An active volcano can have sessions that are more active with seismic activity than others, which makes it difficult for trained volcanologists to predict exactly when the volcano will erupt and how violent the eruption will be in lava flows and pyroclastic debris. It is therefore difficult to restrain activity around a volcano that may or may not erupt over a period of months, if not years. With this type of situation it is critical for administrators to have an effective evacuation and emergency response plan that will address how to contend with the worst-case scenario if the volcano erupted.

Items of Note

There were 57 people killed by the eruption at Mount St. Helens. Over 1.2 billion cubic feet of ash was pushed into the atmosphere from the eruption (USGS, 2005).

Sichuan Earthquake, China, 2008

Stage 1 of the Disaster

You are the emergency manager for Sichuan Province in China. It is May 12, 2008, when your province experienced a major earthquake that measured 7.9 on the Richter scale. You have no communications since wireless and traditional twisted pair wire infrastructure has been damaged immeasurably. Transportation infrastructure, which is still heavily reliant on railways, has also been highly damaged by the quake, and many of the buildings in your province have been leveled (Tan, Washburn, Chorba, and Sandhaus, 2012).

1. *What is your first response to the situation?* You will need to gather up as many volunteers and first responders as possible since there will be many people that are trapped under rubble and will need assistance to get free of the debris. Heavy digging and excavation equipment will be needed for the bigger parts of structures that are sure to have collapsed during the earthquake. Additionally, medical resources will be needed as well as facilities that are still standing to take on patients and become makeshift operating rooms. Challenges will also be found in obtaining sufficient amounts of food, water, and medicine for not only patients, but also first responders and displaced persons.

2. *What is your communication plan?* It will be necessary to reestablish communications with governmental agencies outside the province in order to obtain assistance that will be needed to contend with the casualties from the earthquake, as well as reestablishing critical infrastructure for logistical purposes. Command posts will need to be set up to communicate with the populations of the province, which will require couriers until modern communication infrastructures can be reestablished.

Stage 2 of the Disaster

In spite of the urgent need for medical care, you are unable to get sufficient medical resources to your residents in the province, since it is rural and is more impoverished than urban provinces (Kurtenbach and Foreman, 2008). Additionally, you are finding that many of the schools and buildings that have been constructed over the years have not been built to the same standards as in other developed provinces, which leads to the collapse of many buildings during the earthquake and results in many injuries and fatalities (Kurtenbach and Foreman, 2008). In schools alone there were over 9,000 casualties from the earthquakes (Hays, 2010). In addition, you now have anywhere from 5 to 11 million people without housing (Vervaeck and Daniell, 2011).

1. *What is your plan of action?* The first priority should be to contact governmental officials and organizations such as the International Federation of the Red Cross to assist you with any medical needs. Medical resources are often difficult to obtain due to the scarcity of such resources during times of crisis, and due to the fact that personnel in particular are highly skilled but very few in number, especially in more rural and impoverished areas. Additionally, you will need to obtain as much manpower and equipment as possible to increase the search and rescue efforts. With the widespread path of destruction, it will be necessary to launch several teams for search and rescue of fallen structures. As with any large displacement of residents, temporary housing will be needed for those individuals as well as food, water, sanitation, and medical logistics for those temporary encampments. One method that may be used in place of heavy digging equipment is heavy-lift military helicopters, such as the Mi-6 or Mi-26, which have a maximum payload of 12,000 kilograms and can lift heavy debris if the area is completely inaccessible to earth-moving equipment or cranes.

2. *What resources should you mobilize?* In addition to the search and rescue efforts that are currently underway, you will need to mobilize as many construction workers and engineers as possible to fix any damaged infrastructure as well as inspect buildings that are still erect but which may be structurally unsound for habitation.

Key Issues Raised from the Case Study

Building codes are very important in earthquake zones. If buildings are older, or have not been constructed in accord with building codes suitable for earthquake zones, then the possibility of these buildings collapsing and causing death or injury increases. In this case, a largely undeveloped province of China had buildings that were mostly constructed before the building codes of 1976, codes that were developed to ensure earthquake proofing, and this led to a much greater amount of damage and fatalities. In addition, the damage to infrastructure for transportation meant that both manpower and equipment that could have been deployed to the region quickly were severely limited. Even though modern communications such as wireless communication and traditional twisted pair telephony were part of the infrastructure, the earthquake was devastating enough to render potentially life-saving technology moot, with no apparent redundancy built in for emergency communications if those primary means were disabled.

Emergency managers must plan for redundant means of communications in their disaster response plans.

Items of Note

Over 68,000 people were killed and over 370,000 individuals were injured in the earthquake. The earthquake also formed 34 lakes due to landslides blocking rivers (Vervaeck and Daniell, 2011).

Chapter 7

Case Studies: Disasters from Natural Sources— Other Weather, Animal, and Viral Phenomena

Great Blizzard, 1888

Stage 1 of the Disaster

You are a director of health and human services. It is based on good authority that the northeastern region of the United States is going to have some extremely cold weather. March 11 should be a fairly nice day in most parts of the country; however, you are coiled up in a blanket looking outside your office window as snow is falling at a very alarming rate. The scene is the same in at least three other states and transportation is coming to a standstill (Douglas, 2005).

1. *What is your plan of action?* As director for health and human services it would be important to determine what groups of people are vulnerable to severe cold. Once these groups have been identified, it is important to gather information on what resources are available and how those resources can be

deployed. Motor vehicles are not available and you will have to find some other way to distribute any resources that are needed.*

2. *What is your communication plan?* Electronic communications are extremely limited at this time. You will need to find some other methods of communicating with the population, municipal and state leaders, other agencies, and first responders.

3. *What resources should you mobilize?* With a cold weather emergency on the way, supplies to vulnerable populations (e.g., the very young, the very old, and homeless persons) should be distributed by any means possible as fast as possible. This means an administrator will have to know where to locate supplies and get agreements in place with local agencies in order to distribute the resources to the appropriate groups of people considered to be vulnerable to cold weather. In addition, supplies should be stockpiled in the way of food, fuel for heating, heaters, and water for different groups of people that may get isolated if roads are closed down and they are unable to get required resources. Additionally, an administrator will need to find alternative ways to get supplies to those types of isolated groups of people.

Stage 2 of the Disaster

As the day wears on, reports from the National Weather Service indicate that over 50 inches of snow has fallen throughout the day in different areas of the country (Douglas, 2005). Additionally, your communication infrastructure has faltered and fuel is now very limited (Brunner, 2007).

1. *What is your plan of action?* The time to act is now. You must see if you can get additional supplies brought in from states and areas of the country that are not affected by bad weather. The train would be a good source of transportation to bring in large amounts of supplies quickly. This means that leaders in those areas of the country need to be communicated with and an agreement needs to be put in place to gather up the necessary food, water, and fuel for the residents in snowed-in communities. If possible, shipping may be another possibility to bring in large amounts of supplies from southern states. Additionally, you will need to have adequate resources to keep railroad tracks clear and waterways open for shipping. Temporary shelters need to be identified for those that have no fuel or have no home.

2. *What is your new communication plan?* With electronic means of communication being limited, using couriers in the form of horseback, ships, or trains

---

* The first automobile was invented in 1885 in Germany. The first car in the United States was not produced until 1893. Depending upon the technology of the region, infrastructure condition, and availability of fuel, first responders even in modern times may not have vehicles to utilize for disaster response operations.

will be your main form of communication over any great distance. For communicating locally, a series of couriers could be utilized to send messages to and from local municipality leaders.

3. *How will you mobilize your resources?* The resources will need to be dedicated to logistical efforts of keeping passages open and distributing goods, and a medical plan of action will need to be implemented for patients dealing with starvation and frostbite.

Stage 3 of the Disaster

It is now March 13 and your office is flooded with notifications of people starving to death or freezing to death in their homes (Schmid, 2005). In addition, there are now several people who are being injured due to the fire stations being closed down due to the roads being completely closed, which is leaving fires going unchecked throughout the region (Brunner, 2007).

1. *What is your plan of action?* At this point an administrator will need to take stock of the situation and determine what has been done to alleviate the food shortage situation and what should be done to alleviate the food shortage situation. Resources may have to be reallocated to get logistics where they need to be, and manpower will need to be allocated for hospital staff as well as getting the fire stations back in operational use.

2. *What resources should you mobilize?* You will need to allocate resources toward logistic efforts and getting emergency management services in place. Manpower will be crucial in getting roads, railways, and ship channels clear to receive cargo for food, water, and fuel. Getting skilled personnel to man hospitals and fire stations will prove to be crucial during this phase of the crisis.

Stage 4 of the Disaster

March 14 and the snow is still falling (Brunner, 2007). It has been reported to you that 100 sailors have now died on 200 ships that have been frozen in place along the coastline (Douglas, 2005). The fuel has now been depleted and the unchecked fires have cost the region over $25 million in property damages alone (Brunner, 2007).

1. *What is your plan of action?* Since so many ships are frozen in the harbor, the local administrators should provide shelter for sailors whose ships are stranded in the harbor and potentially use those individuals to provide logistics and clear transit areas. Additional personnel should be allocated to fight fires that are currently roaring unchecked.

2. *What services should you be focusing on at this point?* Your main focus should be to keep the logistical pathways clear; distribute food, water, and fuel to

residents; and fight any fire that is currently active. Additionally, people who are without shelter or fuel should be evacuated to temporary shelters or even out of the region temporarily until logistics have improved.

Key Issues Raised from the Case Study

Having a good logistical plan in place and a reserve of fuel, food, and water can make the difference in surviving this disaster response situation. With adverse conditions, both the very young and very old are susceptible to becoming ill or dying as a result of extreme cold. Administrators need to keep these factors in mind when determining what parts of the population are the most vulnerable and where the resources should be sent as a priority.

There were several areas in the case study that need to be addressed. The biggest issue was failing to store any supplies for an emergency cold spell. It is critical to have a fuel depot on hand for transportation and heating needs in case infrastructure is damaged and people are isolated. Additionally, the communication infrastructure had no redundancy, leaving people without any means to communicate effectively with external entities. An administrator must make plans to use another manner of communication if the primary systems have failed.

Items of Note

The Great Blizzard of 1888 is still known as the worst snowstorm in American history. It isolated the cities of Boston, New York, Philadelphia, and Washington, D.C., for a 2-day period (Brunner, 2007). As a result of not having enough food, water, or fuel, a number of people died who would have been able to survive if the proper resources had been available.

Lions of Tsavo, Africa, 1898

Stage 1 of the Disaster

You are the director of engineering for a public works project to construct a vital bridge that is part of the railroad from Kenya to Uganda. The Uganda Railway project is budgeted for 5.3 million pounds and is supposed to open up trade in valuable commodities like ivory between Kenya and Uganda (Monitor Reporter, 2012). On this project, the British government has spent 1 million pounds on rolling stock and labor from India alone (Monitor Reporter, 2012). The railway has been under construction since 1895, and the British government is anxious for you to get the bridge completed so that the rest of the railway can be completed ahead of any potential competition (*Nairobi Chronicle*, 2008). You have a design for the bridge and are about to begin work when you arrive at Tsavo to oversee the construction. After a week of being on-site, you receive word that two of your best workers have mysteriously disappeared. Some workers believe they had been killed by lions as they slept in their tents (Patterson, 1919).

1. *What is your plan of action?* Your first priority is to take steps to protect your workforce. Even if you are skeptical that they were in fact killed by lions, as opposed to coworkers (Patterson, 1919), you have a duty to take every step possible to ensure the safety and security of your workplace. Having your employees in tents may be an acceptable practice, but if there are marauding lions in the area, you need to make sure that, at minimum, the perimeter around the tents is protected and guarded. After all, you are in the middle of an undeveloped region where the local wildlife can be extremely dangerous. This issue should have been considered before the workers arrived on-site. Additionally, you need to find the bodies of the two workers that disappeared to verify whether the attack was by lions or by a criminal act.

2. *What is your communication plan?* As the director you should communicate with your workforce that action is being taken to not only verify what killed the two workers, but also explain the steps that are being taken to safeguard their lives. This is very important since you expect good, honest, hard work out of your employees and you need to ensure that their physical and mental health is being taken seriously. You should ask your workers to report anything suspicious to you or your managers immediately so that steps can be taken to address the potential danger to the encampment.

3. *What resources should you mobilize?* The workers' quarters should be clustered together so that they can be protected more efficiently and effectively. Armed guards should be employed and a perimeter fencing system should be constructed around the quarters of the employees. Additionally, any items that can attract lions (if this is what killed the two workers) should be placed well away from the employee quarters so that the employees will not attract the attention of marauding animals. You should also have your employees trained in how to avoid problems with the local wildlife (not just lions) to prevent any injury or deaths.

Stage 2 of the Disaster

You have been at Tsavo for 3 weeks and have not found the bodies of your two workers. Additionally, your skepticism that lions killed the two workers prevents you from taking any proactive measures to protect your workforce. However, you now have a third worker that has been seen by his coworkers being dragged out of his tent and devoured by a lion. You have inspected the tent and believe that the man was truly taken by a lion and killed. You and one of your other employees attempt to track down the lion you believe is responsible for the attack. You managed to recover the body of the most recent victim and discover the remains of the other two workers that had been killed earlier. After examination of the bodies, it becomes apparent that there are in fact two lions that are responsible for the attacks (Patterson, 1919).

1. *What is your plan of action?* Now that you have confirmed that there are two lions, you should take action immediately to protect your workforce. You may have an engineering background, but management is the task that should be at hand with a project as big as building a sizable bridge. The individuals that are being killed work for you under your direction. Their safety and security should become your priority, and constructing the bridge should be a secondary concern. You should also contact outside organizations to see if any assistance can be given to address the problems with the lions.

2. *What is your communication plan?* Your workers want to know what you plan to do about the lions as well as how you are going to protect them. As the director, you need to communicate all news of what has occurred so far as well as tell the employees what steps you are taking to address the issues at hand. If this step is not done at this time, your employees will believe that their lives are secondary to the task of completing the bridge and will lose confidence in your ability to manage.

3. *What resources should you mobilize?* Once again, as the director, you should take steps to protect your workforce by situating the employees housing grouped together and making sure that armed guards are on duty at night when the lions are most likely to attack. A temporary security barrier should be along the perimeter of the encampment. Additionally, you should call in a trained expert hunter to go after the lions.

Stage 3 of the Disaster

You decided that you need to rid the problem of the lions yourself. You set up a hunting station that overlooks the tents where the last victim was taken and which your employees are still using as living quarters (Patterson, 1919). In essence, you are using your employees as bait and hoping the lions will reappear. Your hopes are dashed, however, as the lions strike another camp that is half a mile away and kill another employee (Patterson, 1919). Since you still have not clustered the living quarters together the lions have multiple targets to choose from while you are left guessing where they will strike next. This strategy has multiple pitfalls, so what is your next plan of action?

1. *What is your plan of action?* The director should consider calling in an expert hunter since he is supposed to be managing the construction of the bridge. Successfully constructing the bridge means that you need to have employees

that are willing to work on the project. At the rate the director is going currently, he is losing good employees fairly rapidly. Again, safeguarding the employees is paramount, and this issue still needs to be addressed.

2. *What is your communication plan?* You need to communicate with your employees and show them that there are steps being taken to contend with the lions and find the latest victim. Do not tell your employees that you were using them as bait. Your employees would probably not appreciate this tactic very much, and it would erode their confidence in your leadership abilities.

3. *What resources should you mobilize?* Until the lions are dealt with effectively, your efforts to build the bridge across the Tsavo River will be slow in progress. You need to bring in a professional hunter and tracker to kill or capture both lions. You also need to hire armed security to protect your workforce as well as set up better accommodations for your workforce that would be less vulnerable than canvas tents.

Stage 4 of the Disaster

Five workers have now been killed and your strategies for killing the lions have not worked. You have lost many employees while you have experimented with how to hunt these two predators. While you have now started to use goats chained to a tree as bait, the lions are still busy killing your employees that continue to sleep in unprotected tents. You have taken steps to better protect your workers by building a new hospital as well as constructing a new fence. However, you are still attempting to hunt the lions on your own by using a new hunting location in an attempt to bag your quarry (Patterson, 1919). Do you think this strategy will work any better?

1. *What is your plan of action?* The construction of a fence and a new hospital are steps in the right direction, but the director should do far more than this to protect his workforce. A professional hunter and tracker should be brought in so that he can focus on killing these animals and you can do what you are supposed to do, which is build the bridge for the railroad.

2. *What is your communication plan?* So far everything you have tried has failed. Sometimes it is important for your employees to understand that you are attempting to rid them of the problem but have not been successful as of yet. You need to highlight the fact that you are taking steps for their well-being and that the new hospital and fence have been constructed to better protect their lives.

3. *What resources should you mobilize?* Contrary to what the director believes, he is not the best hunter in the world and he should bring in a professional hunter as well as armed guards since these lions are coming into the camps at will and taking their victims with little resistance.

Stage 5 of the Disaster

You have received support to hunt the lions in the form of a hunter and his logistic support personnel (Patterson, 1919). After months of the lions killing your workers, you manage to kill one of the lions (Patterson, 1919). Your employers are concerned that your bridge is not finished and that the entire railway completion date is not on course to finish as originally planned. Your employers have sent someone to inspect the bridge and the consultant has stated that he was satisfied with the progress on the bridge and sympathized with your plight with the lions (Patterson, 1919). However, you still have one lion that is on the loose and your workers are still imperiled.

1. *What is your plan of action?* There needs to be an effort made to get the final lion, but the question is: How are you going to kill it? Will you use a professional or will you attempt to kill the lion by yourself? Either way the workers will continue to be in danger until the last lion is killed. There still needs to be given to the workers safety and security, which have still never really been resolved satisfactorily.

2. *What is your communication plan?* The director needs to highlight the fact that one of the lions has definitely been killed in order to raise worker morale. There also needs to be discussion of the fact that there is an effort currently underway to kill the remaining lion.

3. *What resources should you mobilize?* You have one lion remaining, so a proper amount of resources should be dedicated to killing it. Security guards should still be stationed at night to guard the employees' housing and all precautions should be taken to keep anything that might tempt a lion away from sleeping quarters.

Stage 6 of the Disaster

You have now killed the second lion and are working to complete the bridge (Patterson, 1919). Some of your workers who left earlier are returning to work (Patterson, 1919). The death toll from the two lions is estimated to be 135 railway workers killed over a 9-month period (Field Museum, 2007). You are still having issues with other wildlife (i.e., crocodiles) killing some of your employees (Patterson, 1919).

1. *What is your plan of action?* Your main focus at this point is to finish the bridge. The other item of note is that you need to remind your employees that there are other dangers in the area besides the lions that still exist.

2. *What is your communication plan?* You should communicate with outside organizations that the lion issue has been put to rest and that the work environment is now secure for employees.

Key Issues Raised from the Case Study

This case study takes place in a time during the imperialist age when workers that were imported into a workplace did not have the same value as the host country requiring the work. Therefore, Patterson's decision-making processes were along the lines of workers being somewhat expendable (i.e., using the workers as bait). What should be noted is that eventually Patterson did make adjustments to ensure the safety and security of his employees, only after much blood had already been spilled.

When working in areas that have dangerous wildlife, employers can avert disaster if precautions are taken and the proper resources are put in place. An administrator who is primarily a manager over an engineering project should not have to contend with hunting lions in addition to playing the roles of architect, engineer, and building supervisor. Granted, the authors have hindsight to make their recommendations on what should have taken place, but some of the actions that should have been taken by Patterson would have appeared to be logical precautions in an area where dangerous wildlife was known to exist to ensure his workers' safety. This case study demonstrates that sometimes a professional is needed to resolve an issue. A professional hunter or tracker could have been called in as soon as the problem appeared, which could have prevented the disaster from claiming as many lives as it did in the end.

Items of Note

The lions of Tsavo are both currently (2012) displayed at the Field Museum in Chicago. Contrary to the Hollywood movie *The Ghost and the Darkness*, the lions of Tsavo are both maneless male lions (Field Museum, 2007).

Great White Shark Attacks, New Jersey, 1916

Stage 1 of the Disaster

You are a commander with the U.S. Coast Guard assigned to safeguard the coastline of a state. Your country is not at war presently, but you are under orders that war could erupt at any moment and you may not only have lifeguard duties but also antisub duty as well. Your resources are finite and you have two basic jobs to perform. You have jurisdiction over all waterways in and around this state in times of crisis. It is an unusually hot summer. Most people do not have air-conditioning in their homes because they reside in a northern state that rarely sees warm temperatures during even the summer months, and air-conditioning at this time is very expensive to buy for residential use.* To escape from the heat, the citizens are taking

---

* Central air-conditioning did exist at this time but was extremely expensive to buy and install, which limited how many residences actually had air-conditioning.

to the beaches, rivers, and creeks to cool off and some recreation. You are responsible for the safety of thousands of citizens and you must work with the state and city governments on this issue.

1. *What is your plan of action?* The commander should essentially take an inventory of all personnel and resources and determine how to best deploy them to perform both tasks. For smaller ships that are used for coastal work that are on hand, the Coast Guard could use these resources for patrolling the beaches as well as the major rivers around the areas. For the antisubmarine duties you will be using your larger ships to patrol the coastline for any submarines if war breaks out.

2. *What is your communication plan?* As commander of the Coast Guard around the state, you will work closely with the local community leaders as well as state agencies that may provide additional support to your efforts. You need to ensure that your missions are clear to these officials, and that if war breaks out, antisubmarine warfare duties will be your primary responsibility. In addition, you need to make contact with locals that know the waterways and coastal areas to establish a robust communication network so that information can be collected and distributed.

Stage 2 of the Disaster

On July 2, you are told that on July 1 at 6:45 p.m. (Fernicola, 2001) one person at a resort town had been attacked and killed by "a large animal" as the person was swimming in shallow water. From the eyewitness accounts and evidence of the injuries to the person who was killed, you are convinced that a large shark is responsible for the attack.

1. *What is your plan of action?* You need to meet with local leaders and attempt to persuade them to close the beaches that are close to where the incident occurred. This may just be an isolated incident where if the beaches are closed for a short period of time, the shark may move out of the area when it realizes there is no food in the area. In addition, you need to determine if some of the beaches can be better protected by shark nets and patrols around the most popular beaches. You should attempt to retain the services of a shark behavior specialist to assist you in capturing the shark or in helping you find a shark deterrent to protect swimmers.

2. *What is your communication plan?* Since you are in charge of safety around the state, it would be prudent to issue a press release asking swimmers and locals to be aware of potential dangers as well as keeping their eye out for large and potentially dangerous sharks.

3. *How will you cooperate with other governmental officials?* Closing the beaches is only one way you can hopefully get cooperation from the local officials.

In addition, local officials can dedicate additional resources to locate the dangerous shark. Many of the coastal towns and cities have large fishing boats that can catch such a dangerous creature and can help alleviate your already taxed resources.

4. *How will you allocate your resources?* At this point you should highly consider dedicating some of your smaller boats and their crews to safeguarding the public beaches and swimming areas from sharks. Instead of traditional lifeguarding types of duties and search and rescue missions, your resources will be dedicated to shark hunting activities.

Stage 3 of the Disaster

Even after the attack the beaches remain open and no shark has been caught as of yet. There are various reports from sea captains at large port cities that large sharks are seen swimming in the area. On July 6 another victim was attacked and killed on a resort beach as he was swimming 130 yards from shore (Fernicola, 2001). Panic is now sweeping the state's coastal areas. Local and state officials are worried that the attacks will damage the state's tourism revenues.

1. *What is your plan of action?* Now that a second shark victim has been killed at a resort beach, you have more leverage to use against the local leaders to temporarily close their beaches. Since the shark attacks are becoming more of an issue, you decide that more ships and resources are needed to assist your efforts in finding the shark. You can also continue to try and persuade local leaders to dedicate more resources to hunt the shark down that may be in their areas of operation.

2. *What is your communication plan?* The public should be warned of a second shark attack and the local leaders should ask the fishermen in their communities to notify them if a dangerous shark is seen in the area. This will allow you to have more people looking for the dangerous shark and effectively increase your resources to find and kill the shark.

Stage 4 of the Disaster

Some resorts around certain beaches are installing nets, and you now see that boats with armed men are patrolling coastal areas for sharks. Some beaches are closing altogether. To compound your problems, local mayors and the governor of the state are offering large bounties on sharks that encourage even more people to enter the waterways to hunt sharks (Fernicola, 2001).

1. *What is your plan of action?* Now you will have to dedicate some of your resources to safeguard the influx of shark hunters in the waterway. Some of your resources can be redeployed, however, to areas that do not have shark nets or armed men patrolling the beaches.

2. *What is your communication plan?* Now that there are more men in boats, you will need to provide safety instructions to all new boaters to prevent an increase in accidents. In addition, you should keep up the communication efforts to notify the public that the dangerous shark has still not been caught and that the danger still exists to swimmers.

Stage 5 of the Disaster

You have a new report (July 12) of a local sea captain sighting an 8-foot shark in Matawan Creek that is located on an inland waterway (Fernicola, 2001). Local residents are currently swimming in the creek for recreation and there has never been a shark sighting in this area before.

1. *What is your plan of action?* You should immediately redeploy any small boats and their crews in the area of the river to provide safety to the public and to catch and kill the shark.
2. *What is your communication plan?* You should contact local leaders and have them evacuate swimmers out of the river due to the shark sighting. The local leaders should be encouraged to send resources to catch the shark before it leaves the river and returns to the ocean.

Stage 6 of the Disaster

At 2:00 p.m. on July 12, children spot a dorsal fin and a shark attacks a 12-year-old boy, who is killed in the creek. A second person, who attempted to rescue the boy, is also attacked and killed by the shark (Fernicola, 2001).

1. *What is your plan of action?* The time to act is now. You must get all swimmers out of the river waters. In addition, you should have your men seal off the river with nets in the section of the river that the shark is most likely present. If possible, the bodies of the two victims should be recovered.
2. *What is your communication plan?* You need to talk to locals and get a good estimate on which section of the river the shark was located at the time of attack. In addition, you need to discover what direction the shark appeared to be heading so that you can use your resources efficiently and effectively. All residents along the river should be warned about the shark's presence.

Stage 7 of the Disaster

At 2:30 p.m. on July 12 a third person is attacked in the same creek but is rescued by the locals (Fernicola, 2001). You now have four people killed and one injured from one or more sharks. Not a single shark has been caught that is associated with any of the attacks. The public is scared and demanding action. In addition, the state's resort areas have lost money in tourism and people have left the beaches at various coastal areas (*New York Times*, 1916). The attacks have generated so much press that the president of the United States discussed the issue with his Cabinet (Fernicola, 2001). A massive shark hunt begins off the coastline of several states.

1. *What is your plan of action?* You should send as many resources as possible to the river area since the shark is still actively attacking humans. You now need to retain medical supplies and personnel since an injury has occurred.
2. *What is your communication plan?* You should coordinate efforts with the local fishermen who are actively engaged in hunting the shark. If the effort is not coordinated, the shark could escape out of the area via a location that is not being covered.

Stage 8 of the Disaster

Finally, some good news has arrived. On July 14, two locals caught a 7½-foot great white shark close to the mouth of the river where the attacks occurred (Fernicola, 2001). There were human remains found in the shark's stomach upon examination. After the great white shark is caught, no further attacks occur throughout the year.

Key Issues Raised from the Case Study

Natural disasters do occur and there is little anyone can do to prevent them. The important issue in this case study is that, with proper communication, some of the victims' lives may have been saved if the residents had been told to get out of the river after the first attack had occurred. The biggest failure in this case study is a misunderstanding of how dangerous the shark was to the public. In the case of the river attacks, there appears to be a lack of communication to the people along the river that there was a dangerous shark in the area after the first attack occurred. The reaction was strong from the residents but was ultimately too late to prevent more shark attacks from occurring or to catch the shark before it left the river area.

Items of Note

There were a total of four individuals killed in this shark attack and another was wounded. Additionally, a huge amount of revenue was lost during the tourist season. This incident was the inspiration for the book *Jaws* by Peter Benchley and the movie that was made in 1975 (Fernicola, 2001).

Chicago Heat Wave, 1995

Stage 1 of the Disaster

You are the director of a state agency in the Midwestern United States. It is the first of July and already the state is experiencing a heat wave that is very unseasonable for this part of the country. Many residences do not have central air-conditioning installed since it rarely gets that warm during the summer months. On July 12, the temperature rose over 99°F (Klinenberg, 2004). From experience, you know that the elderly and children are more susceptible to heat exhaustion and heat stroke.

1. *What is your current plan of action?* The director should attempt to get funding that would allow for either buying window air-conditioning units and electric fans or subsidizing the costs. This would allow for some of the impoverished or elderly who are on a fixed income to have some relief from the heat.
2. *What resources do you need?* The director will need personnel to manage such a program and then will need to get funding for such a project. A fund could also be established to assist with the subsidy of electricity bills for those who fall below a certain income level.
3. *What is your communication plan?* To raise funds for such a project, the director should be in contact with nonprofit groups that can identify those in need and possibly provide some funds to carry out the program. In addition, the director will need to establish a manner in which to communicate with the public that such a program exists.

Stage 2 of the Disaster

Between July 13 and 14 the temperatures remain above 99°F and residents are dying or being hospitalized at an alarming rate (Klinenberg, 2004).

1. *What are you going to propose for a plan to prevent death and illness from occurring?* In addition to air-conditioning, water is the other item that people need to prevent dehydration, heat exhaustion, and heat stroke. The director needs to set up watering stations for those who do not have running water. If funding is not forthcoming, then the director should attempt to get temporary shelters that are air-conditioned. If groups of people who lack air-conditioning in their residence, can stay in until the heat wave has passed.
2. *What should your communication plan be to the residents in your state?* The director should urge people who have air-conditioning to use it so that they are not at risk for heat exhaustion or heat stroke or dehydration. If a program can be funded to provide air-conditioning and water to residents, the program should be widely publicized. In addition, it should be communicated to citizens to keep an eye on neighbors that live alone that are at risk for

dehydration, heat exhaustion, or heat stroke, and notify the department with people that appear to be at high risk for such issues.

3. *What other agencies should you think about getting involved in the current crisis in hopes of providing relief to the residents that are suffering from the heat wave?* The director needs to reach out to nonprofit organizations that already assist the impoverished or the elderly. By allying with such organizations, the director has effectively increased the capabilities of his or her department.

Key Issues Raised from the Case Study

Administrators should ensure that alliances are in place with nonprofit organizations that can effectively render aid to individuals that may be at the greatest risk for heat exhaustion. Unlike other areas of the country that traditionally have central air-conditioning for residents (i.e., Arizona, New Mexico, and Texas), northern states, which typically experience mild summers, will be less likely to have air-conditioning in their residential housing.

The inability to get effective assistance to residents that are particularly vulnerable to the excessive heat is the focus for this case study. In addition to the most vulnerable populations (i.e., young and old), there are also populations that are also at risk due to socioeconomic factors. Some residents may have difficulty paying the electric bill or reside in an old, unconditioned dwelling, which further exacerbates the situation.

Items of Note

The Chicago heat wave directly resulted in the death of 485 residents in Chicago and an untold number of people that were hospitalized (Klinenberg, 2004). The heat wave also led to infrastructure damage on roads and some drawbridges that had to be temporarily closed (Schreuder, 1995). The Chicago Board of Health estimated that 733 deaths were directly or indirectly due to the heat wave (Schreuder, 1995).

West Nile Virus, North America, 1999–2004

Stage 1 of the Disaster

You are a director for the Centers for Disease Control for the United States. You are alarmed by the number of cases that are being reported with West Nile virus. Between 1999 and 2001, there were 149 cases of people diagnosed with the illness, and 18 of those people died (Lane County of Oregon, 2008).

1. *What is your plan of action?* The director should see if there is a pattern to where the illnesses are occurring. If a pattern does emerge, then the director

should plan to take action in one particular area to see if the cases of West Nile virus decrease after the plan is put into place. If the plan is successful, then the director should implement it in other areas that have been impacted by the virus.

2. *What is your communication plan?* It is important for the director to communicate with local and state officials where West Nile virus has been documented. Since West Nile virus is carried by a mosquito, the communication plan should state to residents where West Nile virus is common the precautions to take to prevent mosquito bites.

Stage 2 of the Disaster

The year 2003 proved to be even worse than the previous years, as 9,862 cases were reported with West Nile virus, and 264 people died of it (Lane County of Oregon, 2008).

1. *How do you propose to stop the spread of West Nile virus?* To stop the West Nile virus, the director should institute a program to spray for mosquitoes where the West Nile virus has been found. Unless the mosquitoes carrying West Nile virus are killed, the spread of the disease will continue.

2. *How do you plan to interact with local and state officials on this crisis?* The director needs to coordinate any type of spraying effort to kill the mosquitoes with state and local efforts that may already be underway. There may be a possibility to standardize the methods and chemicals used to kill the mosquitoes, which would allow an efficiency gain as well as a cost savings.

3. *What resources will you need to contain the virus as well as medically treat victims of the virus?* The director will need spraying apparatuses available to them as well as pharmaceuticals available to treat anyone that is infected with the virus. The development of a vaccine for West Nile virus would be a long-term goal if the virus becomes more widespread.

Stage 3 of the Disaster

For 2004, the spread of West Nile virus through the population was decreasing, with only 2,470 cases being reported, and the number of deaths had dropped to 88 (Lane County of Oregon, 2008).

1. *To what do you attribute the decrease in West Nile virus among the population at this point?* The decrease could be due to multiple events. There may be more people using mosquito repellant, and spraying for mosquitoes may be proving to be effective. Additionally, the climate may be different, which could

contribute to there being less cases of West Nile virus being transmitted since there could be fewer mosquitoes.

2. *What programs should you continue based on your data that the disease is not spreading as much as it was in 2003?* The programs that target spraying for mosquitoes should be continued in order for the West Nile virus cases to be kept at a low point.

Key Issues Raised from the Case Study

Although viruses can be spread in numerous ways, mosquitoes have been a source of infectious disease since the beginning of time (e.g., malaria, yellow fever, etc.) (CDC, 2007). It is critically important to have an effective plan in place to control the mosquito population and prevent a massive outbreak of infection in densely populated areas. In this case study, health officials appeared to be caught off guard on the spread of West Nile virus. They were unable to have a plan in place that prevented a high number of infected cases from occurring.

Items of Note

North America West Nile virus was first diagnosed in Uganda in 1937 (Lane County of Oregon, 2008).

Killer Bee Attacks, United States, 2008

Stage 1 of the Disaster

You are the director for a state agency contending with agriculture in the southwest United States. On March 25, you receive a report out of San Antonio that a family was attacked by bees inside their home (Sting Shield Insect Veil, 2008). It was later confirmed that the bees were "killer bees" or Africanized bees that are beginning to migrate through the United States from Mexico (Sting Shield Insect Veil, 2008). In addition, you know that these types of bees can cause damage to your state's local honeybee population, which is essential for producing commercial honey and pollinating crops.

1. *What should be the main priority for your agency?* The director should determine the current location of the killer bees and attempt to contain them until a plan is formulated to terminate the bees in the state. A second priority would be to put a plan in place to assist residents who have a killer bees' nest located on their property and are at risk for a bee attack. These types of nests need to be dealt with first and foremost.

2. *What should be your communication plan for government officials and residents of your state?* The director should keep in contact with county and city officials and animal control divisions that could alert the director to the presence of killer bees in their areas. In addition, the director could communicate with the agricultural stations that are run by university and college systems throughout the state to give them an alert of killer bee migration.

3. *What resources do you think you will require at this point?* The director needs to formulate a plan to quarantine the killer bees where they have been sighted and then needs the resources to poison the bees before they can cause harm to humans or agriculture.

4. *What other agencies do you need to contact and coordinate with in contending with the killer bees?* The federal government can provide resources to combat such an invasive and dangerous insect. The federal government has an interest in making sure that the killer bees do not proceed any further into the United States to damage agriculture in other parts of the country. The director will need to coordinate efforts with county and city governments as well as any organization contending with beekeeping and agriculture. In addition, the agriculture programs in state universities and colleges may be able to assist the director in combating the killer bee threat.

Stage 2 of the Disaster

On April 20, a second killer bee attack took place in San Antonio against a man who accidently set his house on fire when attempting to drive the bees away (Sting Shield Insect Veil, 2008).

1. *What is your plan of action?* The director should make sure to take action on killer bee nests when they are discovered. The director should quarantine bee transfers to and from the San Antonio area.

2. *What resources should you mobilize to the affected area of the state?* The director should send any type of resource to the area that can be used to destroy any killer bee nests that are found. In addition, the director may also want to send research scientists to the area to collect data in an effort to analyze what would be the best approach to eliminate killer bees.

3. *What is your communication plan?* The director should make an effort to inform the public on how to act around killer bees and who to notify if killer bee nests are found. By informing the public on what not to do to killer bees, the director could potentially save some lives.

Stage 3 of the Disaster

The presence of killer bees has been verified in 151 counties of your state, and they show no sign of containment. The killer bees have now attacked a family in Abilene and killed their two dogs. On April 29, you received a report that a Corpus Christi retirement home had literally thousands of bees swarming inside it (Sting Shield Insect Veil, 2008).

1. *What is your plan of action?* If the director is unable to stop the flow of killer bees throughout the state, then the federal government should be contacted and requested to provide assistance. The director needs to verify that killer bees are indeed at populated areas, and if so, take action on eliminating killer bee nests.
2. *What is your communication plan?* The director needs to communicate effectively with federal, county, and city officials. The population needs to be kept apprised of the situation as well as anyone involved with beekeeping in the agriculture business.

Stage 4 of the Disaster

It turns out that the attack on the retirement home was caused by ordinary honeybees. However, on May 26, the killer bees claim a 41-year-old victim in Palestine, Texas, who was attacked by hundreds of bees (Sting Shield Insect Veil, 2008).

1. *What is your plan of action?* The director needs to be aggressive about going after killer bee nests to prevent the insects from encroaching on populated areas. The director's efforts need to be coordinated with county and local officials and agencies. In addition, medical supplies to contend with killer bee attacks on people should be kept on hand where killer bees are now known to reside.
2. *What resources should you mobilize to the affected area of the state?* More research should be done on killer bees to get an understanding of what their weaknesses may be in an effort to eliminate them from the state without damaging honeybees, which contribute to the agriculture business.
3. *What is your communication plan?* The director should make a very large effort to continue any public announcement on the dangers of killer bees and educate the public on how to recognize that particular type of bee.

Key Issues Raised from the Case Study

Now that the killer bee colony has been seen in the United States, there is no effective choke point to stop the bees from entering in other states, cities, or counties. Therefore, administrators that face the possibility of killer bees being in their area should have a plan on hand to assist individuals that have been attacked by the killer bees and to protect any industry that may be impacted by the killer bees' presence. The inability to contain the killer bee colony led to people being attacked as well as inflicting harm on the honeybee population, which produces honey for the agricultural industry.

Items of Note

The killer bee attacks resulted in deaths and injuries to people and animals over the years. In counties where killer bee attacks have occurred, numbers of honeybee colonies have been quarantined, impacting the honey industry (Sting Shield Insect Veil, 2008).

MAN-MADE DISASTERS

Chapter 8

Case Studies: Man-Made Disasters— Industrial Accidents and Structural Failure

Monongah Mine Disaster, West Virginia, 1907

Stage 1 of the Disaster

You are the fire chief for a local municipality. At 10:15 in the morning on December 6, you receive a dispatch that there has been an explosion at the local mining operation near your city (Boise State University, 2008).

1. *What is your plan of action?* The fire chief should alert all first responders that there has been an accident at the mine and then locate any type of resource that can assist first responders with digging (e.g., heavy machinery), oxygen, and breathing apparatuses, hazardous materials experts, medical supplies, and personnel, as well as engineers that can assist first responders in getting to any trapped miners in a safe and timely manner.
2. *What is your communication plan?* The fire chief should contact the owners of the mining operation, local government officials, and any other entity that may be able to provide resources for search and rescue operations.

Stage 2 of the Disaster

You have now been told that two mine shafts, numbers 6 and 8, have collapsed and there are over 300 workers trapped in the tunnels where there is presence of poisonous gases. It turns out that none of your first responders have the appropriate breathing apparatuses to contend with the poisonous gases, and therefore the first responders must work in shifts. In addition, the main entrances to the tunnels are completely blocked with two strings of iron ore cars, rock, and twisted metal debris caused by the blast that induced the cave-in (Boise State University, 2008).

1. *What type of resources will you need at this point in the rescue process?* The fire chief needs to acquire appropriate breathing apparatuses from other organizations if they are not available to him currently. The fire chief should also obtain heavy machinery to dig tunnels into the mine to retrieve the miners. This activity should be conducted under the supervision of an engineer to ensure the safety of the first responders and to advise how best to dig the victims out of the rubble. Additional manpower should also be sought from nearby communities in the form of first responders and volunteers. To assist in protecting your first responders, you should limit how long and how many shifts each first responder works at clearing the mine. In addition, you should make sure that there is plenty of water on-site to ensure that the first responders are well hydrated.

2. *What is your communication plan?* The fire chief should be keep in constant contact with the mining company as well as maintain close contact with his first responders on the scene. In addition, the fire chief should also begin to release information about the status of the rescue attempts to keep the families of the trapped miners informed.

Stage 3 of the Disaster

It is now 2 days later, on December 8, and you now are contending with two fires that are hindering your rescue work (Boise State University, 2008). In addition, you now have a large crowd of friends and family members gathering at the front gates to hear news about their loved ones who were trapped in the mines (Boise State University, 2008). Your rescuers are now beginning to bring bodies up from the mine shaft and there is no place to put the bodies.

1. *What is your plan of action?* The fire chief needs to designate a location for the mortuary so that bodies can be identified and families can be contacted or asked to identify the remains. Additionally, the fires will now have to take a priority over any further search and rescue attempt since the fires could jeopardize not only the miners that could still be alive, but also the first responders and support personnel.

2. *What is your communication plan?* The fire chief needs to employ law enforcement for crowd control and continue holding daily public briefings on the search and rescue operations. The city officials should be kept apprised of the ongoing operations and the fire chief should still attempt to contact outside organizations to solicit help for the efforts to rescue the miners.

Stage 4 of the Disaster

You have now set up a temporary morgue to handle the influx of dead bodies that are being brought out from the mine shafts (Boise State University, 2008).

1. *What is your plan of action?* The fire chief should ensure that his first responders are maintaining safe work conditions through the ongoing efforts, and as soon as possible, should begin an investigation into how the explosion at the mine occurred in the first place.
2. *What is your communication plan?* The fire chief should refer the families to the temporary morgue for information on their relatives that were in the mine. At this point in the operation, there is little hope that anyone will be found alive. The operation should now shift to a body recovery operation.

Key Issues Raised from the Case Study

When a specialized industry is located in a community, it is imperative for that community to be prepared for the possibility of an emergency rescue operation by maintaining reserves of specialized personnel and equipment. Having such resources available can make a difference in life or death rescue operations (e.g., the submarine *Kursk* explosion, in which no crew could be saved, and the Oklahoma City bombing). If specialized equipment or personnel are not available, then administrators will need to have a strategy for how they will obtain those resources quickly, which will allow for more effective rescue operations.

Local area first responders lacked the necessary emergency rescue equipment required to clear debris as well as to contend with poisonous gas. This set of circumstances could have only prolonged the ability to get miners out of the collapsed mine shafts, which decreased their chances of survival. The Monongah mine disaster killed 362 men and boys and was the reason for the creation of the U.S. Department of Mines in 1908 to regulate mining safety (Boise State University, 2008).

Items of Note

The Monongah mine disaster was the biggest mine disaster to date (Mine Safety and Health Administration, 2008).

Triangle Shirtwaist Factory Fire, New York, 1911

Stage 1 of the Disaster

You are the mayor of a large metropolitan city. Your code enforcement officer has stated that a clothing manufacturer has been cited for several fire and safety violations.

1. *What is your plan of action?* The plant should be notified that unless it complies with the city codes immediately, the factory will be shut down and the company will be fined on a weekly schedule until compliance is achieved. The city inspectors should be notified that the factory will be inspected on a regular and frequent basis until compliance is achieved.
2. *What resources do you need to carry out your plan?* As the mayor, you have code enforcement officers, city attorneys, and if criminal charges occur, a police department to enforce your will upon the company owners.
3. *What other outside agencies will you contact?* You should contact any regulatory agency that can apply the necessary pressure to make the company compliant, or if the company fails to be compliant, force the company to shut down.

Stage 2 of the Disaster

You have been alerted that a fire has broken out in the clothing factory and that there are over 500 workers trapped in the building (Zasky, 2008). How should you proceed in getting the workers to safety?

1. *What is your plan of action?* You need to deploy your first responders to the scene so that the factory workers can be evacuated safely and the fire can be prevented from spreading to any of the surrounding buildings near the factory. If the factory can be saved that is even better.
2. *What resources will you need?* For a large factory you will need a large amount of fire and emergency medical technicians to put out the fire and evacuate anyone who might be injured in the blaze.

Stage 3 of the Disaster

You have learned that a fire escape has collapsed as the workers have been attempting to flee from the fire out of the building (Zasky, 2008). Do you have a secondary or backup plan to evacuate the workers? What resources do you have on hand to accomplish a different evacuation plan?

1. *What is your plan of action?* You will need to have the fire department create other avenues of escape for the workers. Since you do not have helicopters,

you will need to rely on fire equipment that would consist of ladders long enough to reach the upper floors.*

2. *What resources will you need?* Since you have a large number of people potentially trapped inside a smoky building, you will need more medical assets and firefighters to extinguish the blaze.

3. *What is your communication plan?* You will need to contact any next of kin of any worker that is injured or killed in the fire. Additionally, you will need to mobilize your fire investigators and police department once the blaze has been extinguished.

Key Issues Raised from the Case Study

This case study provides an example of why it is so important to have building codes and enforce them. If building codes had been enforced, then the fire and safety violations would have forced the company to comply with the ordinances, or the city could have had the leverage to close the factory for noncompliance. By having proper building codes in place and enforced, a governmental entity has the ability to limit liability to itself, as well as being able to prevent potential tragedy from occurring in the first place.

The single biggest failure in the case study is the failure to enforce any type of building codes for the factory. Viable avenues of escape were unavailable to workers when the fire broke out, which hindered effective evacuation. The fire lasted 30 minutes and resulted in the deaths of 146 employees (Zasky, 2008).

Items of Note

The Triangle Shirtwaist Factory fire inspired reforms for safety of workers and instituted more government oversight over industrial safety (Zasky, 2008).

Bhopal Industrial Chemical Accident, India, 1984

Stage 1 of the Disaster

You are the director for public safety in Bhopal, India, where an industrial plant owned by Union Carbide Corporation produces a host of chemicals used to make pesticides. The plant was built using money from local shareholders and the government has a 22% share in Union Carbide India Ltd. (a subsidiary of Union Carbide) as well. The plant was built in a light industrial zoned area (not for hazardous industry) with access to a good transportation infrastructure network. The plant was eventually set up to produce raw chemicals as well as refined,

---

* A helicopter that could be mass-produced was not truly feasible until 1938. It was then that Germany introduced its Fw61. The U.S. debuted its R-4 in 1942.

finished pesticides due to competition in the chemical industry. The government has noted that there have been safety shortfalls with the plant, but the company has made no effort to have those shortfalls corrected. Perhaps this is due to the possibility that the fixes may cause the company to shut down the plant, which would have a severe economic impact upon the region (Broughton, 2005).

1. *What is your plan of action?* Your first plan of action should be to note exactly what safety shortfalls exist at the plant and come up with an estimate of the consequences if those safety shortfalls cause a catastrophic failure in a populated area. If the government fails to act upon your report, then prepare an evacuation plan and a containment plan for around the plant. You should forge ties with organizations that can assist your personnel to contain any type of chemical release that may occur. With a large industrial chemical plant, your staff will need additional assistance in containing any leak that may occur, and your staff will need assistance to evacuate the population. In addition, you should prepare an evacuation route plan for the areas around the plant and have your personnel equipped with HAZMAT suits that are rated to handle exposure to volatile, corrosive, or airborne chemicals.

2. *What is your communication plan?* You should brief staff on the potential issues with the chemical plant and ensure that their training with chemical HAZMAT is current. You will need to stay in regular touch with the government on the status of the plant and keep it informed on any changes in status in regard to the safety shortfalls that are noted.

3. *What resources should you utilize to ensure safety codes are being followed?* A series of Geographic Information Systems (GIS) maps should be produced to show the evacuation routes for the population, the potential exposure radius of a leak with certain chemicals, and the location of infrastructure lines that may need to be closed in the event of an emergency. Additionally, you should also maintain an inventory of gas masks, vehicles for evacuation, medical resources, and first responders in case of an emergency.

Stage 2 of the Disaster

At 1:05 a.m. on December 3 you are notified that the plant has had a catastrophic failure in a safety valve that has released a cloud of gas into the atmosphere during the time when most of the community was asleep (Broughton, 2005). You are unsure what type of gas has been released, but you can see the corpses of humans and animals alike lying in the streets of Bhopal. You are now receiving reports that almost 3,800 individuals have died instantly from the mysterious gas cloud (Broughton, 2005).

1. *What is your plan of action?* The first order of business is to equip your personnel with respirator masks so that they can safely evacuate the area where the gas cloud has been released. Second, you will need to find out what type of gas

was released from the plant. If you cannot determine this information, medical staff will have no idea on how to treat patients and you will have difficulty attempting to shut down where the gas cloud is coming from at the plant.

2. *What is your communication plan?* You need to immediately appeal to the population to evacuate the area before they are caught up in the gas cloud. In addition, you will need to contact the plant to see what type of chemical has been released and determine the status of sealing the leak at the factory. Outside organizations will need to be contacted for both medical assistance and to assist with evacuating the populous in the surrounding areas.

3. *What resources should you mobilize at this time?* The director will need to mobilize all medical resources possible as well as any first responders that are properly equipped with respirator gear and vehicles to evacuate the area.

Stage 3 of the Disaster

The disaster is now into its sixth day, and up to 10,000 people have been killed and several thousand left ill due to chemical exposure. Your hospitals are completely full and no one is exactly sure what the chemical effects of methyl isocyanate will be long term on individuals exposed to the chemical (Broughton, 2005).

1. *What is your plan of action?* You will need to locate all types of medical resources that could be needed to combat the effects of the chemical. Furthermore, you will need to get additional first responders on the scene to assist individuals who may be disabled by the chemical.

2. *What is your communication plan?* The director will need to keep in contact with government officials and should convey the needs for medical resources in this time of emergency. Outside agencies and organizations should be contacted as well to seek additional help with medical resources.

3. *What resources should you mobilize at this time?* At this point, medical resources should be the most sought after items as well as facilities that can be converted into hospital space, which is currently in short supply. Additionally, you will need to locate facilities that can also serve as a temporary morgue. The bodies will need to be taken somewhere to isolate the corpses since the chemical will still be present on their clothes and bodies. Anyone who removes or contacts any person (or corpse for that matter) should wear protective gear and respirators when making physical contact with the person.

Key Issues Raised from the Case Study

The government ignored the safety shortfalls at the plant and this played a part in the Bhopal tragedy. For government officials and administrators this case study should demonstrate what can go terribly wrong when safety precautions and safety standards are below industry standards. The full extent of damage will never be known concerning the health and well-being of the citizens of Bhopal. With a plant that has the capacity to produce a deadly by-product, administrators should be prepared for a worst-case scenario and maintain a readily accessible inventory of items like gas masks for anyone in the immediate vicinity of the industrial complex. Additionally, this case study also points out that economic development does not justify tolerating conditions that can be dangerous for the population.

Items of Note

Union Carbide Corporation would eventually pay the Indian government $470 million to compensate the victims of Bhopal (Broughton, 2005). The payment was based on the information that 3,000 people had been killed and another 102,000 had been permanently disabled by the chemical release. Union Carbide Corporation closed the plant at Bhopal but did not clean up the site. The site eventually contaminated the water supply (Broughton, 2005).

Texas City Disaster, 1947

Stage 1 of the Disaster

You are the city manager for a midsized city (16,000 residents) in the Southwest part of the United States. Your city has been a main deep water shipping port for agricultural products and industrial products with railroad line access since 1911. The city has a large chemical and petroleum industry that has several facilities throughout the city (Moore Memorial Public Library, 2007).

1. *What issues should you address for an emergency management plan of action?* It would be essential to know what chemicals exist in the municipality and to have trained teams to contend with such hazards. A starting point would be for the city to map locations where storage tanks and any type of infrastructure that contends with chemicals currently reside. In addition, the city's police and fire departments should carry out training exercises on how to contend with such disasters. Additionally, hospitals should have resources on hand to treat patients with chemical injuries. If the resources are available, the city's fire department should carry out regular safety and compliance inspections on any large plant that handles chemical manufacturing.

2. *What should an emergency management plan have for a communication plan?* The city should have a response plan for industrial accidents and an effective evacuation plan for any businesses and residences near large manufacturing plants.

3. *What resources should you have on hand for the emergencies that you think could possibly occur?* A hazardous materials team should be available to the fire department as well as fireboats and an aerial firefighting plane that can dump large amounts of chemicals on fires.
4. *What agreements should you have in place with other organizations?* A city manager should attempt to make regional agreements with other city managers that in times of crisis, cities will assist each.

Stage 2 of the Disaster

The S.S. *Grandcamp* is currently docked at your port city and is carrying a cargo of small arms ammunition and taking on a cargo of over 2,300 tons of ammonium nitrate fertilizer (Moore Memorial Public Library, 2007).

1. *Does this ship pose a hazard to your city, and if so, what measures will you take to ensure the safety of your city and industrial facilities?* The city manager should be concerned with a ship carrying this type of explosive ordinance combined with a chemical that is a component used to make gunpowder. The city manager needs to ensure that all safety procedures are being followed by the ship's captain and crew while they are in the port.
2. *What policies and procedures should you have in place for ships carrying this type of cargo?* A ship carrying this type of cargo should declare its inventory to the city fire department, type and amount. Furthermore, ships carrying this type of cargo should be berthed in an isolated area of the harbor so that if something does go wrong, it will not impact other ships or infrastructure.

Stage 3 of the Disaster

On April 16, a fire was noticed on board the SS *Grandcamp* while a longshoreman was loading the ship (Moore Memorial Public Library, 2007).

1. *What resources should you mobilize for this emergency?* The fire department should mobilize all of its resources immediately to combat the blaze. Any persons in the area of this ship should be evacuated to a safe location.
2. *What is your communication plan?* The city manager should stay in close contact with the fire department and alert hospitals that a crisis is currently unfolding. In addition, the city manager should seek out assistance from surrounding municipalities and state officials.
3. *What steps can you take to mitigate a potential disaster?* If possible, the ship needs to be moved well away from any infrastructure and other ships. If the ship cannot be moved, then other ships that are in the vicinity need to be moved away from the area.

Stage 4 of the Disaster

The fire is now raging out of control as the longshoremen and sailors have been unable to put it out. Additionally, there is no telephone service since the telephone operators are on strike and there is no one to perform their function. You have dispatched the city's two fire trucks and the volunteer firefighters have arrived on the scene with an additional two fire trucks, but the fire cannot be contained with just water (Moore Memorial Public Library, 2007).

1. *What is your plan of action?* The city manager needs to make sure that the area is cleared of workers and citizens to avoid casualties. If possible, an airplane equipped with fire-retardant chemicals needs to be obtained to help fight the blaze.
2. *What is your communication plan?* Since you have no electronic communications through the telephone system, other means will need be made available, such as setting up runners or getting volunteers with short-wave radios to assist with communication efforts. Since you have no hazardous materials team, local officials and state officials need to be contacted to obtain critical resources that can be used to fight a chemical fire. You need to make a public plea for the telephone operators to come back to work and off strike so that your communication system will be operable.

Stage 5 of the Disaster

The ship's crew had only been able to remove 3 of 16 boxes of small arms ammunition. In an attempt to douse the blaze, the captain of the ship has had steam poured into the cargo hold. Unfortunately, the steam turned the ammonium nitrate into poisonous nitrous oxide gas vapors, which fill the ship. The ship's crew has now been evacuated (Moore Memorial Public Library, 2007).

1. *What is your plan of action?* The area needs to be completely evacuated since the fire is out of control and there is no viable means to fight the fire at this point. All ships need to be cleared of the harbor and chemicals that are in the dock area need to be relocated if at all possible.
2. *What other resources will you need at this point?* Additional first responders will be needed to seal off the area and ensure that all of the evacuations have taken place. Medical personnel and resources will need to be put on full alert.

Stage 6 of the Disaster

The steam has super heated the ammonium nitrate and has caused the ship's fuel and oil tanks to leak, which is feeding the fire. Due to the fire, you now have many bystanders watching the blaze on the SS *Grandcamp* (Moore Memorial Public Library, 2007).

1. *How will you contend with the growing number of bystanders?* The city manager needs to make sure that his police department keeps bystanders away from the disaster site by sealing off roadways leading to the harbor.
2. *What are you going to do about the fire on the SS Grandcamp?* Unfortunately there is not much that the city manager can do at this point since the fire is out of control and the city lacks proper firefighting equipment to take care of the situation. You should evacuate all of your firefighters from the area to avoid any of them getting hurt or killed.

Stage 7 of the Disaster

At 9:12 a.m. an explosion rocks the SS *Grandcamp* and rips the ship apart. Pieces of the ship are sent through the air like shrapnel. Shock waves are felt 250 miles away. The explosion causes flooding around the initial area and also flattens a plant and several buildings in the nearby vicinity. You learn that the fire chief and 27 firefighters were killed, which leaves you with a huge shortage of trained first responders. In addition, you have no operational hospital in your city (Moore Memorial Public Library, 2007).

1. *What is your plan of action?* The city manager needs to contact nearby cities with hospitals to manage anyone who has been injured in the fire or the blast. Search and rescue teams need to be formed to look for survivors in the buildings that were destroyed.
2. *What are you going to do about having no medical facility?* The city manager will need to set up a makeshift hospital with as many medical volunteers as possible to assist with the wounded until those patients can be taken to a proper medical facility.

Stage 8 of the Disaster

The explosion killed hundreds of bystanders, pedestrians, and workers, and obliterated several buildings. Several buildings have fires raging out of control. However, you finally have some good news. The telephone operators have gone back on the job in this time of crisis and have telephoned a number of nearby agencies and municipalities for assistance. You have just received word that the military, local municipals, and medical centers are all sending personnel and resources to assist your city (Moore Memorial Public Library, 2007).

1. *What will be your first priority with these new resources that are available?* The first priority is to put out fires that are now ongoing throughout the cities. The second focus should be on search and rescue of anyone that has been injured.

2. *What is your communication plan?* The search and rescue efforts will need to be coordinated so that every survivor is found and treated. Coordinated communication will be essential between the other municipal first responders, your first responders, and the military.

3. *What other issues could arise?* The city manager will have to monitor how all of the efforts are being coordinated effectively. Medical facilities can easily become overloaded and medical supplies could quickly run out.

Stage 9 of the Disaster

Your city hall and chamber of commerce are now being used as makeshift medical centers. The military is setting up temporary housing and bulldozing as much of the debris as possible. In addition, you are evacuating the wounded to nearby cities whenever possible. Unfortunately, the SS *High Flyer* (which was moored next to the SS *Grandcamp*) has caught fire and is loaded with a large amount of ammonium nitrate and sulfur (Moore Memorial Public Library, 2007). The crew has now abandoned ship.

1. *What are you going to do about the SS High Flyer?* The ship should be moved if possible and should be doused with a chemical fire retardant if available to the first responders.

2. *What are the other risks that are in the port that should be addressed immediately?* If any other ships are in the vicinity of the SS *High Flyer* they should be relocated immediately.

Stage 10 of the Disaster

At 1:10 a.m. on April 17 the SS *High Flyer* explodes, killing two people, and also causes the SS *Wilson B. Keene* to sink. You now know that 500 to 600 people have died and thousands more were wounded by the explosions and resulting fires (Moore Memorial Public Library, 2007).

1. *What is your plan of action?* The plan of action should be to evacuate any people or ships that are still in the harbor. The city manager should now begin focusing on recovery of the bodies and getting any infrastructure repaired that will assist the first responders in tackling fires or shoring up any buildings with structural damage.

2. *What resources do you need at this point?* The city manager may want to consider bringing in engineers to determine the safety of some of the buildings that were hit with the explosions. In addition, pathologists are going to be needed to identify the bodies and families will need to be notified.

3. *What agencies should you ask for assistance?* The American Red Cross should be contacted as well as the governor's office to request assistance in cleaning up the disaster area.

Key Issues Raised from the Case Study

The main point that should be made in this case study concerns the issue of having proper rules and regulations in place to prevent a disaster from occurring. While it may be impossible to stop a fire from breaking out on a single ship, it is possible to limit the damage to that one particular vessel. In the Texas City incident, the disaster was compounded by the fact that the initial explosion destroyed or damaged infrastructure, killed or wounded individuals, and caused fires on other vessels that were laden with chemicals. It would behoove administrators to take note that when contending with certain industries, effective rules and regulations should be in place and reviewed on a regular basis.

The ships that had volatile chemicals on board should not have been allowed near each other and should have been isolated from the harbor facilities until they were ready to completely load or off-load their cargo. Allowing these ships to be in close proximity to each other enabled the fire to spread to other chemical-laden cargo ships when the SS *Grandcamp* caught fire and exploded. A loading facility should be well away from other harbor facilities since a fire or explosion potentially puts those facilities at risk.

There were three ships sunk and numerous people were hurt or killed in the ensuing fire and explosions. During the disaster, a city lost an entire corps of highly trained firefighters, which took years to replace. Until those personnel were replaced, the city had to rely more on outside help to battle any blazes that occurred within its municipality. There were also the additional costs of repairing any infrastructure that was damaged as well as the costs to salvage the ships to clear the port so that other ships could use the docking areas again.

Items of Note

The Texas City disaster had over 150 morticians working to take care of the bodies that were recovered as well as dental students being utilized to help with identification (Moore Memorial Public Library, 2007).

Exxon Valdez, Alaska, 1989

Stage 1 of the Disaster

You are the head of a state agency on the West Coast of the United States. It is March 24 when an oil tanker, the *Exxon Valdez*, has run aground at Prince William

Sound. The accident has caused the oil tanker to release 42 million liters of oil into the Prince William Sound, which harbors several different types of animals and aquatic life (Andres, 1997).

1. *What is your plan of action?* The first step would be to notify the U.S. Coast Guard to determine if it could intervene and contain the oil spill. Second, the Exxon corporation should be ordered immediately to survey the ship and contain the oil that has not already leaked out of it. State wildlife employees should be deployed to the disaster area immediately to protect the indigenous wildlife as much as possible. For those animals or birds that have already been covered in oil, wildlife officials will need to clean the animals as well as possible.

2. *What is your communication plan?* Contact veterinarians and request that they volunteer to assist the wildlife affected by the oil spill. Other state and federal officials should be contacted to obtain resources to contain the oil spill as much as possible.

Stage 2 of the Disaster

The oil is spreading over an 8-mile area around the oil tanker and 1,300 miles of your coastline is now contaminated, and a large amount of wildlife is covered by the oil. It is an environmental disaster of epic proportions. The U.S. Coast Guard, environmentalists, and other emergency workers have been unable to contain or burn off the oil at this point (BBC, 1989).

1. *What is your plan of action?* The only action that can be taken is to repair the rupture in the ship to prevent more oil from leaking and to try to evacuate wildlife from the affected area.

2. *What is your communication plan?* An appeal to volunteers and nonprofit groups for help may bring some assistance in the cleanup of the area and the wildlife that is covered in oil. The situation needs to be closely monitored to see where the oil slick may be expanding to along the coastline. Federal, state, and local officials need to be kept informed on the extent of the disaster, resources that are currently needed, and the progress of the different efforts to contain the oil leakage.

Key Issues Raised from the Case Study

Unfortunately, there is very little that local administrators can do in a situation where it appears that industry standards for safety were less than ideal. However, administrators can mitigate foreseeable ecological disasters by working closely with government agencies that have jurisdiction over shipping and conduct spot checks on the sobriety of the crew on ships that are carrying potentially dangerous cargo. Administrators can also restrict vessels with hazardous materials from traveling near wildlife refuges and inhabited areas.

The resources that administrators called for to contend with the crisis were ultimately insufficient for the disaster that was occurring. The *Exxon Valdez* resulted in the deaths of 250,000 birds, 3,000 sea otters, 250 bald eagles, and 22 killer whales (BBC, 1989). Additionally, the oil spill caused substantial damage to the environment, which in turn negatively impacted commercial fishing, recreational usage, and tourism (Schure, 2010).

Items of Note

Exxon was ordered to pay $4.5 billion for damages inflicted upon the environment (BBC, 1989).

Hyatt Regency Walkway Collapse, Kansas City, 1981

Stage 1 of the Disaster

You are the director of code enforcement for a major metropolitan city. You have been under pressure lately since a structure, the roof of the Kemper Arena, has collapsed. Luckily no one was present during that structure failure.

1. *What is your plan of action?* The first plan of action should be to review what processes were in place in regard to code enforcement that would allow a structure to be approved that was not designed properly. The other major issue would be to review the personnel involved that were instrumental in approving the roof of the Kemper Arena and review the training and the credentials of the inspectors that were involved in that particular project. Last, a departmental review should be undertaken to ensure that all personnel have the correct credentials and training in the code enforcement department.

2. *What resources should you utilize to ensure safety codes are being followed?* An external audit should be undertaken of all code enforcement policies and personnel to ensure that the department can comply with municipal mandates that are necessary for the municipality. A review should be undertaken to ensure that the department is correctly funded for the amount of workload that is placed on the department. If there are too many projects and not enough personnel, there is a potential danger for projects to be approved that would not ordinarily be approved.

3. *What is your communication plan?* You should communicate with your department to take a stricter approach on reviewing construction projects and communicate to contractors and architects working on projects in your city that code enforcement will be stepped up and projects that do not pass rigor will not be allowed to proceed.

Stage 2 of the Disaster

Your office has just overseen an inspection of a newly constructed hotel that is 40 stories high and has a series of walkways suspended over the main lobby area. At 9:00 p.m. on July 17, you receive a call that more than one of the walkways has collapsed onto the lobby floor during a dance and tea party, killing and injuring several people (Martin, 1999).

1. *What is your plan of action?* Your plan of action should be to undertake an external audit immediately as well as interview the employees that worked on the project. Since it may be a construction issue instead of a design flaw, you need to find out all the information you can before taking any further action.
2. *What resources should you utilize to ensure safety codes are being followed?* Depending on the findings of the investigation, you may need more inspectors for your department or more highly skilled inspectors working in the code enforcement department. In addition, there may need to be policy or procedures put in place to prevent this type of accident from occurring in the future.
3. *What is your communication plan?* It is important to keep your assistant city manager and city manager informed of all of your findings in regard to the accident and your department's involvement with the company that built the hotel.

Stage 3 of the Disaster

The accident, caused by a structural failure, has killed 114 people and injured 200 others. Four days after the accident the local media discovers that there was a design change in the walkways during the construction of the hotel. It turns out that even the original design would not comply with the municipal building codes since the structure could only support 60% of the minimum load requirement. The revised design could only support 30% of the mandated weight requirement (Martin, 1999).

1. *What is your plan of action?* At this point you now know that it was indeed a design flaw. You will have to investigate how your personnel failed to detect the problems with the design they approved. Since your office was responsible for approving the design, you may very well be asked to resign from your position.
2. *What resources should you utilize to ensure safety codes are being followed?* A review of all recent building projects should be undertaken, as well as current policies, procedures, and personnel if this task has not already been started.
3. *What is your communication plan?* You need to keep the city administrators well informed about the progress of any investigation as well as reassure the public that safety codes for construction will be strictly enforced on future projects.

Key Issues Raised from the Case Study

Having policies and procedures is important, but it is even more important for administrators to remember that there needs to be a comprehensive process established to ensure that those ordinances are being followed when projects are being formulated and constructed. There was no apparent mechanism in place to ensure that building codes were being followed during the design or implementation stage of construction. Thus, there were no checks or balances to ensure that the design firm or construction company had actually followed existing building codes.

The engineers in charge of the project were convicted by the Missouri Board of Architects, Professional Engineers, and Land Surveyors of negligence. The various judgments and civil lawsuits resulted in $140 million being awarded to the families of the victims (Dubill, 2011).

Items of Note

Texas A&M University uses the Kansas City Hyatt Regency walkway collapse for their engineering ethics courses in the Department of Philosophy and Department of Mechanical Engineering (Texas A&M University, 2009).

Bridge Collapse, Minnesota, 2007

Stage 1 of the Disaster

You are the fire chief for a northern municipality. On August 1, a large bridge carrying traffic across a major river collapses (Wald, 2008).

1. *What is your plan of action?* The first order of business should be to stop all current traffic on the roadway and divert any other vehicles away from the area so that emergency vehicles can gain access to the area much more easily. Second, a search and rescue team should be deployed as quickly as possible to search for cars that contain survivors. Last, a triage should be used to assist medical workers in prioritizing who needs medical treatment immediately versus those individuals that can be treated on-site. The medical facilities could be potentially overloaded if patients are all taken at once to emergency facilities.

2. *What resources do you need to mobilize?* Any type of equipment that can be used for heavy lifting should be mobilized as well as any medical personnel that will be needed to treat injured persons. The fire chief should get all of the available personnel to the site as quickly as possible as well as trained SCUBA divers for any activities that may involve deep water search and rescue efforts.

3. *What other organizations do you need to contact for assistance?* All first responders should be asked for assistance (e.g., police department, sheriff's department, etc.). In addition, the fire chief should also consider obtaining assistance from civil engineers, who may be needed to ensure safety of rescuers since parts of the bridge may have to be removed or cut away to get to victims.

Stage 2 of the Disaster

Your personnel are busy attempting to provide search and rescue around the bridge structure and in the water where several people have been killed or injured (Keen, 2007).

1. *What will you do to ensure the safety of your rescuers?* The fire chief should be extremely concerned that the remaining bridge structure might collapse, thus harming the first responders as well as further endangering victims that are still trapped in their cars or under rubble. Even though time is critical, it would be a wise precaution to have the proper heavy equipment on hand to contend with the remaining structure under the supervision of a civil engineer. In addition, medical personnel should be on-site to treat any first responders who are injured. Additionally, the first responders should have proper safety gear (e.g., helmet, steel-toed work boots) as well as water on hand to keep hydrated properly.
2. *What additional resources do you need at the rescue site?* The fire chief may want to employ barges that can assist in taking debris away from the disaster site so that first responders can more effectively perform search and rescue tactics more quickly.
3. *What is your plan for contending with the increase in medical needs?* The fire chief needs to contact other hospitals that are in the area and employ CareFlight (e.g., Medevac helicopter) as much as possible, since aircraft have better range and speed than land transportation. By using helicopters, the injured victims could be flown in a fairly speedy manner to hospitals that would have the capability to handle incoming wounded persons.

Stage 3 of the Disaster

Several cars and victims were trapped underneath the concrete or water when the bridge collapsed and there is no hope of victims being found alive at this point.

1. *What will you have your personnel focus on at this point?* The operation needs to be changed to a recovery operation instead of a search and rescue operation. The fire chief should have the first responders take their time and use every safety precaution available so that the first responders operate in an environment that is safe as possible.

2. *Different types of resources will now be needed, what will those resources need to be focused on at this stage?* Heavy lifting equipment will now become more important, along with the use of trucks and barges to haul away metal and concrete. Body bags will have to be made available and mortuaries will need to be put on alert so that the remains can be identified and the families notified.
3. *How will you keep your personnel's morale and physical health up at this point?* The fire chief needs to make sure that his or her personnel are rotated in and out of the disaster site. If the personnel are not rested, this could lead to a mistake or, worse, an injury for a first responder.

Key Issues Raised from the Case Study

Government administrators should make sure that a mechanism is in place to evaluate critical infrastructure when modifications are being made to an existing structure. The bridge was initially constructed in 1967 and had been modified several times over the years before it collapsed (CNN U.S., 2008). During the modifications to the structure, the renovation plans should have included an evaluation by engineers concerning whether or not the initial design could support the increased weight from the modifications as well as the increased traffic the bridge was now incurring on a daily basis. The bridge collapsed because the gusset plates used in the bridge's construction were half as thick as required to hold that much weight (CNN U.S., 2008). The Minnesota bridge collapse resulted in 13 deaths and 145 injured (Roy, 2008).

Items of Note

A settlement of $52.4 million was awarded to the victims of the Minnesota bridge collapse in 2010 by USR Corporation, the engineering firm responsible for the inspection of the bridge prior to the bridge collapsing in 2007 (CNN, 2010).

Northeast Blackout, 2003

Stage 1 of the Disaster

You are a director for Homeland Security in the United States. At 4:20 p.m. on August 14, you are notified that the power grid has gone down for the entire eastern seaboard of the United States, leaving 50 million people without electricity (CBS News Online, 2003).

1. *What is your plan of action?* The director needs to find out how the power supply was disrupted in order to determine whether or not the power supply was disrupted intentionally. If the power supply was intentionally disrupted, then a full investigation should be launched to determine the cause and the

criminals involved. The director will need to muster more resources to ascertain whether or not the attack on the power supply is actually a precursor to another strike on a different target. If the power supply failure occurred accidentally, then the director should attempt to identify resources that can be sent to the region to provide relief (e.g., mobile generators, water, etc.). In addition the director will need to put other resources in place to protect certain infrastructures from criminal or terrorist targeting.

2. *What is your communication plan?* The director should keep in close contact with the director of FEMA along with state and local authorities that may have gaps occurring in their operations due to the power failure. The director should also be in contact with other federal officials about having certain military assets used to assist with the monitoring of activities (e.g., Airborne Early Warning & Control [AWACS]).

3. *What are your primary concerns at this point?* The director should be concerned about criminal or terrorist attacks while the power grid is down, thus causing many areas to be vulnerable with only limited resources to protect a vast regional area.

Stage 2 of the Disaster

You have now learned that FirstEnergy's East Lake plant unexpectedly shut down, resulting in power failures along the East Coast. It is now August 15, and only some of the power has been restored (CBS News Online, 2003).

1. *What is your plan of action for entities that are still without power?* For organizations that require security and protection and which still do not have power, the director should highly consider sending organizational assets to cover any gap in security until the power grid is up and running again. The director may want to consider sending or leasing mobile generators for some organizations that could be considered high-value targets.

2. *What areas should you be concerned with that power could be critical for operations to continue?* The director should be concerned about areas that could be damaged or where certain key assets could be stolen and used later, such as certain manufacturers and key transportation hubs.

Stage 3 of the Disaster

It is now August 16, and residents still do not have electricity in certain parts of the area (CBS News Online, 2003).

1. *What is your plan to get power on in critical areas of operation?* The director should see if it would be possible to divert power from other parts of the country to locations that have high security requirements. For those

areas that still do not have power, the director can send either personnel to guard certain installations or mobile generators to power security and alarm systems.

2. *What is your mitigation plan for the next time a blackout of this magnitude occurs?* The director should come up with a plan that would actually use power from other regions of the country for the areas that power has been knocked out. If that is not possible, the director should consider pre-positioning mobile generators that can be used for certain installations temporarily until the power is running again in that region.

Key Issues Raised from the Case Study

Administrators should be wary of allowing critical infrastructure industries to regulate their own standards. One of the biggest problems that occurred in this case study was the administrators had no oversight over the utility company standards (Minkel, 2008). Administrators should also have a workable contingency plan to bring up new electrical resources quickly when infrastructure does shut down. This incident can mimic the effects of a major cyber attack, which can paralyze information technology infrastructure as well as utility grids. To prevent cyber attacks and power grid failures, sufficient resources should be dedicated to upgrade network security capability, information technology, and provide a reliable and redundant set of backup systems for emergency use.

The massive blackout in 2003 was caused by human error and the failure by utility companies to upgrade equipment over the years (Minkel, 2008). When administrators do not enforce standards or mandate equipment upgrades, the chances of having a blackout over an interconnected region increase dramatically. The power failure caused 11 people to lose their lives, cost an estimated $6 billion in damage, and left up to 50 million people without electricity (Minkel, 2008).

Items of Note

The Northeast blackout is the largest blackout in U.S. history (2009) (CBS News Online, 2003). In 2005, the Energy Policy Act of 2005 set standards and policy for the Federal Energy Regulatory Commission to oversee utility companies and ensure that minimum reliability standards are met.

TERRORISM AND CRIMINAL ACTS

Chapter 9

Case Studies: Disasters from Criminal or Terrorist Acts—Bombings

Bomb at Haymarket Square, Chicago, 1886

Stage 1 of the Disaster

You are the police chief of a large Midwestern municipality. It is May 1, and you are concerned about a new law going into effect that will make it mandatory for all workers to work a maximum of 8 hours a day (CBS Chicago.com, 2011). You know that there are factions opposing a pro-worker rally that is scheduled to occur in your municipality for May 1 (CBS Chicago.com, 2011). You expect that events could be heated between the different factions (H2g2, 2001).

1. *What is your plan of action?* The first action should be to gather intelligence on who will be attending the pro-worker rally and get an estimate on how many protesters will be attending the event. This is a potentially volatile situation, and therefore, it is important to gather as much information as possible so that the proper resources can be obtained before May 1.

2. *What is your communication plan?* At this stage, it is important to communicate with the upper city administration as well as law enforcement agencies

at both the state and federal levels and inform them that a potential threat is looming for May 1. In addition, agreements with other agencies and departments should be sought to bolster capabilities of the police department.

3. *What resources should you consider mobilizing?* Depending upon the intelligence that is received, it would be prudent to call in all police officers as well as fire and medical personnel for the May 1 event. In addition, the police officers should be equipped with riot gear and be supported with portable fences that can be used to create temporary holding space. The fire department should be contacted for the use of fire hoses for crowd disbursal.

4. *What other political or civil forces should you coordinate with before the rally?* An attempt should be made to contact both factions that will be at the rally in an effort to defuse a potentially violent event. Leaders on both sides of the rally should be forewarned that violence will not be tolerated, and that if violence ensues, the leaders will be arrested along with any followers that perform any type of behavior that could incite a riot.

Stage 2 of the Disaster

At last count, there were thousands of people participating in the rally and being led by an anarchist. You are feeling uneasy at how tense the situation is becoming, especially when you learn that the workers are now on strike nationwide (H2g2, 2001).

1. *What is your plan of action?* The police and fire personnel should be deployed with all of their riot gear. In addition, if there are other agencies that can provide police personnel to assist the city police and fire departments, those resources should be immediately deployed. The fire hoses should also be held in a position to where the water pressure can break up any riot that is forming.

2. *What is your communication plan?* The police need to coordinate with any outside agency personnel that were brought in to support the police as well as the fire department, since they are manning the hoses that may be needed in case a riot ensues. The local city government and city administrators should be kept informed as the situation evolves.

Stage 3 of the Disaster

On May 3, you are forced to dispatch police forces to the McCormick Harvesting Machine Co. plant when a fight erupts between striking workers picketing the company and strikebreakers crossing the picket line (H2g2, 2001). Your police officers kill four people and several other people are injured before the melee is brought to a stopping point (McCabe, 2009). The police actions have infuriated the local population. You realize there are many more workers than there are police officers (Arvich, 1984).

1. *What is your action plan of action?* In the current situation the police have one of two options. Either the police can send reinforcements that are equipped with riot gear as well as put the fire hoses to use by breaking up the crowds, or the police can withdraw from the area temporarily until the situation calms down. An investigation should immediately be launched into the deaths and injuries to the protesters to see if the killings were justified by the police. Additionally, it would be prudent to take measures to protect infrastructure and critical assets in other industrial areas that might be a site for another protest or riot.

2. *What is your communication plan?* Since the police officers killed four people, it is important to de-escalate the situation by discussing the events with both parties that were involved in the incident as well as announcing to the public that an investigation has been launched into the deaths and injuries of people involved in the fight. The local officials and administrators should be kept informed about the status of the riots and what is suspected that the protesters may do next.

3. *How should you involve your local politicians?* It would be advisable to involve the local politicians to see if they could talk to the local citizens to de-escalate the situation.

Stage 4 of the Disaster

The local anarchists have called for a rally at Haymarket Square, your busiest industrial center, and have made very inflammatory remarks about your police officers killing innocent workers (Arvich, 1984). The situation is getting much worse between the police and the workers.

1. *What is your plan of action?* Since the situation is very tense, you will need as much manpower and resources deployed to the Haymarket Square rally point as possible. All officers should be equipped with riot gear, and as much crowd control equipment should be deployed to the scene as possible. If leaders begin to incite protesters, they should be arrested and detained until the situation calms down with the protesters.

2. *What is your communication plan?* The communication plan should consist of meeting with the protest leaders and stating ahead of time that violence will not be tolerated. The local community leaders should be contacted and advised to encourage people that are in their respective areas of influence to stay home instead of going to the rally. City administrators should be communicated with to advise them of the current situation.

Stage 5 of the Disaster

During the rally you have several police officers monitor the demonstration. Your police officers have seen enough and begin to disperse the crowd by using a line formation. A bomb is thrown from the crowd that results in one police officer being killed. Your police officers respond by opening fire into the crowd of demonstrators (Arvich, 1984).

1. *What is your plan of action?* Police intervention has triggered a collective violence effect. If the police had simply watched and only intervened when an incident occurred, the riot and ensuing violence may well have been avoided. However, since the police did intervene, the situation has deteriorated significantly, which will force the police administration to make some very drastic decisions. If water hoses are available, they should be employed to disperse the crowd. If horseback officers are available, they should be deployed to support the police against any riot that begins to threaten the lives and safety of the police officers. Medical first responders should be dispatched immediately to assist any persons that were wounded in the riot.

2. *What is your communication plan?* The focus should be to keep the police officers from getting any further out of control than their previous actions. The police commanders need to communicate to their subordinates to maintain discipline. Communication also needs to be directed toward the protesters to leave the area peacefully and go home. The message needs to be conveyed that if violence persists, arrests will occur.

Stage 6 of the Disaster

A riot has now ensued, resulting in over 60 police officers getting wounded, 7 police officers being killed, and 4 workers being killed. There are an untold number of workers wounded in the riot (Arvich, 1984).

1. *What is your plan of action?* Medical teams need to be dispatched to the scene to treat any wounded persons. If reinforcements are available to the police, those should be dispatched immediately with riot gear to control the protesters if they are still a threat and cover any medical teams that are attempting to evacuate the wounded. Furthermore, arrests will need to be made at this point to gain control of the situation. Detectives should be dispatched to begin collecting evidence in regard to the killings of both the protesters and the police.

2. *How will you calm the community's fears?* The community needs to be reassured that the local government is in control of the situation. Therefore, it is important to control Haymarket Square and make sure the crowd is completely dispersed. The community leaders and city administrators should be requested to interface with the public and allay their fears.

Key Issues Raised from the Case Study

This case study should illustrate what can go wrong with a large crowd protesting and turning violent quickly. If it is known that large numbers of demonstrators can be potentially violent, administrators need to make sure that adequate manpower is on hand as well as resources that can be used for nondeadly force against protesters. Additionally, it would be prudent to take lead instigators into custody as soon as they begin to incite the crowd to begin acts of violence.

The inability to call in sufficient manpower to handle a crowd that consists of thousands of protesters definitely presented a problem for the police. The police using deadly force only served to incite the crowd further and resulted in a bomb being tossed among the police officers. In modern times, other resources could have been used to disperse the crowd more successfully (e.g., fire hoses, pepper spray, etc.). The police arrested eight people that were held to be responsible for the bombing and rioting at Haymarket Square. Seven of the defendants were later convicted for the crime, with five of the defendants receiving the death penalty (Naden, 1968).

Items of Note

The police chief of Chicago was later convicted for bribery (Arvich, 1984).

Wall Street Bombing, 1920

Stage 1 of the Disaster

You are a police chief of a large metropolitan East Coast city. On September 16 at noon, your police officers notice a wagon that is parked across the street from the headquarters of J.P. Morgan Inc. bank, at one of the busiest corners in the financial district (Barron, 2003). A note is found in a nearby mailbox warning of death unless all political prisoners are freed. The note is signed by the American Anarchist Fighters (Manning, 2006).

1. *What will you tell your officers to do in regard to the wagon?* You will need to tell your officers to seal off the area around the wagon and not let people anywhere near it. You also need to tell your officers to evacuate any buildings that are potentially in the area that could be damaged by a bomb blast from the wagon.
2. *How will you safeguard the public in the financial district?* After the area is sealed off by police, a bomb disposal unit should be deployed to see if the suspicious wagon is in fact dangerous and carrying a bomb. If the bomb can be defused or the wagon can be moved without having the bomb go off, then this action would prevent people from getting killed or injured and prevent the city from being damaged by a blast.
3. *What is your communication plan to your officers?* Your officers need to be vigilant for any type of suspicious activity or suspicious objects. If in fact this

situation is an action by a criminal or terrorist organization, there may be more than just one threat of criminal events that could be carried out against the public.

4. *What is your communication plan to the public?* You need to tell the public to be alert to suspicious activity and report any suspicious activity to the police department immediately. In addition, you need to tell the public to avoid the financial district for the time being.

Stage 2 of the Disaster

In a short time period, the wagon detonates, sending explosives and shrapnel in all directions (Gross, 2001). As a result, 38 people are killed, 400 other citizens are injured (Ivry, 2007), and over $2 million worth of property is destroyed (Barron, 2003).

1. *What is your plan of action?* Your plan of action should be to get medical personnel rushed to the scene to assist with any injuries that have occurred. In addition, you need to have your police investigators seal off the area to begin collecting evidence of the criminal action in an effort to catch the criminal and potentially use the evidence at a later time to convict the criminal if he or she is ever apprehended. Structural engineers should be called in to assess the damage and ensure that the buildings affected by the blast are safe to occupy. If those buildings are not safe to occupy, they will need to be temporarily condemned until they can be made safe.

2. *What is your communication plan?* You need to reassure the public that every action possible is being taken to ensure the public safety. You need to keep your city manager informed about the events that have occurred and make sure your police officers are ever vigilant for new suspicious activity that may occur.

Stage 3 of the Disaster

The public is beginning to panic as a rumor starts that another bomb is located nearby (Manning, 2006).

1. *What is your plan of action?* The only action that can be accomplished at this point is to put more patrols out so that the public can see that the police are in control of the situation. Additionally, if needed, you can call up any reserve forces you may have available to you to alleviate any manpower limitations you may have to contend with the situation.

2. *What is your communication plan?* Since there is no additional threat that you are aware of, you need to reassure the public that the rumor is unfounded and that the police department is in fact on the lookout for any suspicious activity or person that could induce a terrorist or criminal activity.

Key Issues Raised from the Case Study

No matter how remote the possibility is, an administrator should be aware of another explosive device and have a plan to evacuate the area effectively. In modern times, a bomb squad would have been dispatched to the area to contend with the threat. The biggest failure in the case study was not evacuating the area in time. The Wall Street bombing resulted in multiple people being killed or injured, as well as a large amount of property damage from the blast.

Items of Note

The 1920 Wall Street bombing resulted in no arrests or criminal prosecutions. It was suspected that anarchists planted the bomb, but the police did not have a viable suspect or proof that any particular organization was responsible for the crime (Barron, 2003).

Bombing of Boeing 247, 1933

Stage 1 of the Disaster

You are an official for the Aeronautics Branch for the Department of Commerce.* Your position is a relatively new area of responsibility within the federal government. You are in charge of preventing accidents and responding to emergencies with regard to commercial flights. On October 10, you and your staff have just received word that a commercial aircraft has crashed in Indiana at 9:15 p.m. (Plane Crash Info, 2007).

1. *What is your plan of action?* First, you should organize a search and rescue operation for possible survivors. This will require collection of resources in the form of equipment and personnel to work on this search and rescue operation. In addition, you will need medical supplies and personnel dedicated to the task of treating any possible survivors.
2. *Which agencies will you need to cooperate and how will you communicate with the agencies and the population at large?* As a representative of the federal government you will need to gain the cooperation of state and local officials that can assist you with search and rescue operations and securing the crash site for later investigation.

Stage 2 of the Disaster

You and your team arrive on the site of the aircraft wreckage and determine the following: the plane was a United Airlines flight and had seven crew and passengers on board. All of the crew and passengers died in the crash (Plane Crash Info, 2007).

---

* The Aeronautics Branch for the Department of Commerce became the Federal Aviation Agency in 1958.

1. *What is your plan of action?* The operation has now changed from a search and rescue to one of finding out the cause of the crash. You will need your team of investigators to begin reviewing the crash site and collect any evidence that may provide answers on why the crash occurred. Identification of the bodies will also need to be carried out so that the families can be notified.

2. *What is your communication plan?* You should stay in constant contact with state and local officials who can assist in keeping the crash site secure as well as contact officials of United Airlines to begin an investigation on what may have caused the aircraft to crash. You should keep the public informed of very basic information since this could become a criminal investigation at some point, depending on the cause.

Stage 3 of the Disaster

Upon investigation of the wreckage you and your team made a startling discovery. The baggage compartment was blown up by a chemical identified as nitroglycerin (Plane Crash Info, 2007).

1. *What is your plan of action?* The investigation now has a new focus— determining the party or parties responsible for planting the explosives on the plane as well as taking safety measures to prevent another similar bombing.

2. *What resources do you need to carry out and complete your investigation?* You will need cooperation at the federal, state, and local levels of law enforcement to run an effective investigation as to who could have caused the deaths of seven individuals.

3. *What other issues need to be addressed to prevent a similar event from occurring in the future?* The FAA will need to improve security procedures at airports in regard to passengers boarding planes, maintenance crews servicing aircraft, and proper screening of luggage and cargo that are carried on commercial flights.

Key Issues Raised from the Case Study

Operational safety procedures are critically important to ensure the safety of airline passengers and crews. Administrators must perform risk assessments to vulnerable targets on a regular basis to ensure that security measures are keeping up with the latest threats to the transportation industry. This case study demonstrates the danger of not having baggage properly screened for explosive devices, which can result in devastating consequences. The same danger still exists today, as seen by the bombing of Pam Am Flight 103 in Lockerbie, where an explosive device was on board the plane (BBC News, 2001).

Items of Note

The 1933 bombing of Boeing 247 was the first documented case of air sabotage. The bombing resulted in the first death of an airline flight attendant (Deepthi, 2007).

World Trade Center Bombing, 1993

Stage 1 of the Disaster

You are the police chief of a large metropolitan city in the United States. On February 26, an explosion rocks the largest business building in the country, located in your city (FBI, 2008).

1. *What is your first action step?* The police chief needs to determine what resources are available to send to the area. There will need to be crowd control and evacuation efforts, and these are priority. The cause of the explosion will need to be determined quickly in order to judge whether or not the bomb squad should be deployed. If the explosion was caused by an explosive device, the bomb squad will be required since there may or may not be other explosives that will need to be defused.
2. *What organizations do you need to contact for assistance?* First and foremost, the mayor or city manager needs to be contacted to notify him or her about the current situation. The police chief will need to coordinate efforts with other city entities, such as the fire chief, public works director (in case gas, electrical, or water lines need attention), and hospital administrators. In addition, federal and state law enforcement officials should be contacted to coordinate efforts in case the explosion was a terrorist attack or criminal act.

Stage 2 of the Disaster

Several fires resulted from the explosion, and smoke is beginning to fill the corridors and the stairwells (FBI, 2008). This building and the one right next to it generate considerable traffic, as 100,000 people a day work there or visit the business buildings (BBC, 1993).

1. *What is your plan of action?* The building and surrounding areas should be evacuated immediately since at this point you have no information on what caused the explosion. The police chief should coordinate his or her efforts with the fire department so that the resources can be used efficiently and effectively.
2. *What is your communication plan?* The police chief should keep the city officials informed on the status of efforts that are currently being undertaken to evacuate the building.

Stage 3 of the Disaster

Your officers have reported that the explosion was caused by a car bomb, which has created a 100-foot crater with six people killed and over a thousand injured (FBI, 2008).

1. *What should be the focus for your department at this point?* Once the building and surrounding areas have been evacuated, the new focus should be given to making sure all of the explosives have been diffused and ensuring that there are no more explosives that exist anywhere else in the vicinity. The next phase of operations for the police department will be to preserve and gather evidence as well as apprehending those responsible for the car bomb.
2. *What assistance do you think you will need?* A police chief will need to coordinate efforts with state and federal law enforcement in order to apprehend the criminals responsible for the bombing.
3. *What is your communication and coordination plan with other agencies?* The police chief will need to provide any clues to the other law enforcement agencies that could potentially lead to the terrorists' apprehension.
4. *What is your communication plan with the public?* The police chief should address the public on the basic information concerning what has transpired and reassure the public that an investigation is currently underway. In addition, the police chief needs to state to the public that the incident will be investigated and measures will be taken to prevent a similar type of attack in the future.

Key Issues Raised from the Case Study

The World Trade Center became a favorite target of terrorists. This bombing preceded the much deadlier attack on the World Trade Center that occurred on September 11, 2001. This first attack served as a wakeup call to administrators of the dangers posed by car bombs to fairly large buildings, as well as a need for better evacuation plans and procedures for large buildings. It is difficult to protect large structures with a high volume of traffic in parking garages and around the building. The ability to drive a vehicle full of explosives into the parking garage of the World Trade Center highlighted a flaw in the building's security. A nondescript vehicle such as a rental truck (i.e., Oklahoma City bombing of the Alfred P. Murrah Federal Building in 1995) can pack enough explosives to level a mid-sized structure.

Items of Note

The World Trade Center bombing resulted in two terrorist rings being captured and convicted (FBI, 2008).

Oklahoma City Bombing, 1995

Stage 1 of the Disaster

You are the director of a federal agency tasked with emergency management operations. On April 19, your agency is deployed to the scene of the Alfred P. Murrah Federal Building. A truck bomb was detonated in front of the building, resulting in massive damage and casualties (Michel and Herbeck, 2001). Your agency is tasked with search and rescue operations.

1. *What is your plan of action?* As director you will need to determine if available manpower has the necessary skills to perform search and rescue operations in structures that have victims trapped underneath rubble. Once this determination has been made, you will need to ensure that the proper logistics are in place to transport those individuals with their equipment to the location in a rapid manner.

2. *What resources do you need at this time?* Since there is a large amount of debris that is very heavy, digging and excavation equipment will be needed as well as trained dogs with handlers to detect where victims might be located. Any type of equipment that can be used to detect persons trapped under a great deal of rubble, such as ground-penetrating radar or equipment that can pick up sound, should be sent to the area. First responders should have helmets, steel-toed boots, and gloves in addition to the equipment that they are using. In addition, a large supply of water should be on hand to make sure the responders stay hydrated.

3. *What other departments or agencies do you need to coordinate with for the search and rescue mission?* The director should coordinate the agency's efforts with local fire and police departments. Additionally, the director should see if any companies locally could supply support for the first responders in the form of equipment or supplies that may be needed.

Stage 2 of the Disaster

When your department is on site, you notice that there is rubble and debris in every direction, and that there are bodies and injured people lying in almost every area that you can see. You believe that many more are underneath the rubble, some still alive. As the debris is carefully removed and sound listening equipment is used to find survivors, the number of people dead and wounded begins to increase.

1. *What would you do to assist medical personnel and resources?* The agency should attempt to make sure there are pathways cleared out for emergency vehicles to come and go into the emergency area for quicker egress. In addition, as victims are found a triage should be set up for anyone that has been injured so that medical personnel can put a priority on who should go to the hospitals first.

2. *What resources should you request that you could run short of during this crisis?* The director should request food, water, and ice for the first responders since those items will be needed to continue operations. In addition, more first responders will be needed when the initial wave of first responders begin to tire or wear out. If first responders are limited in number, the director should have them work in shifts. Additional lighting and generators should be requested so that operations can continue throughout the nighttime hours.

Stage 3 of the Disaster

Your department is finding survivors with missing limbs, bleeding profusely, badly burned, or horribly disfigured (Michel and Herbeck, 2001). Other victims are found around the building as well as inside the building. Sixteen buildings around the Murrah building have all been damaged by the blast (Michel and Herbeck, 2001).

1. *What is your plan of action?* Once the initial building has been searched thoroughly, the surrounding buildings should be checked for injured persons. When this has been completed, body recovery should commence as well as clearing out roadways around the building so that more heavy equipment can be brought in to look for human remains that are under tons of rubble.
2. *How will you ensure that your department can function safely and effectively in the environment?* The director should be very firm on search and rescue workers having only a set time to perform search and rescue operations. In addition, the director should make sure that a medical doctor is on site to address any injuries that occur with your employees.

Key Issues Raised from the Case Study

As in the World Trade Center disaster, a truck laden with explosives was used to attack a building. In this case, not only was the building actually destroyed completely, but several surrounding buildings were also damaged. This attack would have been difficult to prevent due to the fact that the truck was actually outside the building on the street and not in a controlled parking area. Government buildings that can be considered high-valued targets to terrorist organizations or militants should be constructed in areas that are far removed from densely populated areas and can have controlled access to and from the governmental facility.

Items of Note

The Oklahoma City bombing of the Alfred P. Murrah Federal Building caused the death of 168 people and the injury of 509 others (Michel and Herbeck, 2001).

After the explosion, the Oklahoma National Memorial and Museum was constructed. This memorial has an empty chair for every victim that was killed in the blast (Oklahoma National Memorial and Museum, 2011).

Centennial Olympic Park Bombing, Atlanta, 1996

Stage 1 of the Disaster

You are in charge of public security and safety at a major international sporting event that is being held in a very large metropolitan area. There are several venues that occur in public parks and arenas. With the threat of terrorism ever present, you have an extremely difficult task of ensuring public safety and security to thousands of people attending ceremonies and public sporting events.

1. *What is your plan to ensure security and safety for the sporting event?* Certain sites, facilities, and venues will obviously need more security than other areas. In the 1972 Munich games, Israeli athletes were taken hostage at their dormitory by terrorists, so obviously athletes' quarters will need special and added security to provide adequate protection to all athletes that are competing in the Olympics. Other venues, such as arenas, will need screening of patrons at entrances to ensure that no weapons are taken inside. Open-air areas will be much more difficult to guard and will require the use of technology to assist in securing certain areas.

2. *What resources will you need for securing the event?* Security will need to be tight and plentiful by having as many police and security guarding venues and open areas as possible. For open-air areas, security cameras can be used to supplement the use of security forces. A set of dogs and dog handlers will be required to sweep the venues for explosives. The local SWAT team should be on standby as well as the local police department's hazardous materials response unit and bomb squad. For venues that have restricted access, electronic card readers and security cameras should be installed to reduce the chance of an intruder gaining access. Barriers should also be erected in front of certain venues that could be vulnerable to car bombs since these types of attacks can cause massive casualties as well as property damage.

3. *What is your coordination plan with other agencies?* A plan needs to be formulated that can incorporate the use of local, state, and federal law enforcement and emergency response teams. A person should be designated as a liaison officer to coordinate between the different organizations. In addition, an effort should be made to use the same communication equipment and procedures in case interdepartmental cooperation does occur.

Stage 2 of the Disaster

On July 26, a concert is being held at the Centennial Olympic Park, which is expected to draw several thousand spectators to the nighttime event. At 12:30 a.m., a security guard points out an unattended green knapsack to law enforcement officers that are at the event (Noe, 2008).

1. *What is your plan of action?* The park needs to be evacuated in an orderly manner. Once the park has been evacuated, the local police department bomb squad needs to be summoned immediately and the park needs to be secured.
2. *What is your communication plan?* The units from the bomb squad need to be contacted to respond to a suspicious-looking package and local security forces should be ordered to work in tandem with the local police department to secure the facilities and look for any suspicious persons.
3. *What resources should you mobilize at this point?* If an explosive sniffing dog team is available, it should be employed to sweep the other areas for bombs, since there may be other suspect packages in the area. The security forces should begin to review security camera footage of the park to see if anyone can be identified that left the package.

Stage 3 of the Disaster

The area is immediately evacuated by law enforcement and the bomb squad is called in to contend with the suspicious-looking package. There has been an anonymous call stating a bomb would explode in the park in 30 minutes. In addition, you are having problems getting some of the people to leave because they had been consuming alcohol at the event (Noe, 2008).

1. *What is your plan of action?* Since there are quite a few inebriated people, more manpower should be brought in to ensure that everyone is evacuated in a timely fashion. Just because someone stated that the bomb will go off at a certain time does not mean that it will not go off earlier. A medical team should also be called in as a precautionary measure.
2. *What is your communication plan?* Law enforcement organizations in the vicinity should be in contact with one another and kept apprised of the situation as it unfolds. Local government officials should also be notified of the potential issues.

Stage 4 of the Disaster

At 1:20 a.m. the bomb exploded, sending shards of metal in multiple directions. More than 111 people were injured and 2 people died due to the blast (one of those died from a heart attack induced from running from the explosion) (Noe, 2008).

1. *How will you contend with the medical needs?* The security and law enforcement personnel should attempt to provide first aid to as many people as possible since many of the injured will have cuts and puncture wounds from the shrapnel. A triage should be formed so that the medical personnel can concentrate on the patients that are in dire need of medical help.
2. *How will you ensure the rest of the patrons have evacuated safely?* Security and law enforcement officers should go through the park and make sure that everyone that is wounded is found and treated and to escort the uninjured out of the park.
3. *How will you ensure that there are no other explosives in the area?* When the bomb squad arrives it will need to make a sweep of the area to ensure that no other explosive devices are in it. If an explosive sniffing dog team is available, it should be deployed to the park area to ensure that no explosives remain.

Key Issues Raised from the Case Study

It is difficult to control an open-access area that would have allowed any number of people to plant different destructive devices in the park. That being stated, there potentially could have been additional security and safety measures taken to control the area before a big event occurred. In many sporting areas, bag checks and metal detectors are routinely used when individuals enter a venue. In this particular case the entire area could have been fenced off and a security checkpoint could have been installed to control egress to and from the park area. Portable perimeter fences and temporary checkpoints could be installed on events that are high profile (making them inviting targets for terrorist or criminal activity) or will have large numbers of people present.

Items of Note

The bombing of the Atlantic Olympic Games marred the overall tone of the event. The perpetrator was not apprehended until years later. The Centennial Olympic Park bombing was carried out by Eric Rudolf, who was arrested, convicted, and sentenced to life in prison without the possibility of parole (Noe, 2008).

Chapter 10

Case Studies: Disasters from Criminal or Terrorist Acts— Other Terrorist Events

Rajneeshee Cult Salmonella Attacks, Oregon, 1984

Stage 1 of the Disaster

You are a director in a state law enforcement agency. It is September and you have learned there has been an outbreak of Salmonella in a northwestern state that has sickened 30 individuals (Ayers, 2006).

1. *What is your plan of action?* As the director, you should immediately contact the Centers for Disease Control (CDC) to have them investigate the situation. Until it is determined what caused the Salmonella outbreak, there is very little law enforcement can do but contact the local health inspector and request that any business that has been linked to the outbreak of Salmonella be investigated and temporarily closed until the cause of the outbreak can be determined.
2. *What resources will you need?* An increase in food and health inspectors will be needed to investigate the restaurants that have been linked to the outbreak thoroughly. Medical care assets should also be identified in case the outbreak becomes more epidemic among the population.

3. *What is your communication plan?* As director of a state law enforcement agency it is important to maintain contact with other federal, state, and local departments to discover the root of the problem as well as determine if this issue is occurring anywhere else in the country. The director should keep in constant contact with the medical community since at this point no one knows where the next outbreak may occur and how many resources will be needed to contain another Salmonella outbreak in the state.

Stage 2 of the Disaster

Your investigation has led you to believe that several restaurants in one city have been intentionally poisoned with Salmonella. In late September, you learn that another outbreak of Salmonella has occurred, and this time approximately 1,000 people had been infected from 10 different restaurants. In addition, local medical officials are concerned that their resources are taxed to the limit with the large amounts of new cases that are flooding their medical facilities (Ayers, 2006).

1. *What is your plan of action?* As a director, you will need to coordinate with local law enforcement agencies to investigate the method used by perpetrators to spread Salmonella throughout the restaurants and find out who is behind the terroristic act. It will also be important to determine the motives behind the poisonings, which may help law enforcement catch the criminals behind them. Additionally, you will need to recruit doctors and obtain more medical resources for people that become infected with the biotoxin.
2. *How will you coordinate with medical officials, politicians, and other law enforcement agencies?* As director of a state law enforcement agency, you will need to have data to support your position on what was occurring and documentation of your actions to provide proof that more resources are needed. An administrator has a much better chance of gaining resources if adequate documentation is present, which will give a politician or another administrator justification to provide resources to your effort in containing the Salmonella outbreak.

Stage 3 of the Disaster

The Centers for Disease Control and local state health officials are now working with your agency to discover the source of the Salmonella outbreak. The investigators have determined that the salad bars at the restaurants have been contaminated with Salmonella. You have received reports from county officials that they believe a local cult is behind the contaminations. Two county officials previously became ill after visiting the cult compound and had symptoms similar to those of the victims of the Salmonella poisoning (Ayers, 2006).

1. *What is your plan of action?* You will need to obtain a warrant and search the compound for any type of biotoxins or laboratory equipment that could be used to manufacture biotoxins. If those items are present, then you should arrest anyone that could be remotely involved with using biotoxins to poison the public. After the arrests are made, an investigative team should be sent to collect evidence for the prosecutor's office.

2. *How will you proceed with protecting the public from another outbreak?* Arresting any cult member that could potentially launch a bioattack is the only solution that would work at this point in the case study. If biotoxins are found, then law enforcement can impound those items and attempt to get cult members to tell investigators where other stockpiles of the biotoxin are located. Unfortunately, there is no way to protect the public from a biotoxin attack that is low tech and carried out in a covert fashion. The best law enforcement can hope for is that for this type of situation, residents may notice suspicious behavior that will lead to an arrest. Otherwise, law enforcement will usually be unable to take action until after the attack has occurred.

Key Issues Raised from the Case Study

A biotoxin attack can incapacitate a large portion of the population quickly, which can overload medical resources as well as other first responders. Salmonella is not as deadly as other biotoxins (e.g., small pox, Ebola, etc.), but it can render individuals very ill. Administrators should be encouraged to contact other organizations that have expertise in the field and ask for their assistance to stop the infections as quickly as possible.

The Rajneeshee Cult Salmonella attacks were carried out to affect local elections by incapacitating non-Rajneeshee Cult members during election time (Ayers, 2006). Being the first type of bioweapon attack carried out, it is understandable why so many people were infected in such a short timeframe. The key to successfully stopping such an attack is finding out the common link on how people are being infected (weapon delivery) and then attempting to find some way to prevent dispersal of any more biotoxin.

Items of Note

A search warrant was carried out at the cult compound. Deadly biotoxins, in addition to the Salmonella strains, were being actively cultured for the purpose of bioterrorism (Ayers, 2006).

Subway Attack by the Aum Cult, Tokyo, 1995

Stage 1 of the Disaster

You are the director of public safety for the transit authority of a large metropolitan city in Japan. The subway system is extremely large and transports about 5 million people per day (Bellamy, 2008). With that type of volume, you have several areas that you need to be concerned with in regard to safety and security. Furthermore, the city in which the subway operates is also known to be prone to have earthquakes.

1. *What is your plan to prevent or reduce casualties in case of an emergency?* The director of public safety should plan an effective evacuation in case of a natural disaster or other type of emergency. An effective communication system should be installed that will assist first responders in communicating to citizens evacuation notifications and directions. In addition, there should be first aid medical supplies on the subways and in the stations.
2. *What should your plan comprise of for protection of the subway infrastructure?* If possible, the director of public safety should have security cameras posted at key areas, active transit security personnel stationed at key areas inside the subway stations, and roaming security personnel inside the subways themselves. If the resources are available, screening should be set up for passengers' bags and personal items that are going through the subway system.
3. *What organizations should you have agreements in place with for the three different types of crises that could occur?* The director of public safety should have agreements in place with the local officials where subway stations are located. These agreements will allow the director of public safety to send first responders to act in a more coordinated manner with transit security personnel as well as being able to use local medical personnel and facilities. In addition, the director of public safety should make sure that they have adequate resources on hand to contend with any type of hazardous material incident or explosives.

Stage 2 of the Disaster

On March 20 between 7:00 a.m. and 8:00 a.m., your security forces reported several suspicious men (who appear very nervous) who are carrying knapsacks and taking several subway routes that all converge on Kasumigaseki station. Not only is Kasumigaseki station a large hub for commuters, but at 8:00 a.m. the station will be teaming with rush-hour commuters (Bellamy, 2008).

1. *What is your plan of action?* The director of public safety should have his transit security forces interdict the men carrying the backpacks to investigate

why the individuals are so nervous, where their final destination is, and what they are carrying. If security camera feed exists, the footage should be reviewed by security personnel to determine if any additional threats are in the area.

2. *What is your communication plan?* The security forces need to communicate with one another on this issue to determine if it is just one individual that could cause a problem, several that are converging on one target (or several targets), or if it is just a coincidence of individuals acting strangely. If something is found to be a potential threat, an evacuation plan should be enacted, with communication going to all of the passengers that are in the danger area.

3. *What resources need to be mobilized at this point in time?* If a problem is found, the hazardous materials personnel, bomb squad personnel, and medical resources should all be put on standby to respond to an emergency. Additional security personnel may be required to search for other individuals that may be a threat to safety and security in and around the subway stations at other locations.

Stage 3 of the Disaster

The suspicious individuals are seen dropping their knapsacks, puncturing those knapsacks with sharpened umbrella points, and leaving the subway cars quickly (Bellamy, 2008).

1. *What is your plan of action?* If an evacuation plan exists, it needs to be enacted immediately. Medical personnel and hazardous materials response teams need to be summoned immediately. Evacuation of the area should take a top priority.

2. *What is your communication plan?* The passengers in the station need to be informed to make way to the nearest exit and stay calm. As the director of public safety, you need to stay in close touch with your security forces as well as your other teams responding to the crisis. In addition, local leaders and other provincial officials should be kept informed of the status of the situation as it unfolds.

Stage 4 of the Disaster

The subway cars and station are crowded with people as the toxic fumes begin to be emitted from the knapsacks and passengers are seen coughing and vomiting. Panic is striking the commuters, as passengers are either collapsing or running for the exits. Medical, police, and military are arriving on scene, but at this point there is no telling exactly what the issues are for the personnel arriving on the scene (Bellamy, 2008).

1. *At this point what do you do about the safety of the passengers on the subway?* The assessment by the director of public safety is that a chemical weapon

has just been released inside the subway cars. To protect the passengers and other citizens, the trains and station should be evacuated quickly to open-air areas. A hazardous materials response team should then be sent into the station and subway cars to contend with the chemical weapons. If possible, a sample of the toxin needs to be gathered and sent to a laboratory for analysis. A determination of what type of toxin was used could be vital to successfully treating patients effectively. At a minimum, medical teams should be advised that a chemical was used on the passengers that appears to be airborne and can induce vomiting and coughing.

2. *What do you do about the individuals that were seen fleeing the scene?* Security forces should pursue and detain any individuals that are seen fleeing from the subway station that were suspected of leaving the chemical weapons around the subway cars or station.

3. *What other organizations do you need to contact for assistance at this time?* Local hospitals should be contacted so that they can admit patients who need immediate medical attention. The national police need to be contacted and communicated with as well as provincial and national government officials.

Stage 5 of the Disaster

There are now 12 people who have been killed and over 5,500 people who have been injured by the gas attack. There is no sign of the five individuals that were seen puncturing the knapsacks. The military has told you that sarin gas was used for the chemical attack (Bellamy, 2008).

1. *What resources do you need at this point?* Medical personnel and medical resources to treat patients for sarin gas effects will be critical. A hazardous materials team will be needed to sterilize the subways and the subway station of any residual chemicals as well as look for any parcels that failed to disperse the poison. Investigators need to be called in to track down the suspects responsible for the attack as well as determining how the suspects obtained the chemicals in the first place.

2. *What is your communication plan?* The next of kin should be notified about victims who were killed in the attack, as well as families whose loved ones were treated or are being treated for sarin gas exposure. The director of public safety needs to be in contact with the hazardous materials team to ensure that all chemical agents have been cleared out of the subways and subway stations before the transit line can be reopened to the public.

3. *What is your plan to locate the five individuals seen leaving the scene?* Any evidence will now need to be turned over to law enforcement as well as any security camera footage available. Any eyewitness accounts will need to be collected on the incident by the investigators.

4. *How will you reassure the public that your public transportation is safe from terrorist attack?* The director of public safety should make a public announcement on the events that have occurred and positively reinforce the notion that all steps are being taken to apprehend the terrorists responsible for the attacks. In addition, the director of public safety needs to state to the public that steps will be taken to enhance the public's safety on the subway system.

Key Issues Raised from the Case Study

A large-scale chemical attack is difficult to prevent on a major transportation hub. On critical transportation resources, chemical detectors could be deployed to warn passengers to the danger of certain types of air dispersal chemicals being released into the air. Additionally, administrators and government personnel should perform training for such an emergency so that proper resources can be deployed quickly in case of an actual event. As a result of the release of sarin gas, there were a number of people injured as well as the 12 individuals that were killed. This attack illustrated how a major transportation hub was vulnerable to attack from low-technology devices using unconventional weapons.

Items of Note

The Tokyo subway sarin gas attack by the Aum Cult led to the arrest of Shoko Asahara, who was ultimately sentenced to death (Bellamy, 2008).

Amerithrax, 2001

Stage 1 of the Disaster

You are a director for the Centers for Disease Control in the United States. Your office receives reports that on September 19, five major media organizations received letters through the U.S. Postal Service laced with a white powdery substance. This substance was later determined to be weaponized anthrax (Raimondo, 2005).

1. *What agencies should you contact to coordinate efforts to locate the source of anthrax and stop the distribution in the mail?* The director should work closely with the U.S. Postal Service to identify the origin of the letters and who could have sent them. Since the matter is criminal in nature, the FBI should be involved in finding the source of the substance. Since this substance has been identified as weaponized anthrax, the Department of Defense should be involved as well.

2. *What resources do you need to mobilize to contain the anthrax threat?* The director will need many investigators at his or her disposal since there will be many leads to check out for possible sources of anthrax. In addition, there will be a need for laboratory work performed on samples that come in for testing.

Stage 2 of the Disaster

Over the next few weeks, people continue to receive letters laced with anthrax. Twenty-two people are infected and five die (Raimondo, 2005). In many cases, people are reporting the presence of anthrax that turns out to be a false alarm. Your department's resources are completely overextended at present.

1. *What is your plan of action?* The director will need to prioritize the cases that come in to determine which leads may best point to the person who is distributing the anthrax. It is also imperative that medication for treating anthrax is available to hospitals and medical treatment centers that may need it for anyone infected.
2. *What is your communication plan?* The communication plan is to keep in contact with the other federal agencies as well as state and local officials. It is important for the director to reassure the public that the issue is being investigated and that medication for contending with anthrax is being disbursed to medical centers.

Stage 3 of the Disaster

Two letters that have a more refined grade of anthrax are mailed to U.S. senators, which results in the Capitol building being evacuated and sanitized (Raimondo, 2005).

1. *What is your plan of action?* The director should see if the sample of anthrax sent to the senators has the same characteristics as the earlier samples. Furthermore, the director needs to work with the U.S. Postal Service to determine if there is any method or equipment that can be used to detect biotoxins in the U.S. mail.
2. *What is your communication plan?* The communication plan consists of keeping in contact with the FBI, Department of Defense, U.S. Postal Service, and state and local officials. The director must give the public regular updates on the investigation and serve to reassure the public that the government is conducting a full investigation on the matter.

Key Issues Raised from the Case Study

There were a few shortcomings evidenced in this case study. The absence of controls at the laboratory where the weapons-grade anthrax was taken from has to be a primary question for governmental officials. How did someone remove the bio-toxin from the laboratory without detection, and what controls should have been in place to prevent this action from occurring? If proper controls were in place, were they being adhered to appropriately? The case study scenario also shows how vulnerable a critical infrastructure was to a biotoxin attack. By using the U.S. Postal Service, the perpetrator essentially used a public mode of delivery to launch an unconventional weapon attack across a large segment of the country.

Administrators need to ensure not only that proper controls are in place, but also that they are being followed. With dangerous items that can be weaponized, inventory control is vital in order to protect the research facilities and personnel, but also to protect the public at large. It is difficult to protect the U.S. Postal Service from an attack such as a biotoxin, since it is difficult to detect (unlike radiation or certain types of chemicals). Therefore, it is prudent to have on hand medical resources to contend with such an event since there is a possibility for individuals to be infected if a biotoxin of that nature is present.

A number of people died from anthrax infections and more than 20 people were infected by the select agent. Additionally, there were a number of times where detection of anthrax led to shutdowns of different government buildings (i.e., U.S. post offices and Capitol building). The threat of anthrax infection was enough to stop all business at these government facilities until the locations were sanitized.

Items of Note

The anthrax attacks were also known as Amerithrax and resulted in no one ever being charged with the criminal activity (FBI, 2009). One suspect, Dr. Bruce Ivins, committed suicide before officially being charged with the Amerithrax attacks (FBI, 2009).

September 11, 2001

Stage 1 of the Disaster

You are a federal administrator for an agency that is responsible for responding to a terrorist attack. On September 11 at 8:20 a.m., you receive a message that American Airlines Flight 11 has had at least two flight attendants stabbed and that a chemical agent has been used to clear out the first-class passengers. At 8:34 a.m., Otis Air National Guard base in Massachusetts is alerted to Flight 11's potential hijacking status. NORAD is not alerted to the potential hijacking until 8:37 a.m. (Ahlers, 2004). At 8:46 a.m., Flight 11, loaded with passengers and jet fuel, crashes into the North Tower of the World Trade Center, killing all passengers (BBC News, 2007b).

1. *What is your communication plan?* The administrator needs to make sure that all aircraft currently in the air are accounted for. If a plane is not responsive, this information needs to be relayed to military bases where fighter planes are located, and the executives in the federal government need to be notified immediately that a potential situation exists where terrorists may have hijacked more than one aircraft.
2. *What resources do you require at this point?* The administrator needs to establish communication links to the aircraft currently flying. In addition, the administrator needs to confirm and verify that he or she has authority to take action in case terrorists have taken over a flight.
3. *What agencies should be communicating and sharing information?* The administrator should contact the Department of Defense and the Federal Aviation Administration (FAA) about the current situation, as well as the White House.
4. *What is your plan of action?* The administrator should establish the status of all flights. If current status cannot be verified or confirmed, the administrator should verify the authority he or she has to contend with such a situation. If the authority is given to contend with the situation, then fighters should be sent to intercept any aircraft that cannot be contacted. Until the situation is resolved, all flights should be kept on the ground until further notice.

Stage 2 of the Disaster

Two F-15s are scrambled to intercept Flight 11, but this plane has already hit the World Trade Center. The F-15s are sent into a holding pattern around New York when Flight 11 cannot be located. Around 8:50 a.m., United Airlines Flight 175 has become uncommunicative with the flight controllers and the transponder codes have been changed. A call from a flight attendant at 8:52 a.m. states that both pilots have been killed and a flight attendant has been stabbed. The flight attendant believes that the hijackers are in control of the plane. At 8:56 a.m., American Airlines Flight 77 is unresponsive to communication and the plane's transponder has been turned off (National Institute of Standards and Technology, 2005).

1. *What is your communication plan?* The different agencies of the federal government should be contacted as well as the Department of Defense to request an intercept of Flights 175 and 77 by fighters that are currently on standby over New York.
2. *What is your plan of action?* The administrator will need the proper authority to take action on the flights that are suspected of being hijacked. Since there are at least two known flights that are suspected of having the crew killed, there will need to be fighters to intercept this aircraft immediately.

Stage 3 of the Disaster

At 9:02 a.m., United Flight 175 hits the South Tower of the World Trade Center, killing all occupants of the plane. People are stumbling out of both World Trade Center buildings and in some cases are jumping out of windows due to the fires that are raging out of control. At 9:03 a.m., the FAA contacts NORAD about Flight 175 being hijacked. At 9:04 a.m., Boston Air Route Traffic Control Center stops all departing flights from New England and New York. At 9:08 a.m., the FAA stops all departing flights that are going through New York airspace and bans flights from entering New York airspace. At 9:13 a.m., the F-15s are ordered to Manhattan airspace. At 9:24 a.m., NORAD is informed that American Airlines Flight 77 and United Airlines Flight 93 have been hijacked (National Institute of Standards and Technology, 2005). At 9:26 a.m., the FAA grounds all flights across the country. At 9:28 a.m., Flight 93 is taken over by hijackers. At 9:34 a.m., the FAA notifies the Secret Service, which in turn evacuates the White House when Flight 77 turns toward Washington, D.C. At 9:37 a.m., Flight 77 has crashed into the Pentagon, destroying an entire section of the building, killing all passengers and 125 military personnel inside the Pentagon (National Commission on Terrorist Attacks upon the United States, 2004).

1. *What is your communication plan?* The administrator should keep attempting to contact any aircraft that are still in the air and have the crews be alert for a possible hijacking. The White House should be notified about the actions that have transpired and notified that Flight 93 appears to be under terrorist control.
2. *What is your plan of action?* The administrator should make every effort to find out what aircraft can land at the nearest location to get as many planes out of the sky as possible. This will allow the administrator to focus on only aircraft that could have been potentially taken over by terrorists as a threat. The aircraft that do not respond can then have fighter jets intercept them to either force them to land or shoot them down.

Stage 4 of the Disaster

Around 10:00 a.m., United Airlines Flight 93 crashed in Pennsylvania and around the same time the South Tower of the World Trade Center collapses. Around 10:30 a.m., the North Tower of the World Trade Center collapses. There are an untold number of dead and injured, and yet there could be more attacks that could occur (BBC News, 2007b). You have a number of people that are trapped in rubble and the debris (National Institute of Standards and Technology, 2005). Additionally, you still have a credible threat of terrorism that may yet occur.

1. *What is your plan of action?* At this point the administrator should have a very clear count on how many aircraft are still in the air that could be a potential threat. International flights should be escorted in via fighter jets since there

may or may not be enough time to verify if the aircraft are under control of the crews and most of the international flights head toward big cities with major landmarks.

2. *What is your communication plan?* The federal agencies that are impacted by air travel should be briefed on the situation. The administrator should also brief the public on the events as they have unfolded and assure the public that an investigation is underway to prevent occurrences of this nature from happening in the future.

Key Issues Raised from the Case Study

In part, poor controls of student visas granted to international students allowed for several of the terrorist students to stay in the United States past the deadline of their visa expiration dates. Whether or not active tracking of those individuals by the government would have averted this particular crisis will always be debatable. What is not debatable is that a small number of individuals were able to take over four different airlines using an assortment of weapons (e.g., box cutters). The failure to detect the makeshift weapons was a clear defect in airport security screening, which gave the individuals on board a commercial aircraft the means to take control of four airliners.

Aircraft being used by terrorists as a terror weapon was a new concept to public officials. Instead of terrorists using the passengers as hostages, as had been done in previous hijackings, terrorists were now seeking out a method to extract massive amounts of casualties and damage at a very low cost. This new approach also illustrated how vulnerable transportation infrastructure could be to takeover and used as a very large and powerful weapon.

Items of Note

The 9/11 terrorist skyjacking and suicide attack left 2,974 people dead (excluding the 19 hijackers), 24 missing and presumed dead, and over 6,000 injured (Spektor, 2007). In 2011, Osama Bin Laden, the man behind the 9/11 attacks, was killed by the United States in a nighttime raid in Pakistan by a team of Navy Seals (Goldman, 2011).

JFK International Airport Terror Plot, 2007

Stage 1 of the Disaster

You are in charge of a public safety department at a large municipal airport. You have reports from your security force that three or four suspicious men have been seen taking pictures of the airport.

1. *What are the possible concerns for public safety that you might have?* The possible concern that one should have in this situation is that the airport is being reconnoitered for a possible terrorist infiltration or attack on the airport, planes, or passengers.
2. *What resources do you need to mobilize at this time?* You need to mobilize your local security assets at this point and secure the perimeter of the airport from potential penetration by persons unknown. In addition, any area where the men were seen taking pictures needs to have additional security sent to that location.
3. *What other organizations should you contact for assistance?* Federal agencies such as Homeland Security and the FBI should be contacted as well as any local law enforcement agencies that can assist in tracking down any potential terrorists.

Stage 2 of the Disaster

It turns out that one of these four men was a former cargo worker at the airport and has been arrested by the Federal Bureau of Investigation after contacting an informant about a plan to attack the jet fuel pipeline to the airport (BBC News, 2007a).

1. *What is your plan of action?* As part of an ongoing investigation, it would be very prudent to begin investigating any coworkers or employees with whom this individual had regular contact who could be a potential threat to the airport. Additionally, extra security precautions should be given to the infrastructure of the airport since these areas are potentially vulnerable to attack.
2. *What resources do you need?* You may need additional security personnel as well as security assets such as cameras to better protect the airport from an attack. A study should be undertaken to see if the infrastructure could have additional safety and security measures built in to the pipelines in an effort to provide better protection.
3. *What is your communication plan to the governmental agencies and the public?* It is extremely important to turn over any information to law enforcement agencies so that any terrorists involved in the plot to attack the airport can be captured. The public should be reassured that all proper steps were taken to apprehend the terrorists and that the airport was never in danger from the terrorists.

Key Issues Raised from the Case Study

Preventing the attack at JFK Airport shows that administrators and federal officials maintained good intelligence work and took appropriate steps to prevent the terrorist attack, effectively arresting the suspects. By anticipating the plan that was being considered, administrators could reinforce potentially vulnerable targets by putting in additional safety or security measures to prevent future terrorist attempts.

Items of Note

The JFK International Airport terror plot never got beyond the planning stage and resulted in the arrests of three of the four terrorists planning the attacks (BBC News, 2007).

Chapter 11

Case Studies: Disasters from Criminal or Terrorist Acts— Shootings and Riots

University of Texas at Austin, Charles Whitman, 1966

Stage 1 of the Disaster

You are president of a prestigious university located in a midsized town. Your university has a very large student population and a large campus with numerous buildings. You have just been notified that the university police have cited a student for dragging a deer carcass through the dormitory and for skinning the deer carcass in the dormitory shower. The student had shot and killed the deer during a hunting trip (Lavergne, 1997). You find out that the student is not performing well in his academic pursuits.

1. *What is your plan of action?* The president should ask the dean of the student's academic program to intervene to improve his academics. The dean of students should also be contacted since the student should be interviewed to find out if there are any problems the student is having outside of school that is causing behavior not deemed to be normal in the university setting. If the dean of students senses something is wrong, the student should be referred to a counselor in the student health services.

2. *What resources might you want to acquire?* This incident would appear to be a reminder to university officials that a review of security measures is probably warranted. Additionally, the police department needs to have proper equipment and manpower to contend with a wide variety of issues since the university is the size of a municipality.

Stage 2 of the Disaster

It has been reported to you that a student seeing a university doctor and a university psychiatrist has made remarks to the effect that he wanted to "start shooting people". You realize that this is the same student that was cited earlier by the university police for the deer in the dormitory. Your staff member has uncovered information that the student in question had a U.S. Marine Corps scholarship for the mechanical engineering program, but it was cancelled the previous year (Lavergne, 1997). You have one of your staff members do further investigation about the student.

1. *What is your plan of action?* The mental stability of the student is in question at this point and should be taken very seriously. The president should make sure that the dean of students is aware of and abreast of the situation. The president should empower the dean of students to suspend the student from school if the student appears to be a threat to himself or others. In addition, an effort should be made to get the student to seek more medical assistance.

2. *What is your communication plan?* The president should communicate the issues to his police chief as well as his dean of students. Due to medical privacy issues, there is very little else you can communicate to anyone else at this point.

Stage 3 of the Disaster

It has been reported to you that several people have just seen a suspicious person wearing a green jacket, khaki coveralls, and jeans (Lavergne, 1997) pushing a dolly with a trunk across the campus (Macleod, 2007b). A security guard remembers giving the person (who was identified as a research assistant by his ID card) a parking pass after the student claimed he was making a delivery. Unfortunately, no one seems to remember what direction the person was heading (Macleod, 2007b).

1. *What is your plan of action?* An order should be given to the campus police to find the suspicious person immediately. Additionally, the president can direct the police to find the vehicle the person was driving and thus determine who the person is and where they may be going on campus.

2. *What is your communication plan?* The president should keep in close contact with the chief of police to monitor the situation. Additionally, if the situation continues much longer, department heads should be contacted to see if any suspicious persons have been seen in their areas.

Stage 4 of the Disaster

One of your employees just ran into the student at the university tower as he was taking the elevator to the top floor. He had his dolly and trunk in tow (Lavergne, 1997).

1. *What concerns do you have about the student's actions?* Since there are no research facilities in the university tower, the person has no business (as a research assistant) bringing a trunk into the building.
2. *What is your plan of action?* The president should contact the university police and have them dispatched to the university tower immediately. If any employees are in the university tower, they should be alerted to the fact that a suspicious person is in the building and told to be cautious being around the person.

Stage 5 of the Disaster

Shots are heard ringing out from inside the university tower. You receive a call from the municipal police department stating that sniper fire has commenced from the tower and several of your students have been shot (Macleod, 2007c). Panic is now rushing over the campus and students are fleeing in every direction (Lavergne, 1997).

1. *What is your plan of action?* The president should direct the university police to evacuate the area immediately. If any students have been wounded, the police should be directed to get them out of harm's way as fast as possible. The president should direct his chief of police to coordinate efforts with local police to apprehend the sniper.
2. *What is your communication plan?* Students should be directed to stay indoors and away from windows to stay safe. If students are out in the open, they should be directed to seek shelter in nearby buildings. The president should stay in constant contact with his police chief as well as the municipal police department to monitor the situation.

Stage 6 of the Disaster

You now have state police officers, county sheriff's deputies, and municipal police officers on the campus grounds attempting to shoot at the tower. You have local citizens entering the fray and firing at the student with high-power hunting rifles that are in their vehicles (Macleod, 2007c). The police have informed you that only one person is at the top of the tower acting as a sniper. You now have wounded and dead littering the campus courtyards and anarchy is present (Macleod, 2007c).

1. *As a university president, what are your priorities at this point?* The priority is to do anything possible to prevent anyone else from getting killed or wounded. Anyone that has been wounded needs to be evacuated to a hospital as soon as possible.
2. *What resources might you want to acquire?* For anyone that is wounded, obtaining any type of armored car to protect first responders would be preferable. This type of transportation will allow for first responders to safely evacuate wounded persons to a hospital.

Stage 7 of the Disaster

Armored cars and ambulances are now attempting to reach the wounded to evacuate them to a nearby hospital (Lavergne, 1997). A plane is flying overhead to draw fire from the sniper and distract him from shooting down on the campus (Zeman, 1999). You now receive word that three police officers are in the tower and there are people that have been trapped in the bottom of the tower for several minutes, afraid to risk getting shot by the sniper (Macleod, 2007c).

1. *What is your plan of action?* Try to communicate with anyone located at the base of the tower and advise him or her to tell the others to stay there since the sniper fire is coming from an observation deck, and that help is going to arrive. Once the wounded have been evacuated and everyone else is in a building that is safe from rifle fire, the university police need to be directed to help other law enforcement officials in getting the sniper.
2. *What is your communication plan?* The president needs to stay in contact with law enforcement officials as well as municipal officials. In addition, the local hospitals should be notified that there are still some wounded persons that may be coming to their facilities.

Stage 8 of the Disaster

A green towel is being waived from the tower's observation deck by police to indicate the sniper has been neutralized (Lavergne, 1997). Police have informed you that three people were found dead inside the tower close to the observation deck (Lavergne, 1997). A total of 13 people were killed instantly by sniper fire, with another 33 people wounded, with 2 of those being in critical condition (Court TV Online, 1999).

1. *What is your plan of action?* There will need to be a reassessment on how security forces keep track of individuals on campus and how they react to suspicious persons. Unfortunately, the university tower will have to be monitored concerning who has access to the observation deck, and additional dedicated security for that particular building will need to be employed. The monitoring of students that have bizarre or incongruent behavior needs to be improved, as well as having an emergency plan of action in place.

2. *What resources might you want to acquire?* The university will need to have an emergency plan of action formulated as well as develop agreements with other entities to provide the university with law enforcement resources (e.g., a SWAT team) when unusual situations arise. Furthermore, there needs to be joint training between the municipal law enforcement officers and the university police officers.

3. *What measure could you put in place to prevent an occurrence in the future?* In the university tower, metal detectors could be put in place near the entrance to the elevator that provides access to the observation deck. In current times (2011), several electronic devices can be used, such as security cameras, card readers, and modern alarm systems, to potentially mitigate this type of incident from occurring.

Key Issues Raised from the Case Study

It is often difficult to contend with issues such as students that are violent and mentally ill. Often there has to be a threshold of erratic behavior before intervention can be taken with a student that may have mental health issues. Clearly, administrators should act if a student is making statements that he or she is going to "start shooting people." The shootings at other higher education institutions that occurred after this case study follow similar patterns (e.g., Virginia Tech, a disturbed student loner). For administrators it is important to take precautionary measures and ensure that structures on campus offer law enforcement officers a clear field of fire and afford a sniper protection, and they should have adequate security, preventing armed individuals from going into such structures with weapons (e.g., security guards and metal detectors). Unfortunately, there may be very little administrators can really do to prevent such an incident from occurring if a perpetrator begins shooting in a dense or crowded area.

On large college or university campuses, which have open access, it is difficult to determine who should and should not be on a campus legitimately. In this case, the sniper was a student attending the university, and this makes it impossible to prevent him from being on campus grounds. However, having no security in the tower and the campus security failing to question him on what and where he was delivering an item provided the hole in security that the sniper took advantage of by moving his weapons across campus unabated.

Items of Note

It was discovered that the student's wife and mother were stabbed to death before he began his shooting spree from the tower (Macleod, 2007a). The observation deck at the tower was closed for 2 years after the incident and was eventually closed permanently in 1974. In 1999, the observation deck tower reopened under tight restricted access overseen by tour guides (Heimlich and Edwards, 1998).

Los Angeles Riots, 1992

Stage 1 of the Disaster

You are the top administrator for a large metropolitan city on the West Coast of the United States. On April 29, in response to a court decision, a riot begins to erupt in your downtown area (Gray, 2008). Several fires have been started, looting is rampant, and your city firefighters' lives are being threatened while they are attempting to put out several of the fires (Delk, 1992).

1. *What is your plan of action?* The city manager should direct the police department to deploy all available manpower to protect the firefighters and contain the riots in the downtown area. Nonlethal riot gear should be employed quickly to not only quell the rioters, but also get anyone safely out of the area.
2. *What resources do you need?* The city manager will need to call in all first responders available to contend with the fires and riots. Depending on how big the riot is, the city manager should also consider asking nearby cities to send additional first responders to assist with the fires and riots.
3. *What is your communication plan?* The city manager should appeal to the public to stay calm and avoid coming near the downtown area. The city manager should also be in communication with state and other local officials to get assistance with getting the riot under control and putting out fires that are currently burning.

Stage 2 of the Disaster

The riot has now spread to 45–50 square miles and your state's National Guard has been called up by the governor. At this point, there have been 9 deaths and over 150 injuries so far in the riot. You are now faced with over 50,000 people taking to the streets with weapons (Suburban Emergency Management Project, 2004). Looting is increasing and you have not brought order to the city as of yet.

1. *What is your plan of action?* The first priority should be to get injured persons out of danger and into a hospital to be treated. The city manager should

request that the National Guard go to the worst areas of rioting so that certain sectors can be nullified of violence. The police department can then be redeployed to other areas more cohesively to combat rioters in other sectors of the city. In this manner, the rioters will be faced with two well-trained and coordinated forces that should be able to gain control of the situation.

2. *How will your resources integrate with the National Guard?* The city manager should set up a command post that can provide a liaison officer between the police department, fire department, and National Guard that can coordinate the different efforts.

3. *What resources do you need at this point in the crisis?* Since there are 50,000 rioters, the city manager should highly consider asking for more manpower as well as armored vehicles to contain the rioters. The city manager will also need food and water delivered to his or her employees that are currently contending with rioters.

Stage 3 of the Disaster

Your highway patrol has just dispatched 300 officers to protect the firefighters and try to control the outskirts of the rioting. On top of everything else, the sheriff (top law enforcement officer in the area) and the mayor are feuding. Also, the sheriff and chief of police cannot seem to agree on how the National Guard troops should be deployed, and consequently, the National Guard troops have not been deployed (Suburban Emergency Management Project, 2004).

1. *How will you contend with the political situation between your chief of police, sheriff, and mayor?* The city manager should call a meeting among these officials to develop a consensus quickly on how to deploy the National Guard troops. The longer the National Guard troops are inactive, the longer that the riot will continue since the city lacks the number of police officers that are needed to control the riot. The city manager does have leverage over the chief of police, and if the plan he or she wants to use is not workable, the city manager should consider replacing him or her temporarily with another person that can be a team player.

2. *How should the National Guard troops be deployed?* The National Guard should be deployed to the worst of the rioting since they are better equipped to combat a large number of persons in riot gear in addition to the small arms that the National Guard troops have been issued.

Stage 4 of the Disaster

The latest report received is that over 1,000 people have been injured and 31 people have been killed in the rioting. A new problem has arisen because the medical facilities are becoming overrun and patients are being shipped to hospitals that are farther away (Suburban Emergency Management Project, 2004).

1. *What will you do about the current shortage for medical resources?* The city manager should inquire if the National Guard can provide Medevac support in the form of helicopters. If the National Guard can provide this support, the city manager should set up a landing zone for helicopters to take wounded persons to hospitals that are capable of treating injuries sustained in the riot. If possible, the city manager should ask the Navy if the hospital ship USNS *Mercy* can be brought to the city to provide additional medical support.
2. *What other shortages are you currently facing?* Even with the National Guard, 50,000 rioters will need to be controlled by more manpower than is currently available. In addition, holding cells for rioters that have been arrested along with people to guard them will be in short supply.

Stage 5 of the Disaster

Due to all of the confusion, the governor, after 2 days of rioting, has now asked for 3,500 federal troops to be deployed from Fort Ord. The troops are finally deployed on May 2 (Suburban Emergency Management Project, 2004).

1. *What is your plan of action at this point?* The city manager should see if the additional troops can be sent to areas where the rioting is the worst and be integrated with the National Guard's efforts to combat the rioters.
2. *What is your recovery plan?* To rebuild such a broad area will take time and money. Funds will need to be raised and budgets will need to be adjusted to clear out debris and repair infrastructure. The first order of business will be to find shelter and provide supplies to those that are now homeless. A second focus will be to find those responsible for the rioting, arrest them, and prosecute them to the fullest extent of the law.

Key Issues Raised from the Case Study

A major metropolitan city should have an effective organizational structure in place to contend with such an occurrence. The decision-making process should be seamless when dealing with a rioting crowd, and plans should be in place to obtain more resources and make the most use of those resources quickly. As seen in this case study, the command and control center was not unified, which led to an even more dysfunctional situation in responding to the rioting. By not deploying the National Guard troops in a timely fashion, the administrators allowed for more devastation to occur to more parts of the city.

Items of Note

The Los Angeles Riots ultimately cost the lives of 53 people (Gray, 2008). The riots also destroyed over 1,100 buildings and left 2,300 people injured (CNN, 2002).

Columbine High School Massacre, Colorado, 1999

Stage 1 of the Disaster

You are the superintendent of a suburban school district in the United States. On April 20, at 11:45 a.m., you receive a phone call stating that there are two gunmen rampaging through your high school (*Boulder News*, 1999).

1. *What is your plan of action?* The superintendent needs to immediately have the local police dispatched to the high school and make sure that students, staff, and teachers are being evacuated out of the school. The superintendent needs to provide the police and fire department with an accurate floor plan of the high school that may help the first responders contend with the emergency more effectively.
2. *What organizations do you need to coordinate with at this point in the crisis?* The superintendent should be coordinating efforts with the local police department, fire department, and hospitals to provide medical support if it is needed.
3. *What resources do you need to mobilize?* The superintendent at this point cannot really do much except request the local police department to mobilize units to the high school. In addition, the hospitals must be contacted to provide medical services, and the fire department may be needed in case the gunmen have more than just firearms for weapons (i.e., explosive devices).
4. *What is your communication plan?* The communication plan will be limited since there is little information for the superintendent to relay to anyone. All that is known at this point is that two gunmen are in the high school.

Stage 2 of the Disaster

At noon, the SWAT and bomb disposal teams arrive to disarm several bombs around the high school campus and secure the perimeter while ambulances evacuate wounded students (*Boulder News*, 1999). At 12:30 p.m., the SWAT team enters the high school in search of the gunmen and to rescue any students that may still be inside (*Boulder News*, 1999). Gunshots are still being heard outside the high school from the second floor around where the library is located (Steel, 2008).

1. *What is your plan to account for the student population of the school?* The superintendent will need to find as many teachers and administrators as possible to account for students that were in their classes at the time of the attack. Hopefully, the superintendent can get an accurate head count of who may still be in the high school from teachers and staff.
2. *What type of resources do you need at this point?* Medical resources will be needed badly at this point in the crisis. In addition, the superintendent will need to have some mechanism in place to notify families of their child or employee's condition in case they were hurt or killed by the gunmen. A public affairs official for the district should be on hand to report the status of the situation to the parents and community.

Stage 3 of the Disaster

SWAT is evacuating students, staff, and teachers from the high school as they go room to room looking for the gunmen (Steel, 2008). An additional problem for SWAT is that they are defusing homemade bombs as they proceed cautiously through the high school (Steel, 2008). At this point, you know there are some students and teachers that have been killed or wounded by the gunmen. At 4:00 p.m., the SWAT team has finally secured the high school (*Boulder News*, 1999).

1. *What is your plan of action at this point?* The superintendent is going to have to come up with a plan to move forward after this tragedy has occurred. What to do about the high school will be a very emotional decision after an occurrence like this has unfolded. The superintendent will also need to address security policies, precautions, and procedures that are currently in place at the district's other schools in order to reevaluate their effectiveness.
2. *What is your communication plan?* The superintendent will need to make a public statement on what occurred at the high school and what will happen going forward. The superintendent needs to make sure that the public is aware that change will be coming to make the schools safer in the future from having such a situation occur again.

Key Issues Raised from the Case Study

There is very little that a public school can do in the event of such an occurrence except to have an effective evacuation plan in case an armed gunman enters the school. In this case the problem is complicated by the fact that the gunmen were students and it would have been extremely difficult to detect their intentions by school employees until it was too late since they were outside the building when their explosive devices detonated.

Unless early warning signs are heeded that students may have mental illness and could possibly be violent, administrators run the risk of a violent incident occurring in their organization. If action is taken proactively against potential violent individuals, a crisis can potentially be averted.

Items of Note

The Columbine High School massacre resulted in 13 students and teachers killed and 25 injured. The gunmen both took their own lives (Steel, 2008).

Beltway Sniper Attacks, 2002

Stage 1 of the Disaster

You are a governor for an East Coast state in the United States. Your office has just received a report that on September 5 at 10:30 p.m., a person was shot several times while locking up his restaurant (Dao, 2003). On September 21, two more people are shot, one injured and the other person killed in front of the liquor store that they managed (CBC News, 2004).

1. *What is your plan of action?* Since the killings appear to be the act of a single killer, the state police need to be notified to keep a lookout for any suspicious activity. The state police and local police departments need to coordinate efforts in an attempt to find the gunman or gunmen responsible.
2. *What resources do you need at this point?* The resource needed at this point is an analysis from the crime scenes to determine and verify if the victims were all killed in the same manner, and if so, what type of weapon was used. In addition, manpower needs to be deployed to begin hunting the perpetrators down that are responsible for this crime.
3. *What agencies should you coordinate with at this time?* The FBI should be contacted to see if a criminal profiler could be assigned to assist in the investigation effort. The state police force should work with county and local law enforcement agencies in an effort to track down the gunman or gunmen responsible for the attacks.
4. *What is your communication plan?* The population should be informed of the situation and asked for their assistance in trying to capture the wanted criminals.

Stage 2 of the Disaster

On October 2 and 3, six more people are shot and killed along the Beltway (CBC News, 2003). All of the killings on those 2 days were caused by a bullet shot from a great distance by a sniper (Mansbridge, 2003). Between October 7 and October 22, four victims were shot and killed and two other victims were wounded by the sniper in a state that borders yours to the south (CBC News, 2003).

1. *What is your plan of action?* The sniper is apparently very mobile and elusive. Therefore, more resources are going to be needed to capture the sniper. The governor should request the FBI to assist in the investigation since the sniper is now committing crimes across state lines. Another appeal to the public should be made in an effort to capture the sniper to provide information that may assist law enforcement.
2. *What resources do you need to mobilize against the sniper?* Federal, state, and local police officers will be needed to capture the sniper. In addition, resources such as security cameras, helicopters, and aircraft need to be used to observe areas where the sniper appears to operate. In addition, checkpoints can be set up along the Beltway to check for the sniper.

Key Issues Raised from the Case Study

This case study is an example of how deadly a sniper can be when he or she is a skilled marksman, has an accurate and reliable weapon, and is highly mobile. This type of attack is almost impossible to prevent if the sniper has the initiative and there is no basis to detect this type of individual from bringing a weapon into the area. If a sniper takes a shot from a long distance away, the individual could be gone from the entire area before first responders appear on the scene. It may have taken a while for law enforcement to catch the snipers in this case, but overall this case study demonstrates how law enforcement must use patterns to interdict and arrest such individuals.

Administrators need to be aware that attempting to apprehend such individuals may take time, patience, and a good search strategy. Administrators must also be aware that attempting to apprehend such individuals will take quite a few resources to perform a search and set up checkpoints on major roadways.

Items of Note

The Beltway sniper attacks resulted in 10 people killed and 3 people injured (CBC News, 2003). Police arrested John Allen Muhammad and Lee Boyd Malvo in a car with a Bushmaster AR-15 rifle that had been used in the attacks (CBC News, 2004). John Allen Muhammad was sentenced to death and executed, while his accomplice, Lee Boyd Malvo, was sentenced to life in prison without parole in 2003 (Calvert, 2009).

Virginia Tech Massacre, 2007

Stage 1 of the Disaster

You are a university administrator at a large public university. On Monday, April 16, at 8:00 a.m., you receive a report that two students have been shot and killed in one of the resident halls on campus (Office of Governor Timothy M. Kaine, 2007). It is 9:00 a.m. and you are now receiving reports that there was no gun found at the scene of the crime and the university police have no one in custody. At 9:26 a.m. the university sends an email to its students stating that two students have been killed in an apparent domestic altercation (Office of Governor Timothy M. Kaine, 2007).

1. *What is your plan of action?* The administrator should prepare for the worst-case situation at this point and assume there is at least one gunman on the campus grounds roaming around. The administrator needs to have the university police keep searching for the gunman and should consider calling in the local police department for assistance. Any security tapes of the dorm area should be reviewed to see if any suspicious persons are captured by the camera.

2. *What is your communication plan?* A message should be sent out immediately dismissing the students from class for the day since the gunman is still potentially in the area. The administrator should apprise the local government officials that there is a potential problem on campus that still has not been resolved.

3. *What resources do you require at this point?* There needs to be a concerted effort to determine where the gunman is, so that he or she can be taken into custody. To accomplish this task, the administrator will need as many law enforcement and security personnel as possible to assist in the search for the person who is still at large. The local police department should be asked to provide assistance.

Stage 2 of the Disaster

At 10:00 a.m., the university administration receives a call from a faculty member at Norris Hall that a note was attached to the exterior doors stating that any attempt made to gain entrance through the locked door would cause a bomb to go off. Meanwhile, gunshots are heard coming from Norris Hall's second floor (Office of Governor Timothy M. Kaine, 2007).

1. *What is your plan of action?* The administrator should have the police converge on Norris Hall. Since there is the potential of an explosive device, the local police department bomb squad will need to be summoned.

2. *What is your communication plan?* The administrator needs to notify people on campus immediately to stay in their buildings (with the exception of Norris Hall) until police have secured the area.

Stage 3 of the Disaster

The police are having difficulty breaking through the barricaded doors. After 5 minutes, the police finally gain entrance into the building. The last shot has just been fired. In Norris Hall there are multiple dead and wounded. High wind conditions dictate that CareFlight cannot be used to transport the wounded. Transportation of the wounded will have to occur by other means (Office of Governor Timothy M. Kaine, 2007).

1. *What is your plan of action?* The administrator should have every vehicle that can take wounded to the hospital commandeered so that evacuation can occur as quickly as possible. The police will need to make sure that the building is swept clean for explosive devices or other gunmen that could be hiding in Norris Hall. Medical supplies that can be used should be disbursed to treat the wounded, and anyone able to administer first aid should be requested to do so until proper medical help arrives or the person is evacuated.

2. *What is your communication plan?* The administrator needs to communicate to the public what has occurred and what steps are being taken to take care of the wounded. For people that have been killed, the administrator should take steps to notify the next of kin.

Key Issues Raised from the Case Study

Events are not always as they seem and administrators should not be hesitant about deploying additional resources to a situation that could be potentially more dangerous than initial observations indicate. The killer in this case hit two different areas of the campus at different times, which misled authorities on what was actually occurring. It would have been difficult to determine from the initial crime scene that a killer was still on the loose after police found the first two students that had been murdered, which could have appeared to be a murder-suicide.

Administrators in higher education institutions must also keep in mind that maintaining an open-access campus results in less effective security because large, open areas cannot be covered by the number of police officers or security forces that are typically on hand at a college campus. Other methods, such as security cameras and card keyed locks, can be used to supplement the existing security forces on a higher education campus.

Items of Note

The 2007 Virginia Tech massacre resulted in 27 students being killed, 5 faculty members being killed, and 23 people injured or wounded during the killing spree. The gunman took his own life when the police moved into Norris Hall (Office of Governor Timothy M. Kaine, 2007).

Chapter 12

Case Studies: Man-Made Disasters—Nuclear, Biotoxins, or Chemicals

Donora, Air Pollution, 1948

Stage 1 of the Disaster

You are the governor of a large, industrial eastern state in the United States. There are several big industrial centers located around a large city in your state. People have begun to become ill in Donora from the toxic fumes billowing from the factories (Gammage, 1998).

1. *What is your communication plan?* You need to contact city officials in the large city and ask them what they are doing to investigate the issue of health problems of citizens related to the industrial base. Second, you should contact federal, state, and local health agencies and ask them for assistance and information on industrial waste-related illnesses on human populations.
2. *How will you contend with the company owners?* Factory owners need to be contacted and told that inspections will occur at their factories, and that if pollutants are found to be coming out of their factories beyond a certain threshold, the factory owners will be held accountable for reducing the amount of pollutants being expelled in the soil, water, and air. If factory owners do not comply, you will need to begin administrative actions on those companies by levying fines.

3. *What policies and procedures should you put in place?* As an executive member of state government, you should contact the legislature and ask for policies and procedures be put into law that would make factories safer and cleaner for the residents of the communities in your state. Administratively, you can ask various state agencies to formulate new guidelines that will force factories to be more environmentally sound.

4. *What resources should you mobilize?* You will need to begin mobilizing your state agencies regarding health and safety to combat the problem of pollutants causing illnesses to your residents. Additionally, you need to be prepared to move citizens out of certain contaminated areas if the health situation deteriorates any further. You need to provide temporary shelter and logistics if this situation arises.

Stage 2 of the Disaster

Donora, a town of 14,000 people, now has 7,000 people ill from pollution inhalation. Twenty people have been asphyxiated and died (Gammage, 1998).

1. *What is your plan of action?* The situation is increasingly getting worse. You will need to seriously consider relocating some citizens as well as heavily fining or shutting down any noncompliant factory owners. You will also need to bring in any medical assistance either within the state or external to state agencies. The federal agencies should be contacted and a request for assistance should be sent to agencies such as the Centers for Disease Control.

2. *What resources will you need?* Medical supplies and logistics will need to be inventoried before an implementation of any action plan can occur. If you decide to move some of the citizens, you will need to provide them with more than just shelter. Any displaced citizens will need food, water, and money to provide a stable means of living until the situation stabilizes and they are allowed to go home.

Key Issues Raised from the Case Study

The government is responsible for ensuring the health and well-being of its citizens. This case study clearly shows that inaction can lead to long-term issues for the community and its residents. The inability to control pollution is a failure due to not having proper policies or enforcement mechanisms in place to contend with such an issue. Administrators and government officials were not proactive in keeping pollution levels down from the industrial areas, which resulted in severe air pollution. The consequences are potentially long term for many residents whose health has been impacted by the poor air quality of their community.

Items of Note

The Donora incident resulted in legislation being passed for clean air and environmental protective acts (Gammage, 1998).

Love Canal, Niagara Falls, 1970

Stage 1 of the Disaster

You are the city manager of a large city. Your city has two large bodies of water surrounding the area. The citizens are blue-collar, industrial workers who work in the factories that comprise your city's economy. The city's population is expanding rapidly, which necessitates a large development program for new housing. The local school board needs additional land and has selected a site that was previously a chemical dump owned by a corporation (Stoss and Fabian, 1998). Even though the school board members were told that the land was not suitable for use, the corporation sells the land since they are threatened with eminent domain confiscation of the land by the school board.

1. *What problems could arise?* The city manager should be very concerned that chemicals could get into the water supply if construction is undertaken in the area of the former dump site. The city manager should not allow any type of residential construction in the area of the former chemical dump site by denying permits to construction companies for new housing developments.
2. *What steps should you take to ensure safety of the population?* The city manager should contact the school board and school district superintendent and voice his or her concerns about constructing a new school on the chemical dump site. In addition, the city manager should insist on an environmental impact study before any such construction is undertaken.
3. *What resources may you need to contend with this issue?* The city manager may very well need to have legal representation to stop construction before it begins. The city manager may also need to voice concerns to state and federal agencies that oversee environmental and health concerns.
4. *What is your communication plan?* The city manager should stay in close contact with the city council as well as school district officials.

Stage 2 of the Disaster

The school board has begun construction of a new school located on the property that was used as a landfill, even after the corporation that sold them the property stated sternly that it was not safe to build on the site (Zuesse, 1981). The school had to relocate the construction site of the new school due to the discovery of two pits filled with chemicals. You have also learned that chemicals have begun to seep into the sewer system that is next to the school construction site. This area is filled with lower-income residences (Davids, 2009).

1. *What is your plan of action?* If the school district keeps proceeding with the construction project, a legal injunction should be sought. In addition, the city manager should put more pressure on state and federal officials to be more involved with a project that appears to be impacting the sewer system as well as having the potential to contaminate the water supply for the entire municipality.
2. *What is your communication plan?* The issues that are now being created by the construction of the school need to be communicated effectively to the elected officials and residents.
3. *How are you going to contend with the media?* The media needs to be involved in order to put public pressure upon the school district to abandon the project and that poisoned track of land.

Stage 3 of the Disaster

The residents of the homeowners association have begun to notice severe health problems with their children, including epilepsy and severe asthma (Turmoil and Fever, 2007). You now understand that the entire subdivision of housing was built upon 21,000 tons of chemical waste (Goldman Environmental Foundation, 2007). Due to the lack of action by city officials (your employees), residents have organized into a coalition to alert the media and government officials to the increasing number of illnesses and birth defects that have occurred in the subdivision (Beck, 1979).

1. *What is your plan of action?* The city manager needs to show that he or she will take action on this issue. City employees that have been reluctant to take action on this issue need to be reprimanded, reassigned, or terminated from their positions. Anything that the city can do for the residents should be implemented (e.g., testing of local water supplies). The company that dumped the chemicals should be forced, through legal or legislative means, to clean up the chemical dumping site.
2. *What is your communication plan?* The city manager should contact state and federal officials in a coordinated effort to resolve this issue. The public should be kept reassured that steps are being taken to resolve the issue and that the city will do everything in its power to correct a serious environmental oversight.

Stage 4 of the Disaster

The school that was built on top of the landfill has been demolished, but the school board and the corporation are refusing to admit any liability (University of Buffalo Libraries, 2007). The president of the United States has just declared the neighborhood a federal emergency and has relocated all residents out of the subdivision (University of Buffalo Libraries, 2007). The government not only relocated residents, but also purchased the houses.

1. *What is your plan of action?* The city manager should be active in coordination of all activities in relocating residents to temporary housing that is satisfactory, as well as working closely with federal officials in resolving the crisis.
2. *What resources should you begin to allocate?* Money will need to be allocated to a legal fund that will be used to not only hold the school district and company liable for negligence, but also protect the city from lawsuits.

Stage 5 of the Disaster

Congress has just passed the Comprehensive Environmental Response, Compensation and Liability Act (CERCLA) that requires corporations to be accountable for damage that is incurred by pollutants under their auspices (Local Government Environmental Assistance Network, 2007). The Environmental Protection Agency (EPA) successfully sued the corporation for $129 million to provide cleanup of the subdivision area (U.S. Department of Justice, 1995).

1. *What is your new plan of action?* The city manager needs to figure out if the land can be used for any useful purpose other than residential. If the land can be used for something other than residential, a budget needs to be formulated in an effort to revitalize an area that has been so devastated by the chemical dumping incident.
2. *How will you assist the government in its investigation?* The city manager should provide government investigators any information that is needed.
3. *What will you do to safeguard other areas of your city?* In the future the city manager should ensure city inspectors have a very strict building code that must be signed off on by the building inspection department as well as having an environmental impact study prior to construction.

Key Issues Raised from the Case Study

Administrators have an ethical and professional duty to protect their citizenry from items that can potentially produce health-related problems. Administrators and local officials should never ignore or deny that a problem exists. Administrators should take their residents' concerns seriously and investigate legitimate concerns that could negatively impact their community. If issues are found, administrators should act decisively to resolve any issues favorably.

Not holding the industry accountable for disposal of waste was the initial failure that would later haunt the community. Additionally, the school board ignored warnings of the chemical company, building a school on top of a chemical dumping ground, which set the stage for the tragic illnesses that residents blamed upon the chemicals that had been buried in that location. The high number of birth defects and illnesses that appear to be linked to the chemical dumping at Love Canal have had long-term health effects upon the residents. In short, the public was not safeguarded by the local government as it should have been from the chemical company's disposal process.

Items of Note

The residential houses have almost all been demolished in the Love Canal area and new development has been occurring since the 1990s.

Three Mile Island, Pennsylvania, 1979

Stage 1 of the Disaster

You are a director of the Nuclear Regulatory Commission (NRC) and are responsible for overseeing the safety and security of nuclear power plants. One power plant in particular is located close to where over 25,000 people reside (*Washington Post*, 1999). You have received a report that a main feed water pump critical for cooling the reactor has failed at this nuclear power plant (Cantelon and Williams, 1982).

1. *What is your plan of action?* An emergency response team should be sent to the reactor to determine how to get the water pump back online quickly. However, the director should also mandate an evacuation of residents that could be impacted by a potential radioactive leak if the power plant had a meltdown and radioactive isotopes escape into the atmosphere.
2. *What is your communication plan?* The director should inform federal, state, and local officials of the problem and keep those individuals informed as events transpire. The public should be informed on the status of the power plant and the potential dangers that could impact residents nearby.
3. *What resources should you allocate to this crisis?* A team of engineers should be called in quickly to either repair the water pumps or find an alternative way of cooling the reactor.

Stage 2 of the Disaster

Due to the failure of the main feed water pumps, the steam generators have been unable to extract the heat from the reactor. This leads to the turbine and the reactor completely shutting down (Cantelon and Williams, 1982). The pilot-operated pressure relief valve, which is needed to reduce pressure in the reactor, is stuck in an open position (U.S. Nuclear Regulatory Commission, 2007). Due to this problem the reactor has begun to overheat (American Chemical Society, 1986).

1. *What is your plan of action?* The director needs to ensure that if the regular cooling method has failed or is inoperable, then an alternative way of cooling the reactor will need to be found by the engineers. Since a meltdown is possible, any employees working in the power plant need to be issued protective gear and radiation detection badges. Nearby hospitals should be notified of the potential meltdown and requested to have supplies on hand to treat radiation poisoning.
2. *What is your communication plan?* The director should keep in close contact with federal, state, and local officials to keep them aware of the situation as it unfolds.

Stage 3 of the Disaster

Two of five valves for your backup feed water pumps have been closed at the reactor due to human or administrative error. The backup feed water valves have now been opened for the emergency coolant and your reactor is now receiving coolant. However, due to an incorrect system water indicator, your operators at the plant have shut down emergency core cooling pumps. Radioactive coolant is leaking into the general containment building (American Chemical Society, 1986). Temperatures are rising in the reactor core as the top of the reactor core is exposed due to low water levels. The reaction has damaged the zirconium nuclear fuel rod cladding, which has resulted in an apparent explosion in the containment building (Three Mile Island Alert, 2007).

1. *What is your plan of action?* Water will need to be flooded into the reactor core to cool down the core to safe levels. Readings should now be taken on air samples to see if radioactive material has leaked out to the atmosphere.
2. *What is your communication plan?* Any nearby area that could possibly be impacted by radioactivity should be told to evacuate since the containment building has possibly been compromised. Federal, state, and local officials should be notified of the situation since a radioactive leak could affect many regions and parts of the country.

Stage 4 of the Disaster

The plant is contaminated with high levels of radiation. At 7:00 a.m., you declare the plant a site area emergency (Cantelon and Williams, 1982). Thirty minutes later you upgrade the situation to the most serious category of general emergency (President's Commission on the Accident at Three Mile Island, 2006). Most of the core of the reactor has melted. To alleviate the steam and hydrogen from the reactor, a recombiner is used along with venting radioactive noble gases straight into the atmosphere (Three Mile Island Alert, 2007).

1. *What is your plan of action?* The director should primarily worry about the reactor being cooled off enough to prevent any more damage from occurring. The second area of focus is to ensure that radioactive material has not escaped from the facility.
2. *How will you contend with the public?* The director should be open and up front about the meltdown. The director should be very proactive about taking radioactivity tests around the plant in the surrounding communities to allay the public's fear of nuclear power plants.

Key Issues Raised from the Case Study

With technology that can induce damage on such a wide scale, redundant systems are necessary since the personnel operating such technology will need to have different methodologies to measure the system accurately in case one of the measurement methods fail. In addition, administrators that contend with such technology should have a set of experts on standby that can be called in during times of crisis to alleviate the problem if necessary.

The causes of the failures in this case study were from both equipment and human errors. Errors from equipment (i.e., gauges reading incorrectly) should have had a redundant method to get accurate measurements. In addition, the human errors could have been induced by either stress or not having enough training on what to do if particular situations arose.

Items of Note

The cleanup of Three Mile Island cost $973 million, and it was necessary to remove 100 million tons of radioactive fuel (Uranium Information Centre Ltd., 2001). Three Mile Island is the worst commercial reactor accident in U.S. history (USNRC, 2011).

Chernobyl, Ukraine, 1986

Stage 1 of the Disaster

You are a nuclear science administrator in the Soviet Union responsible for the oversight of all nuclear power stations. One of the nuclear power plants is located in the Ukraine close to both the Russian and Belarus borders. The personnel at the plant are not well trained and the power plant itself is a flawed design that was built with four nuclear reactors. The population density around the Chernobyl plant is 115,000 to 135,000 citizens living within a 30-kilometer radius (World Nuclear Association, 2012). On April 26, 1986, you receive a phone call indicating that two explosions have occurred at the Chernobyl power plant.

1. *What is your plan of action?* The most important action to take is to deploy first responders and nuclear engineers in HAZMAT protective gear to the power plant, and determine whether a radioactive incident has occurred. If a leak has occurred or the reactor has failed, then the proper resources need to be deployed to shut down the facility and stop any flow of radioactive isotopes into the air, water, or soil around the plant. Second, you will need to have an evacuation plan for residents around Chernobyl if radioactive isotopes have leaked out of the power plant and entered the atmosphere. Third, you will need to compile an inventory of all medical resources and evacuation vehicles in the area that can be made available should the need arise.

2. *What is your communication plan?* It is critical that you ascertain the condition of the plant and what the status of the radioactive material is at this point in time. Until that information is known, it will be impossible to come up with an effective plan for remediating the situation as well as determining whether the residents need to be evacuated. Both the central and local governments need to be apprised of the situation so that they may issue the appropriate statements to the public as well as obtaining resources that you will need to contend with the reactor.

3. *What resources should you allocate to this crisis?* Any personnel that have a working knowledge of nuclear engineering should be mobilized as well as medical resources and firefighters with the correct protective gear. Vehicles that can be used for evacuation purposes as well as what facilities could be used for medical personnel in times of an emergency should also be identified at this time.

Stage 2 of the Disaster

You have now been informed that reactor 4 has been destroyed by the explosion, resulting in the death of two workers as well as radioactive material being released into the atmosphere. Additionally, six firefighters who were combating the initial fires have all died of radiation poisoning. To combat the radioactive material from further disbursing, water has been flooded into the reactor and 5,000 tons of boron, dolomite, sand, clay, and lead have been dropped directly on the reactor core by helicopters. The meltdown and explosion of the reactor have led to the largest release of uncontrolled radioactive material by a civilian operation into the atmosphere (World Nuclear Association, 2012).

1. *What is your plan of action?* The evacuation of the residents around Chernobyl should have been well underway at that point. With the large amount of radioactive material that was released into the atmosphere, residents anywhere near the plume of radioactive material release should be evacuated and relocated. Medical triages should be set up in cities and

towns outside the potential radioactive release area, and as many helicopters that can be found to evacuate residents for radioactive illness should be utilized. In addition, there will need to be a plan formulated on how to stop the leakage of radioactive material from occurring from the open reactor core.

2. *What is your communication plan?* The government should now inform the public as well as any other country that is in the vicinity of the radioactive material plume that has been thrown into the atmosphere. Additionally, other surrounding countries should be contacted to gain assistance in treating anyone with radiation poisoning, as well as asking for assistance in containing the radioactive material from the open reactor.

3. *What resources should you allocate to this crisis?* By this point in the crisis medical personnel and facilities will be in high demand as well as medications that can be used for cases of radiation poisoning. There will also be a need to obtain as many vehicles as possible for transporting individuals to hospitals or to temporary housing that will now need to be established for refugees escaping the area. These temporary shelter areas will need food, water, and sanitation infrastructure to contend with the residents that have been evacuated.

Stage 3 of the Disaster

The residents have now been evacuated and the radioactive material has now been contained by constructing a large cofferdam over the reactor, which will still leave reactors 1, 2, and 3 operational for power needs. The cofferdam construction has been quickly erected, however, there will eventually need to have a more permanent solution in place since there are still radioactive materials present inside the destroyed reactor core (World Nuclear Association, 2012).

1. *What is your plan of action?* You will need to devise some type of strategy for contending with relocating the residents that have been displaced from the Chernobyl area. Second, there will need to be a plan for long-term medical care for those exposed and affected by the radioactive materials leaking into the atmosphere. Finally, there will need to be an inspection made of all reactors that are currently online to see if their designs are defective. If defects are found, you will need to plan on modifying those reactors so that they are not conducive to a meltdown like Chernobyl.

2. *What is your communication plan?* The government should be informed on what the issues are with the design flaws of the reactor, and it should be informed that the cofferdam constructed hastily will eventually need to have a more permanent solution emplaced in the near future.

3. *What resources should you allocate to this crisis?* Nuclear engineers will be needed to determine whether other power plants are in need of modification

or closure to ensure that another meltdown will not occur in the future. Better training is needed by personnel operating nuclear power plants, so there will need to be some money allocated for this purpose as well. The drain on medical resources will be a very long-term issue since so many people were exposed to radioactive material.

Key Issues Raised from the Case Study

This case study contends with a closed society that was isolated from the culture of safety for its nuclear reactors. Between the personnel that were inefficiently trained at the nuclear power plant and the flaw in the power plant's design, the question was not whether a disaster would occur, but when. Mobilizing first responders, engineers, medical personnel, and their associated resources quickly is necessary if a disaster occurs on such a wide scale. This disaster affected not only the immediate area around the power plant, but also several countries bordering the power plant host country (World Nuclear Association, 2012).

Items of Note

The human toll from Chernobyl years later is still impacting the Ukraine, Belarus, and Russia. The impact on the Ukraine has been significant. About 8,000 people have died and 125,000 individuals have had their health impacted by the radiation. Similarly, Belarus has an estimated 2 million citizens with health issues that can be traced to the radioactivity they were exposed to in 1986. Over 370,000 Russians are estimated to have some type of illness related to radioactive material exposure (Gunter, 1995).

Biological Hazardous Material Violation, Texas A&M University, 2007

Stage 1 of the Disaster

You are an investigator with the Centers for Disease Control and Prevention (CDC). You have just received documentation from a hospital that a laboratory worker from a large university has been infected with a strain of bacteria during an aerosol chamber mishap (Sunshine Project, 2007). This incident occurred a year ago and your federal guidelines clearly state that the incident should have been reported 7 days after the worker was exposed to the bacteria. The worker was on antibiotics for at least 2 months due to the exposure (Sunshine Project, 2007). These incidents were tied to federally funded research. Coincidentally, this university is vying for a $450 million biodefense federal grant (Brainard and Fischer, 2007).

1. *What is your plan of action?* As an investigator your duty is to investigate the university thoroughly in regard to its operational practices, written procedures, and personnel, as well as reviewing any type of select agent (biotoxin such as anthrax) that is reportable to the federal government by the university. To perform such an audit, an investigation must review all archival documents and interview all researchers that handle select agents as well as university administrators that have supervision over research that involves biotoxins. The personnel exposed to the select agents must be interviewed to determine how they believe they were exposed to the select agent to supplement information from their medical records, if possible.

2. *What is your communication plan?* The investigative team needs to communicate with any agencies that may be involved with a research contract or grant (if applicable) as well as keep in contact with upper university officials.

3. *How will you ensure the safety of the population in the university and the surrounding populous around the university?* Until the investigation has been completed and all of the evidence has been gathered, any research with biotoxins should be suspended pending the outcome of the investigation. All research personnel that are authorized to handle select agents at the university should have their authorization revoked until further notice. Additionally, all federal contracts and grants that have research proposals that are open and use select agents cannot be applied for until further notice.

Stage 2 of the Disaster

You have just been notified that three researchers at the same university have been exposed to Q-fever, which is designated by the CDC as a highly restricted select agent (Hill, 2007). This incident apparently occurred 2 months after the bacteria exposure that you had just been notified about earlier. You are still awaiting the paperwork from the university on this incident, which occurred over a year ago (Hill, 2007). Again, 7 days is the maximum amount of time that an institution is supposed to report the incident to the CDC.

1. *What is your plan of action?* As an investigator, you should make it clear to the university that the current lack of documentation is completely unacceptable. You can further recommend to your agency that if the investigators do not receive the paperwork you have requested from the university, along with a full disclosure of events, your agency will recommend that all federal contracts and grants will be suspended for all areas of research. At this time, you should start compiling a list of personnel that could be facing criminal or civil litigation and begin to gather evidence on not only violation of federal statutes, but also obstruction charges.

2. *What is your communication plan?* Communication should be maintained with the upper administration of the university being investigated, as well as keeping your department informed of the status of the investigation.

Stage 3 of the Disaster

You are very upset at hearing that the issue was known to the university and the university chose not to report the incident to the CDC (Sunshine Project, 2007). The interim president of the university has stated that he believed that the university was in compliance with CDC policies since none of the researchers that were exposed to Q-fever became ill (Schnirring, 2007). You have decided that you must send a team of investigators from your Select Agent and Toxins Division to inspect the laboratory facilities at the university (Schnirring, 2007). Your investigators have uncovered that several researchers and administrators knew of the exposures and yet did not file a report to the CDC as required by law. In addition, your 18-person inspection team has found the following:

■ Three vials of microbes missing from inventory
■ Research being undertaken on a regulated bacterium without CDC approval
■ Laboratory workers not wearing correct safety clothing or masks to prevent infection
■ Improper decontamination procedures
■ At least seven instances of employees being given access to restricted bioelements before the CDC granted those employees access (Brainard and Hermes, 2007)

1. *What is your new plan of action?* Until the university can show changes in its research activity and select agent handling procedures to take into account the CDC findings, the university research programs that work with biotoxins and select agents should be shut down indefinitely. In addition, any researcher that was working with select agents that was in violation of federal statutes should not be allowed to have access to biotoxins until the CDC has cleared him or her to do so, no matter what higher education institution or research center employs him or her.

2. *What is your new communication plan?* It needs to be communicated to the university that obstruction and self-interpretation of the federal mandates is completely unacceptable. Research productivity should never compromise safety or take precedence over federal mandate. To ignore these two criteria will potentially result in severe consequences to the researchers, administrators, and university.

Key Issues Raised from the Case Study

If an incident occurs, administrators should report infractions as required by statute. Administrators of higher education institutions should also work with federal officials in resolving any potential violations or safety infractions. Failure to cooperate with federal officials can result in injury or death to faculty, staff, and students and can expose administrators to charges of criminal violations, sanctions, and civil litigation.

The single biggest failure was not reporting the exposures to the federal government as required by law. The second biggest failure was not recognizing that the institution was bound by federal statute. Instead, administrators took the stance that the biosafety guidelines were simply recommendations.

Texas A&M was suspended from federal grants relating to biological research for at least 2 months ($18 million worth of research funding affecting 5 different research laboratories and 120 employees) and banned from performing research on any select agents—the first type of research ban in the United States (Brainard and Fischer, 2007). Texas A&M University was fined $1 million and the university lost out on the $450 million biodefense bill (Cox, 2008; Schnirring, 2008).

Items of Note

The Environmental Health and Safety (EHS) director resigned, stating that he did not have the authority to perform his duties effectively, and the vice president for research also resigned (Haurwitz, 2007).

FINAL THOUGHTS IV

Conclusion

All of the disaster scenarios reported in this case study book are true. We have reported all the facts surrounding each disaster exactly as they happened—to capture the sequence of events as they unfolded. While we can capture and analyze the facts, and thus provide a context in which the decision-making process can be scrutinized, we cannot possibly hope to portray, even remotely, the stress, emotion, and exceedingly difficult decisions that administrators had to make during the actual disaster response. Naturally, it is easy for someone to second-guess what individuals could have or should have done in a disaster response situation, especially with the benefit of hindsight. Unfortunately, in real-life disaster events decision makers are faced with incomplete or inconsistent information, and yet they must still act in response to the event. This lack of information, or perhaps even misinformation, may have influenced the decision makers that were actually on scene and were confronted with the disaster in real time. This book was written to enable public administrators and first responders to consider how events might have been resolved if conditions were different, or if key information had been known.

These case studies present unique challenges that the administrators who were on scene had never encountered before. The reader should remember that every situation is different and that no two problems will be alike. Routine situations such as a building fire or a hostage situation can usually be handled by local first responders. It is the unusual situations that administrators need to keep in mind when they draw up plans for disaster responses. These may require unique solutions and flexible decision making.

Administrators should generally take stock of what risks can adversely impact their community. For example, administrators in California can be impacted by earthquakes since quite a few communities sit on fault lines where earthquakes have been known to occur. Other administrators that have communities on coastlines must contend with other threats, such as hurricanes, floods, and tsunamis, and would not likely confront an earthquake. In short, administrators need to account for what threats are most likely to impact their organizations and plan for resources to contend with those types of threats. As these case studies have demonstrated, improper planning can result in administrators losing control of the situation and being forced to react defensively to survive. With proper planning, adequate resources, foresight, and ingenuity, administrators can anticipate and mitigate the damage that may occur and perhaps even prevent the disaster from occurring altogether.

References

9-11 Research. 2008. The victims. Who was killed in the September 11 attack. Retrieved November 22, 2008, from http://911research.wtc7.net/sept11/victims/index.html.

Ahlers, Mike M. 2004. 9/11 commission hears flight attendant's phone call. CNN Washington Bureau. Retrieved January 28, 2004, from http://edition.cnn.com/2004/US/01/27/911.commis.call/index.html.

American Chemical Society. 1986. *The Three Mile Island accident. Diagnosis and prognosis.* American Chemical Society.

Andres, Brad. 1997. The *Exxon Valdez* oil spill disrupted the breeding of black oystercatchers. *Journal of Wildlife Management*, vol. 10. Retrieved January 13, 2009, from http://www.jstor.org/stable/3802132?&Search=yes&term=exxon&term=valdez&list=hide&searchUri=%2Faction%2FdoBasicSearch%3FQuery%3Dexxon%2Bvaldez%26gw%3Djtx%26prq%3Dchilean%2Bearthquake%26hp%3D25%26wc%3Don&item=1&ttl=1130&returnArticleService=showArticle.

Angelfire. 2005. Havoc created from Hurricane Katrina. Retrieved August 29, 2005, from http://www.angelfire.com/ia3/katrina/USATODAY.

Arsenault, Mark. 2003. Great White: Performing again is the right thing. Retrieved July 31, 2003, from http://www.projo.com/extra/2003/stationfire/archive/projo_20030731_jackr31.55c1.html.

Arvich, Paul. 1984. *The Haymarket tragedy*. Princeton University Press.

Associated Press. 1980. Man who defined volcano gets marriage proposals. LexisNexis. Retrieved April 26, 1980, from http://www.lexisnexis.com/us/lnacademic/results/docview/docview.do?docLinkInd=true&risb=21_T5376184980&format=GNBFI&sort=null&startDocNo=1&resultsUrlKey=29_T5376186586&cisb=22_T5376186585&treeMax=true&treeWidth=0&csi=304478&docNo=1.

Associated Press. 1988. Few know about North America's deadliest fire. LexisNexis. Retrieved October 08, 1988, from http://www.lexisnexis.com/us/lnacademic/results/docview/docview.do?docLinkInd=true&risb=21_T5367979222&format=GNBFI&sort=RELEVANCE&startDocNo=1&resultsUrlKey=29_T5367979225&cisb=22_T5367979224&treeMax=true&treeWidth=0&csi=304478&docNo=7.

Associated Press. 2005a. Bush chooses new FEMA director. MSNBC. Retrieved September 13, 2005, from http://www.msnbc.msn.com/id/9315184/.

Associated Press. 2005b. Coastal evacuation in Texas. Fox News. Retrieved September 20, 2005, from http://www.foxnews.com/story/0,2933,169845,00.html.

Associated Press State and Local Wire. 2006. Some past moves by Alaska native villages. LexisNexis. Retrieved December 26, 2006, from http://www/lexisnexis.com/us/lnacademic/results/docview/docview/docview.do?risb=21_T23030588 25&format=GNBFI&sort=RELEVANCE&startDocNo=1&resultsUrkey=29_ T2303058828&cisb=22_T2303058827&treeMax=true&treeWidth=0&csi=304481 &docNo=7.

Australian Broadcast Corporation. 2012. Black Saturday. Retrieved May 30, 2012, from http://www.abc.net.au/innovation/blacksaturday/#/stories/mosaic.

Ayers, Shirley. 2006. Bioterrorism in Oregon. Emergency Film Group. Retrieved January 6, 2009, from http://www.efilmgroup.com/News/Bioterrorism-in-Oregon.html.

Barnes, Allen. 2008. City manager of Sachse, TX.

Barron, James. 2003. After 1920 blast, the opposite of never forget, no memorials on Wall Street for attack that killed 30. *New York Times*. LexisNexis. Retrieved September 17, 2003, from http://www.lexisnexis.com/us/lnacademic/results/docview/docview.do?docLinkInd=true&risb=21_T5368032022&format=GNBFI&sort=RELEVANC E&startDocNo=1&resultsUrlKey=29_T5368032025&cisb=22_T5368032024&tree Max=true&treeWidth=0&csi=6742&docNo=1.

BBC. 1989. *Exxon Valdez* creates oil slick disaster. March 24. Retrieved January 13, 2009, from http://news.bbc.co.uk/onthisday/hi/dates/stories/march/24/newsid_4231000/4231971.stm.

BBC. 1993. World Trade Center bomb terrorizes New York. February 26. Retrieved January 14, 2009, from http://news.bbc.co.uk/onthisday/hi/dates/stories/february/26/newsid_2516000/2516469.stm.

BBC News. 2001. Libyan guilty of Lockerbie bombing. Retrieved November 29, 2011, from http://news.bbc.co.uk/2/hi/in_depth/1144893.stm.

BBC News. 2007a. Four charged over JFK bomb plot. June 3. Retrieved January 14, 2009, from http://news.bbc.co.uk/1/hi/world/americas/6715443.stm.

BBC News. 2007b. America's day of terror: Timeline. Retrieved September 12, 2001, from http://news.bbc.co.uk/2/hi/americas/1537785.stm.

BBC Weather. 2007. Great storms—Hurricane 1775. Retrieved December 12, 2007, from http://www.bbc.co.uk/weather/features/storms_hurricane2.shtml.

Beck, Eckardt. 1979. The Love Canal tragedy. U.S. Environmental Protection Agency. Retrieved December 17, 2008, from http://www.epa.gov/history/topics/lovecanal/01.htm.

Bellamy, Patrick. 2008. False prophet: The Aum cult of terror. TruTV Crime Library. October 30. Retrieved January 15, 2009, from http://www.trutv.com/library/crime/terrorists_spies/terrorists/prophet/19.html.

Berkley Seismological Lab. 2007. Where can I learn more about the 1906 earthquake? Retrieved August 22, 2007, from http://seismo.berkeley.edu/faq/1906_0.html.

Boise State University. 2008. Disasters: My darling Clementine. Retrieved January 6, 2009, from http://www.boisestate.edu/history/ncasner/hy210/mining.htm.

Boston Globe. 2010. The big picture: Remembering Katrina, five years ago. August 27. Retrieved March 8, 2011, from http://www.boston.com/bigpicture/2010/08/remembering_katrina_five_years.html.

Boulder News. 1999. Tragedy and recovery. April 20. Retrieved January 15, 2009, from http://www.boulderdailycamera.com/shooting/22chronology.html.

Brainard, Jeffery, and Fischer, Karen. 2007. Agency halts risky research on microbes at Texas A&M. *The Chronicle*. Retrieved July 13, 2007, from http://chronicle.com/weekly/v53/i45/45a00101.htm.

Brainard, Jeffery, and Hermes, J.J. 2007. Texas A&M faulted for safety violations. *The Chronicle*, vol. 54, no. 3, p. A19.

Broughton, Edward. 2005. The Bhopal disaster and its aftermath: A review. *BioMed Central: Environmental Health*, May 10. Retrieved May 29, 2012, from http://www.ncbi.nlm. nih.gov/pmc/articles/PMC1142333/.

Brown, Aaron. 2005. Hurricane Katrina pummels three states. CNN. Retrieved August 29, 2005, from http://transcripts.cnn.com/TRANSCRIPTS/0508/29/asb.01.html.

Brown, R.J. 2008. The day the clowns cried. History Buff. October 1. Retrieved January 12, 2009, from http://www.historybuff.com/library/reffire.html.

Brunner, Borgna. 2007. The great white hurricane. The blizzard of 1888: March 11–March 14, 1888. Information Please database. Retrieved December 4, 2007, from http://www.infoplease.com/spot/blizzard1.html.

Bullock, Jane A., Haddow, George D., and Haddow, Kim S. 2009. *Global warming, natural hazards, and emergency management*. Boca Raton, FL: Taylor and Francis Group.

Calvert, Scott. 2009. D.C.–area sniper John Allen Muhammad is executed. *Los Angeles Times*, November 11. Retrieved January 3, 2012, from http://articles.latimes.com/2009/nov/11/nation/na-sniper11.

Cantelon, Philip L., and Williams, Robert C. 1982. *Crisis contained*. The Department of Energy at Three Mile Island. Southern Illinois University, Carbondale, Illinois.

CBS Chicago.com. 2011. 125th anniversary for Haymarket Square conflict. CBS Chicago. com. May 4. Retrieved January 5, 2012, from http://chicago.cbslocal.com/2011/05/04/today-marks-the-125th-anniversary-of-haymarket-square-conflict/.

CBC News. 2003. Timeline: The attacks. CBC News: In Depth: Sniper Attacks. October 21. Retrieved January 3, 2012, from http://www.cbc.ca/news/background/sniper/timeline_attacks.html.

CBC News. 2004. Sniper attacks. CBC News: In Depth: Sniper Attacks. March 10. Retrieved January 3, 2012, from http://www.cbc.ca/news/background/sniper/index. html.

CBS News Online. 2003. Introduction. August 20. Retrieved January 15, 2009, from http://www.cbc.ca/news/background/poweroutage/.

CDC. 2007. Infectious disease information—Mosquito-borne diseases. National Center for Infectious Diseases. Retrieved November 21, 2011, from http://www.cdc.gov/ncidod/diseases/list_mosquitoborne.htm.

Chen, Pauline W. 2010. Tending to patients during a hurricane. *New York Times*, September 2. Retrieved March 8, 2011, from http://www.nytimes.com/2010/09/02/health/views/02chen.html?pagewanted=1&_r=1.

Chicago: City of the Century. 2003. People and events: The great fire of 1871. PBS Online. Retrieved December 19, 2008, from http://www.pbs.org/wgbh/amex/chicago/peopleevents/e_fire.html.

Cline, Isaac M. 2000. Converging paths: A man and a storm. The Weather Doctor. September 1. Retrieved December 19, 2008, from http://www.islandnet.com/~see/weather/history/icline2.htm.

Cooper, Bruce. 2011. A brief illustrated history of the palace hotel of San Francisco. Retrieved January 4, 2012, from http://thepalacehotel.org/.

CNN. 2002. Los Angeles riot still echoes a decade later. April 28. Retrieved November 29, 2011, from http://articles.cnn.com/2002-04-28/us/la.riot.anniversary_1_riot-white-truck-driver-lapd?_s=PM:US.

CNN U.S. 2008. NTSB: Design flaw led to Minnesota bridge collapse. November 14. Retrieved November 23, 2011, from http://articles.cnn.com/2008-11-14/us/bridge. collapse_1_gusset-plates-bridge-collapse-bridge-designs?_s=PM:US.

CNN U.S. 2010. Settlement reached in Minnesota bridge collapse case. August 23. Retrieved November 29, 2011, from http://www.cnn.com/2010/US/08/23/minnesota.bridge. settlement/index.html.

Court TV Online. 1999. Community reels in the aftermath of Colorado school massacre. April 21. Retrieved December 19, 2008, from http://www.courttv.com/archive/ national/1999/0421/shooting_pm_ap.html.

Cox, Kevin. 1997. Devastating storm could happen again: Forecasters fear the kind of hurricane that swept up from the West Indies in 1775 killing thousands. The system actually grew stronger as it moved northward. *The Globe and Mail* (Canada). LexisNexis. Retrieved March 29, 1997, from http://www.lexisnexis.com/us/ lnacademic/results/docview/docview.do?docLinkInd=true&risb=21_T53761016 92&format=GNBFI&sort=RELEVANCE&startDocNo=1&resultsUrlKey=29_ T5376101695&cisb=22_T5376101694&treeMax=true&treeWidth=0&csi=30383 0&docNo=1.

Cox, Stan. 2008. Bidding war for biowarfare labs: The germs next door. Counterpunch. March 26. Retrieved June 17, 2010, from http://www.counterpunch.org/cox03262008. html.

Dallaire, Elise. 2004. Storm of 1913—November 7 to 12, 1913. Storm is the greatest ever to strike the lakes. Retrieved January 12, 2009, from http://elisedallaire.com/44/the_ storm_of_1913.htm.

Dan, Suri. 2003. Dan, Dan, the weatherman's world weather trivia page. July 28. Retrieved December 19, 2008, from http://www.dandantheweatherman.com/wortrivmay.html.

Dao, James. 2003. Polite but dogged, sniper suspect offers defense. *New York Times*, October 23. Retrieved January 3, 2012, from http://www.nytimes.com/2003/10/22/us/polite-but-dogged-sniper-suspect-offers-defense.html?partner=rssnyt&emc=rss.

Davids, Gavin. 2009. The Love Canal chemical waste dump. MSN.News. February 12. Retrieved January 4, 2012, from http://news.in.msn.com/gallery. aspx?cp-documentid=3460600&page=6.

The Day the Sky Turned Black. 2012. About Black Saturday. Retrieved May 30, 2012, from http://www.thedaytheskyturnedblack.com/#/about-black-saturday/4542166439.

Debartolo, Anthony. 1998. Who caused the great Chicago fire? A possible deathbed confession. March. Retrieved December 19, 2008, from http://www.hydeparkmedia.com/ cohn.html.

Deepthi. 2007. Terrorism history timeline 1931–1940. Retrieved December 12, 2007, from http://history-timeline.deepthi.com/terrorism-history-timeline/terror-timeline-1931-1940.html.

Delk, James. 1992. The 1992 Los Angeles riots military operations in Los Angeles. California Military Museum, California State Military Department. September. Retrieved January 13, 2008, from http://www.militarymuseum.org/HistoryKingMilOps.html.

Diamond, Christine S. 2005. Hurricane zaps East Texas's power. Cox News Service. LexisNexis. September 25. Retrieved December 19, 2008, from http://www.lexisnexis. com/us/lnacademic/results/docview/docview.do?docLinkInd=true&risb=21_T53761 08742&format=GNBFI&sort=RELEVANCE&startDocNo=1&resultsUrlKey=29_ T5376108745&cisb=22_T5376108744&treeMax=true&treeWidth=0&csi=157001 &docNo=1.

Douglas, Paul. 2005. *Restless skies: The ultimate weather book*. New York: Barnes & Noble Books.

Dubill, Christina. 2011. A look back at the Hyatt Regency skywalk disaster. nbcactionnews. com. July 13. Retrieved January 4, 2012, from http://www.nbcactionnews.com/dpp/news/local_news/a-look-back-at-the-hyatt-regency-skywalk-disaster.

Duke, Martin. 1960. The Chilean earthquakes of May 1960. JSTOR. December 16. Retrieved January 13, 2009, from http://www.jstor.org/stable/1706763?&Search=ye s&term=earthquake&term=chilean&term=1960&list=hide&searchUri=%2Faction% 2FdoBasicSearch%3FQuery%3Dchilean%2Bearthquake%2B1960%26gw%3Djtx% 26prq%3Dchilean%2Bearthquake%26hp%3D25%26wc%3Don&item=10&ttl=27 2&returnArticleService=showArticle.

Easton, Pam. 2005. Hurricane Rita becomes a 175 mph monster, 1.3 million evacuated. Associated Press. LexisNexis. September 22. Retrieved December 19, 2008, from http://www.lexisnexis.com/us/lnacademic/results/docview/docview. do?docLinkInd=true&risb=21_T5376122070&format=GNBFI&sort=RELEVANC E&startDocNo=1&resultsUrlKey=29_T5376122079&cisb=22_T5376122078&tree Max=true&treeWidth=0&csi=304478&docNo=3.

Eberwine, Donna. 2005. Disaster myths that just won't die. *Perspectives in Health—The Magazine of the Pan American Health Organization*, vol. 10, no. 1. Retrieved January 4, 2012, from http://www.paho.org/english/dd/pin/Number21_article01.htm.

Evans, Blanche. 2007. 1906 San Francisco earthquake. Housing is valuable piece of history. *Realty Times*. Retrieved September 27, 2007, from http://realtytimes.com/rtpages/20060418_quakehistory.htm.

Falkenrath, Richard A., Newman, Robert D., and Thayer, Bradley A. 1998. *America's Achilles' heel: Nuclear, biological, and chemical terrorism and covert attack*. Cambridge, MA: The Belfer Center for Science International Affairs, John F. Kennedy School of Government, MIT Press, Cambridge, MA.

FBI. 2008. First strike: Global terror in America. U.S. Department of Justice. February 26. Retrieved January 14, 2009, from http://www.fbi.gov/page2/feb08/tradebom_022608. html.

FBI. 2009. Amerithrax investigation. Retrieved January 15, 2009, from http://www.fbi.gov/anthrax/amerithraxlinks.htm.

FEMA. 2010. Prepare for a disaster: Water. Retrieved March 14, 2011, from http://www.fema.gov/plan/prepare/water.shtm.

Fernicola, Richard G. 2001. *Twelve days of terror: A definitive investigation of the 1916 New Jersey sharks attacks*. Guilford, CT: Lyons Press.

Field Museum. 2007. Lions of Tsavo. Retrieved May 29, 2012, from http://archive. fieldmuseum.org/exhibits/exhibit_sites/tsavo/maneaters.html.

Fortili, Amy. 2003. Horrific fire stuns Rhode Island, tops headlines in 2003. *Boston News*, December 27. Retrieved December 19, 2008, from http://www.boston.com/news/specials/year_in_review/2003/articles/ri_top_stories/.

Frank, Neil L. 2003. The great Galveston hurricane of 1900. Retrieved December 19, 2008, from http://www.agu.org/pubs/booksales/hurricane/Chapter_05galveston.pdf.

Galveston Newspapers. 2007. An island washed away. Retrieved December 12, 2007, from http://www.1900storm.com/storm/storm3.lasso.

Gammage, Jeff. 1998. 20 died. The government took heed. In 1948, a killer fog spurred air cleanup. *Philadelphia Inquirer*, October 29. Retrieved January 13, 2009, from http://www.depweb.state.pa.us/heritage/cwp/view.asp?a=3&Q=533403&PM=1#marker.

Gold, Scott. 2005. Trapped in the Superdome: Refuge becomes a hellhole. *Seattle Times*, September 1. Retrieved March 8, 2011, from http://seattletimes.nwsource.com/html/hurricanekatrina/2002463400_katrinasuperdome01.html.

Goldman Environmental Foundation. 2007. Lois Gibbs. Retrieved October 2007 from http://www.goldmanprize.org/node/103.

Goldman, Julianna. 2011. Bin Laden killing by U.S. forces praised as officials ready for reprisals. *Bloomberg*, May 2. Retrieved December 1, 2011, from http://www.bloomberg.com/news/2011-05-02/osama-bin-laden-killed-in-u-s-operation-obama-says-in-address-to-nation.html.

Gray, Madison. 2008. The L.A. riots: 15 years after Rodney King. Time in partnership with CNN. October 28. Retrieved January 13, 2009, from http://www.time.com/time/specials/2007/la_riot/article/0,28804,1614117_1614084,00.html.

Greene, R.W. 2002. *Confronting catastrophe: A GIS handbook*. Redlands, CA: ESRI.

Greer, William. 1986. As people move to forest, threat from the fires is rising. *New York Times*. LexisNexis. Retrieved December 19, 2008, from http://www.lexisnexis.com/us/lnacademic/results/docview/docview.do?docLinkInd=true&risb=21_T5398704491&format=GNBFI&sort=RELEVANCE&startDocNo=1&resultsUrlKey=29_T5398704497&cisb=22_T5398704496&treeMax=true&treeWidth=295&selRCNodeID=54&nodeStateId=411en_US,1,53&docsInCategory=43&csi=6742&docNo=3.

Gross, Daniel. 2001. Previous terror on Wall Street. A look at a 1920 bombing. September 20. Retrieved December 19, 2008, from http://www.thestreet.com/comment/ballotdance/10001305.html.

Gunter, Paul. 1995. Reactor Watchdog Project: Chernobyl: Basic facts. Nuclear Information and Resource Service. Retrieved May 30, 2012, from http://www.nirs.org/reactorwatch/accidents/cherfact.htm.

H2g2. 2001. How May Day became worker's holiday. October 4. Retrieved December 19, 2008, from http://www.bbc.co.uk/dna/h2g2/A627662.

Haurwitz, Ralph K.M. 2007. A&M lab safety chief resigns: Campus president to address federal report on shortcomings today. *Austin American–Statesman*. Retrieved September 6, 2007, from http://www.statesman.com/news/content/news/stories/local/09/06/0906am.html.

Hays, Jeffrey. 2010. Facts and details. Sichuan earthquake, poorly-built schools, activists and parents. Retrieved May 31, 2012, from http://factsanddetails.com/china.php?itemid=1020&catid=10&subcatid=65.

Hays, Kristen. 2005. Houstonians rethinking storm preparedness. Associated Press. September 27. Retrieved January 13, 2009, from http://www.wfaa.com/sharedcontent/nationworld/hurricaneRita/stories/092705ccRitawchouprep.d2ac3308.html.

Heimlich, Janet, and Edwards, Bob. 1998. University may reopen tower. NPR Morning Edition. LexisNexis. November 11. Retrieved December 19, 2008, from http://www.lexisnexis.com/us/lnacademic/results/docview/docview.do?docLinkInd=true&risb=21_T5376162105&format=GNBFI&sort=RELEVANCE&startDocNo=1&resultsUrlKey=29_T5376162120&cisb=22_T5376162119&treeMax=true&treeWidth=0&csi=8398&docNo=3.

Hill, Michael. 2012. Black Saturday. *Wildfire Magazine*. Retrieved May 30, 2012, from http://wildfiremag.com/tactics/black-saturday-bushfire-lessons-200905/.

Hill, Todd. 2007. Biological agent infects A&M scientists … again. Burnt Orange Report. Retrieved June 27, 2007, from http://www.burntorangereport.com/showDiary.do?diaryId=3728.

Hipke, Deana C. 2007a. The great Peshtigo fire of 1871. Retrieved November 30, 2007, from http://www.peshtogofire.info/gallery/burntmap.htm.

Hipke, Deana C. 2007b. The great Peshtigo fire of 1871. Retrieved November 30, 2007, from http://www.peshtigofire.info/gallery/birdseye1871.htm.

Homeland Security. 2011c. Creation of the Department of Homeland Security. Retrieved December 1, 2011, from http://www.dhs.gov/xabout/history/gc_1297963906741.shtm.

Hurricane Headquarters. 2007. Hurricane Rita. CNN News. Retrieved December 12, 2007, from http://www.cnn.com/SPECIALS/2005/hurricanes/interactive/fullpage.hurricanes/rita.html.

Ishman, Zach. 2001. Newspaper coverage of the tri-state tornado ravage of Murphysboro. Illinois Periodicals Online, Northern University Libraries. December 11. Retrieved January 12, 2009, http://www.lib.niu.edu/2001/ihy011210.html.

Ivry, Benjamin. 2007. Sacco and Venzetti: Murders or martyrs? *Washington Times*. LexisNexis. August 24. Retrieved December 19, 2008, from http://www.lexisnexis.com/us/lnacademic/results/docview/docview.do?docLinkInd=true&risb=21_T53762 17695&format=GNBFI&sort=RELEVANCE&startDocNo=1&resultsUrlKey=29_ T5376219000&cisb=22_T5376217699&treeMax=true&treeWidth=0&csi=8176&d ocNo=2.

Jeter, Jon. 1997. Letter from Chicago, putting a myth out to pasture. *Washington Post*. LexisNexis. October 29. Retrieved December 19, 2008, from http://www.lexisnexis.com/us/lnacademic/results/docview/docview.do?docLinkInd=true&risb=21_T53986 00316&format=GNBFI&sort=RELEVANCE&startDocNo=1&resultsUrlKey=29_ T5398600319&cisb=22_T5398600318&treeMax=true&treeWidth=0&selRCNodeI D=64&nodeStateId=411en_US,1,63&docsInCategory=4&csi=8075&docNo=3.

Johnstown Flood Museum. 2012. The complete story of the 1889 disaster. Johnstown Flood Museum. Retrieved January 6, 2012, from http://www.jaha.org/FloodMuseum/history.html.

Joint Australian Tsunami Warning Center. 2008. The 1 April 1946 Aleutian earthquake and tsunami. Bureau of Meteorology. October 7. Retrieved January 12, 2009, from http://www.bom.gov.au/tsunami/tsunami_1946.shtml.

Karl Kuenning RFL. 2005. Great White fire. January 30. Retrieved December 19, 2008, from http://www.roadiebook.com/greatwhitefire.htm.

Keen, Judy. 2007. Minn. Bridge warning issued in 1990. *USA Today*, August 6. Retrieved January 14, 2009, from http://www.usatoday.com/news/nation/2007-08-02-minneapolis-bridge_N.htm.

Klinenberg, Eric. 2004. Heat wave of 1995. Encyclopedia of Chicago. Retrieved January 14, 2009, from http://www.encyclopedia.chicagohistory.org/pages/2433.html.

Knabb, Richard D., Brown, Daniel P., and Rhome, Jamie R. 2006. Tropical cyclone report Hurricane Rita. National Hurricane Center. March 17. Retrieved January 3, 2012, from http://www.nhc.noaa.gov/pdf/TCR-AL182005_Rita.pdf.

Kurtenbach, Elaine, and Foreman, William. 2008. China quake shows flaws in building boom. *USA Today*, May 14. Retrieved May 31, 2012, from http://www.usatoday.com/money/economy/2008-05-14-3651640224_x.htm.

Landy, Marc. 2008. *Mega-disasters and federalism*. Public Administration Review, American Society for Public Administration, suppl. to vol. 68. Hoboken, NJ: John Wiley & Sons.

Lane County of Oregon. 2008. The history of West Nile Virus. November 10. Retrieved January 15, 2009, from http://www.lanecounty.org/CAO_PIO/westnilevirus/2_History.htm.

Lavergne, Gary M. 1997. *A sniper in the tower: The Charles Whitman murders.* Denton, TX: University of North Texas Press.

Lester, Paul. 2006. *The great Galveston disaster.* Denton, TX: The University of North Texas Libraries, Pelican Publishing Company.

Local Government Environmental Assistance Network. 2007. Comprehensive Environmental Response, Compensation and Liability Act. Retrieved October 2007 from http://www.lgean.org/html/fedregsguide/ve.cfm.

Long, Merritt. 2008. History of the Great Chicago Fire of 1871. *My Firefighter Nation,* February 3. Retrieved January 4, 2012, from http://my.firefighternation.com/group/firefightinghistorymyths/forum/topics/889755:Topic:341669.

Louisiana Homeland Security and Emergency Preparedness. 2007. 2006 Louisiana citizen awareness and disaster evacuation guides. Retrieved August 2, 2007, from http://www.ohsep.louisiana.gov/evacinfo/stateevacrtes.htm.

Macaulay, Tyson. 2009. *Critical infrastructure: Understanding its component parts, vulnerabilities, operating risks, and interdependencies.* Boca Raton, FL: CRC Press, Taylor and Francis Group.

Macleod, Marlee. 2007a. Charles Whitman: The Texas tower sniper. Court TV Crime Library. Retrieved November 9, 2007, from http://www.crimelibrary.com/notorious_murders/mass/whitman/preparations_4.html.

Macleod, Marlee. 2007b. Charles Whitman: The Texas tower sniper. Court TV Crime Library. Retrieved November 9, 2007, from http://www.crimelibrary.com/notorious_murders/mass/whitman/battle_5.html.

Macleod, Marlee. 2007c. Charles Whitman: The Texas tower sniper. Court TV Crime Library. Retrieved November 9, 2007, from http://www.crimelibrary.com/notorious_murders/mass/whitman/tower_6.html.

Madigan, Erin. 2004. Nightclub fire prompts new fireworks laws. Stateline. July 3. Retrieved December 19, 2008, from http://www.stateline.org/live/ViewPage.action?siteNodeId=136&languageId=1&contentId=15304.

Manning, Lona. 2006. 9/16: Terrorists bomb Wall Street. *Crime Magazine,* January 25. Retrieved December 19, 2008, from http://crimemagazine.com/06/wallstreetbomb,0115-6.htm.

Mansbridge, Tara. 2003. Viewpoint: A city hiding in fear. CBC News: In Depth: Sniper Attacks. October 10. Retrieved January 3, 2012, from http://www.cbc.ca/news/background/sniper/mansbridge_viewpoint.html.

Martin, Rachel. 1999. Hyatt Regency walkway collapse. Kansas, Missouri. July 17, 1981. December 6. Retrieved December 19, 2008, from http://www.eng.uab.edu/cee/faculty/ndelatte/case_studies_project/Hyatt%20Regency/hyatt.htm#Causes.

McCabe, Scott. 2009. Crime history—Haymarket Square bomb kills 8 in Chicago. *Washington Examiner—Crime Reports.* Retrieved June 18, 2012, from http://washingtonexaminer.com/local/crime/2009/05/crime-history-haymarket-square-bomb-kills-8-chicago/106907.

McLeod, Jaime. 2011. The big blow: The Great Lakes blizzard of 1913. *Farmer's Almanac,* October 31. Retrieved January 5, 2012, from http://www.farmersalmanac.com/weather/2011/10/31/the-big-blow-the-great-lakes-blizzard-of-1913/.

Michel, Lou, and Herbeck, Dan. 2001. *American terrorist: Timothy McVeigh and the Oklahoma City bombing.* New York: Regan Books.

Mine Safety and Health Administration. 2008. 1907 Fairmont Coal Company mining disaster: Monongah, West Virginia. U.S. Department of Labor. September 24. Retrieved from http://www.msha.gov/disaster/monongah/monon1.asp.

Minkel, J.R. 2008. The 2003 northeastern blackout—Five years later. *Scientific American*, August 13. Retrieved November 23, 2011, from http://www.scientificamerican.com/ article.cfm?id=2003-blackout-five-years-later.

Monitor Reporter. 2012. The Uganda railway that had death and method to its lunacy. *Daily Monitor*, April 27. Retrieved May 29, 2012, http://www.monitor.co.ug/SpecialReports/ ugandaat50/-/1370466/1394816/-/uicvf8z/-/index.html.

Moore Memorial Public Library. 2007. The Texas City disaster: April 16 and 17, 1947. April 2. Retrieved January 13, 2009, from http://www.texascity-library.org/ TCDisasterExhibit/index.html.

MSNBC. 2005. New Orleans major orders looting crackdown. Thousands feared dead from Katrina's wrath, stadium evacuation begins. September 1. Retrieved December 19, 2008, from http://www.msnbc.msn.com/id/9063708.

Mufson, Steven. 1997. Three gorges: China floods the Yangtze. *Washington Post*, November 9. Retrieved May 31, 2012, from http://www.washingtonpost.com/wp-srv/inatl/long- term/yangtze/yangtze.htm.

Naden, Corinne J. 1968. *The Haymarket affair, Chicago, 1886. The "great anarchist" riot and trial*. New York: Franklin Watts.

Nairobi Chronicle. 2008. Kenya-Uganda railway: A short history. August 9. Retrieved May 29, 2012, from http://nairobichronicle.wordpress.com/2008/08/09/kenya-uganda-railway- a-short-history/.

NASA. 2011. Sequence of major events of the *Challenger* accident. *Challenger* STS 51-L-Accident. Office of Communications. Retrieved March 10, 2011, from http:// science.ksc.nasa.gov/shuttle/missions/51-l/docs/events.txt.

National Commission on Terrorist Attacks upon the United States. 2004. We have some planes. August 21. Retrieved December 19, 2008, from http://www.9-11commission. gov/report/911Report_Ch1.htm.

National Institute of Standards and Technology. 2004. Interim report on WTC 7. June 2004. Retrieved December 19, 2008, from http://wtc.nist.gov/progress_report_june04/ appendixl.pdf.

National Weather Service. 2007. Tropical weather summary—2005 web final. January 25. Retrieved December 19, 2008, from http://www.nhc.noaa.gov/archive/2005/tws/ MIATWSAT_nov_final.shtml.

National Weather Service, Paducah, Kentucky, Forecast Office. 2010. NOAA/NWS 1925 tri-state tornado web site—Startling statistics. March 2. Retrieved January 5, 2012, from http://www.crh.noaa.gov/pah/?n=1925_tor_ss.

Navarro, Peter. 2008. Earthquake repercussions spur rethinking of China's dam building strategy. *Asia-Pacific Journal: Japan Focus*, vol. 8, no. 12. Retrieved May 31, 2012, from http://japanfocus.org/-Peter-Navarro/2774.

Nelson, Stanley. 2004. The great Natchez tornado of 1840. *The Sentinel*, December 13. Retrieved November 21, 2011, from http://www.natchezcitycemetery.com/custom/ webpage.cfm?content=News&id=75.

New York Times. 1906. Over 500 dead, $200,000,000 lost in San Francisco earthquake. Retrieved January 4, 2012, from http://www.nytimes.com/learning/general/onthisday/ big/0418.html#article.

New York Times. 1916. Shark guards out at beach resorts. July 8. Retrieved January 3, 2012, from http://query.nytimes.com/mem/archive-free/pdf?res=F60A1FFE355B17738DD DA10894DF405B868DF1D3.

New York Times. 2005. Former FEMA director testifies before Congress. September 27. Retrieved December 19, 2008, from http://www.nytimes.com/2005/09/27/national/nationalspecial/27text-brown.html?pagewanted=all.

NOAA Celebrates. 2007. The great Galveston hurricane of 1900. August 31. Retrieved December 19, 2008, from http://celebrating200years.noaa.gov/magazine/galv_hurricane/welcome.html#pred.

Noe, Denise. 2008. The Olympics bombed. TruTV Crime Library. October 30. Retrieved from http://www.trutv.com/library/crime/terrorists_spies/terrorists/eric_rudolph/1.html.

Office of Governor Timothy M. Kaine. 2007. Report of the Virginia Tech Review Panel. December 12. Retrieved December 19, 2008, from http://www.governor.virginia.gov/TempContent/techPanelReport.cfm.

Office of Public Affairs. 2005. Department of Energy response to Hurricane Katrina. September 2. Retrieved December 19, 2008, from http://www.energy.gov/print/1707.htm.

Ohio Historical Society. 2006. November 9–11, 1913: Great Lakes Hurricane. Severe weather in Ohio. Retrieved January 12, 2009, from http://www.ohiohistory.org/etcetera/exhibits/swio/pages/content/1913_hurricane.htm.

Oklahoma National Memorial and Museum. 2011. One city, one nation, one resolve. Retrieved November 29, 2011, from http://www.oklahomacitynationalmemorial.org/.

Pararas-Carayannis, George. 2011. Chile earthquake and tsunami of 22 May 1960. Disaster Pages of Dr. Pararas-Carayannis. Retrieved January 3, 2012, from http://www.drgeorgepc.com/Tsunami1960.html.

Parker, Paul Edward. 2007. Tally of a tragedy: 462 were in the station on the night of fire. December 3. Retrieved December 19, 2008, from http://www.projo.com/extra/2003/stationfire/content/STATION_FIRE_LIST_12-03-07_QL81OLD_v55.2a82be5.html.

Patterson, John Henry. 1919. *The man-eaters of Tsavo.* London: Macmillan and Co., Ltd. Retrieved May 29, 2012, from http://robroy.dyndns.info/tsavo/tsavo.html#chap1.

Perrow, Charles. 1999. *Normal accidents: Living with high-risk technologies.* Princeton, NJ: Princeton University Press.

Perrow, Charles. 2007. *The next catastrophe: Reducing our vulnerabilities to natural, industrial, and terrorist disasters.* Princeton, NJ: Princeton University Press.

Petersen, Jim. 2005. The 1910 fire. *Evergreen Magazine,* winter edition 1994–1995. Idaho Forest Products Commission. Retrieved January 6, 2009, from http://www.idahoforests.org/fires.htm.

Plane crash info. 2007. Accident details. December 12. Retrieved December 19, 2008, from http://www.planecrashinfo.com/1933/1933-16.htm.

Preparation for Hurricanes. 2007. Hurricane Katrina. December 5. Retrieved December 19, 2008, from http://www.preparationforhurricanes.com/hurricanekatrina.html.

President's Commission on the Accident at Three Mile Island. 2006. Account of the accident. Wednesday, March 28, 1979. Retrieved December 19, 2008, from http://www.pddoc.com/tmi2/kemeny/wednesday_march_28_1979.htm.

PR Newswire US. 2006. Reliving the gripping tale of America's most catastrophic earthquake in National Geographic channel's the great quake. Two hours HD special marks the 100 year anniversary of the epic 1906 San Francisco earthquake the destroyed three quarters of the city. LexisNexis. March 27. Retrieved December 19, 2008, from http://www.lexisnexis.com/us/lnacademic/results/docview/docview.

do?docLinkInd=true&risb=21_T5398624577&format=GNBFI&sort=null&startD ocNo=1&resultsUrlKey=29_T5398625929&cisb=22_T5398625928&treeMax=true &treeWidth=0&csi=8054&docNo=1.

Raimondo, Justin. 2005. Covering the tracks of the anthrax attacks. What, where, why—who. September 19. Retrieved January 15, 2009, from http://www.antiwar.com/justin/?articleid=7312.

Rainey, Sarah. 2011. Dambusters hero "killed by friendly fire." *The Telegraph*, October 10. Retrieved November 21, 2011, from http://www.telegraph.co.uk/news/newstopics/world-war-2/8817932/Dambusters-hero-killed-by-friendly-fire.html.

Richmond Then and Now. 2007. Richmond theatre fire—December 26, 1811. Two lovers perished together in the burning of Richmond theatre. December 5. Retrieved December 19, 2008, from http://richmondthenandnow.com/Newspaper-Articles/Richmond-Theatre-Fire.html.

Ricks, Truett A., Tillett, Bill G., and Van Meter, Clifford 1994. Principles of Security: Third Edition. Anderson Publishing Company, Cincinatti, Ohio.

Rodriguez, Havidan, Quarantelli, Enrico L., and Dynes, Russell R. 2007. *Handbook of disaster research*. New York: Spring Science + Business Media. "The role of geographic information systems/remote sensing in disaster management." In Havidan Rodriquez, Enrico L. Quarantelli, and Russell R. Dynes (eds.), *Handbook of disaster research*. New York: Springer.

Roy, Jennifer. 2008. Design flaw identified in Minnesota Bridge collapse. *Design News*, January 15. Retrieved January 14, 2009, from http://www.designnews.com/article/1790-Design_Flaw_Identified_in_Minnesota_Bridge_Collapse.php.

Rozell, Ned. 2009. Steward devastated during 1964 earthquake. Sit News: Stories in the News—Alaska Science. April 10. Retrieved February 1, 2012, from http://www.sit-news.us/0409news/041009/041009_ak_science.html.

Ruffman, Alan. 1996. The multidisciplinary rediscovery and tracking of "the Great Newfoundland and Saint-Pierre et Miquelon Hurricane of September 1775." Retrieved January 4, 2012, from http://cnrs-scrn.org/northern_mariner/vol06/tnm_6_3_11-23.pdf.

Schmid, Randolph E. 2005. Engrossing account of tragic 1888 blizzard. Associated Press. LexisNexis. January 31. Retrieved December 19, 2008, from http://www.lexisnexis.com/us/lnacademic/results/docview/docview.do?docLinkInd=true&risb=21_T53985 94066&format=GNBFI&sort=RELEVANCE&startDocNo=1&resultsUrlKey=29_ T5398594072&cisb=22_T5398594071&treeMax=true&treeWidth=0&csi=304478 &docNo=1.

Schnirring, Lisa. 2007. CDC suspends work at Texas A&M biodefense lab. CIDRAP. July 3. Retrieved December 19, 2008, from http://www.cidrap.umn.edu/cidrap/content/bt/bioprep/news/jul0307bioweapons.html.

Schnirring, Lisa. 2008. Texas A&M fined $1 million for lab safety lapses. CIDRAP. February 21. Retrieved June 17, 2010, from http://www.cidrap.umn.edu/cidrap/content/bt/bioprep/news/feb2108biolab-jw.html.

Schreuder, Cindy. 1995. The 1995 Chicago heat wave. *Chicago Tribune*, July 13. Retrieved November 21, 1995, from http://www.chicagotribune.com/news/politics/chi-chicagodays-1995heat-story%2C0%2C4201565.story.

Schure, Teri. 2010. *Exxon Valdez* oil spill: 21 years later. June 15. Retrieved February 1, 2012, from http://www.worldpress.org/Americas/3571.cfm.

Sheahan, James, and Upton, George. 1871. *The great conflagration. Chicago: Its past, present and future*. Chicago: Union Publishing Company.

Siddaway, Jason M., and Petelina, Svetlana. 2009. Australian 2009 Black Saturday bushfire smoke in the lower stratosphere: Study with Odin/OSIRIS. Retrieved May 30, 2012, from http://www.thedaytheskyturnedblack.com/#/about-black-saturday/4542166439.

Solar Navigator. 2007. Hurricane Katrina. September 2005. December 5. Retrieved December 19, 2008, from http://www.solarnavigator.net/hurricane_katrina.htm.

Spektor, Alex. 2007. September 11, 2001 victims. December 18. Retrieved December 19, 2008, from http://www.september11victims.com/september11victims/STATISTIC.asp.

Steel, Fiona. 2008. The Littleton school massacre. TruTV. November 7. Retrieved January 15, 2009, from http://www.trutv.com/library/crime/notorious_murders/mass/littleton/index_1.html.

Sting Shield Insect Veil. 2008. Archive: 2004 AHB News reported in the media. October 28. Retrieved January 14, 2009, from http://www.stingshield.com/2004news.htm.

Stone, Jamie. 2006. The world's deadliest storms. Ezinearticles. October 24. Retrieved December 19, 2008, from http://ezinearticles.com/?The-Worlds-Deadliest-Storm&id=337559/

Stoss, Fred, and Fabian, Carole. 1998. Love Canal@25. University of Buffalo. August. Retrieved December 19, 2008, from http://library.buffalo.edu/libraries/specialcollections/lovecanal/about.html.

Struck, Doug, and Milbank, Dana. 2005. Rita spares cities, devastates rural areas. *Washington Post*, September 26. Retrieved March 6, 2009, from http://www.washingtonpost.com/wp-dyn/content/article/2005/09/25/AR2005092500335.html.

Suburban Emergency Management Project. 2004. The flawed emergency response to the 1992 Los Angeles Riots Part C. November 30. Retrieved January 13, 2008, from http://www.semp.us/publications/biot_reader.php?BiotID=144.

Sullivan, Casey. 2009. USS Squalus submarine tragedy, rescue was 70 years ago. *Herald Sunday*, May 24. Retrieved March 10, 2011, from http://www.hampton.lib.nh.us/hampton/history/ships/usssqualus/USS_Squalus_70yearsagoHS20090524.htm.

Sunshine Project. 2007. Texas A&M University violates federal law in biodefense lab infection. April 12. Retrieved December 19, 2008, from http://www.sunshine-project.org/publications/pr/pr120407.html.

Tan, Kenneth, Washburn, Dan, Chorba, Pete, and Sandhaus, Derek. 2012. Earthquake 7.9 on Richter scale hits Sichuan, tremors felt across China, more than 10,000 dead, thousands more trapped under rubble. *Shanghaiist*. Retrieved May 31, 2012, from http://shanghaiist.com/2008/05/12/earthquake-hits-wenchuan-sichuan.php.

Texas A&M University. 2009. Engineering ethics—Negligence and the professional "debate" over responsibility for design." Department of Philosophy and Department of Mechanical Engineering. Retrieved November 23, 2011, from http://ethics.tamu.edu/ethics/hyatt/hyatt1.htm.

Texas State Historical Association. 2001. Indianola hurricanes. June 6. Retrieved December 19, 2008, from http://www.tshaonline.org/handbook/online/articles/II/ydi1.html.

Texas State Historical Association. 2002. Galveston hurricane of 1900. March 8. Retrieved December 19, 2008, from http://www.tshaonline.org/handbook/online/articles/GG/ydg2.html.

Thevenot, Brian, and Russell, Gordon. 2005. Report of anarchy at Superdome overstated. September 26. Retrieved December 19, 2008, from http://seattletimes.nwsource.com/html/nationworld/2002520986_katmyth26.html.

Think Progress. 2007. Katrina's timeline. December 7. Retrieved December 19, 2008, from http://thinkprogress.org/katrina-timeline.

Thomas, Deborah S.K., Ertugay, Kivanc, and Kemec, Serkan. 2007.

Three Mile Island Alert. 2007. Three Mile Island nuclear accident, March 28, 1979. November 26. Retrieved December 19, 2008, from http://www.tmia.com/accident/28. html.

Tilling, Robert, Lyn, Topinka, and Swanson, Donald. 1990. Eruptions of Mount St. Helens: Past, present, and future. U.S. Geological Survey Special Interest Publication. December 27. Retrieved December 19, 2008, from http://vulcan.wr.usgs.gov/Volcanoes/MSH/Publications/MSHPPF/MSH_past_present_future.html.

Timberline Drive Bed & Breakfast. 2007. All about Girlwood, Alaska. October 19. Retrieved December 19, 2008, from http://www.timberlinedrivebnb.com/girlwood.html.

Times Picayune. 2005a. The latest news from the *Times Picayune.* August 28. Retrieved December 19, 2008, from http://www.nola.com/newslogs/breakingtp/index.ssf?/mtlogs/nola_Times-Picayune/archives/2005_08_28.html#074657.

Times Picayune. 2005b. Evacuations to hotels come with own set of hazards. August 20. Retrieved December 19, 2008, from http://www.nola.com/hurricane/t-p/katrina.ssf?/hurricane/katrina/stories/083005_a15_hotels.html.

Tornado Project. 2007a. The top ten U.S. killer tornadoes. December 12. Retrieved December 19, 2008, from http://www.tornadoproject.com/toptens/toptens.htm.

Tornado Project. 2007b. The top ten U.S. killer tornadoes. December 12. Retrieved December 19, 2008, from http://www.tornadoproject.com/toptens/2.htm#top.

Townsend, Mark, Helmore, Edward, and Borger, Julian. 2005. U.S. relieved as Rita rolls past: She was no Katrina, but there are still millions stranded, four days of torrential rain expected and growing anger over the evacuation. *The Observer.* LexisNexis. Retrieved September 25, 2008, from http://www.lexisnexis.com/us/lnacademic/results/docview/docview.do?docLinkInd=true&risb=21_T5398588214&format=GNBFI&sort=RELEVANCE&startDocNo=1&resultsUrlKey=29_T5398588217&cisb=22_T53985882 16&treeMax=true&treeWidth=0&csi=143296&docNo=1.

Turmoil and Fever. 2007. Lois Gibb. Environmental activist. Retrieved October 2007 from http://www.heroism.org/class/1970/gibbs.html.

United Press International. 1996. Anniversary of nation's deadliest fire. October 2. Retrieved December 29, 2008, from http://www.lexisnexis.com/us/lnacademic/results/docview/docview.do?docLinkInd=true&risb=21_T5398571217&format=GNBFI&sort=RELEVANCE&startDocNo=1&resultsUrlKey=29_T5398571222&cisb=22_T53985712 21&treeMax=true&treeWidth=0&selRCNodeID=49&nodeStateId=411en_US,1,46, 17&docsInCategory=29&csi=8076&docNo=1.

University of Buffalo Libraries. 2007. Love Canal collection. October 5. Retrieved December 19, 2008, from http://ublib.buffalo.edu/libraries/projects/lovecanal/introduction. html.

University of Texas at Austin. 2006. Historic fires. December 13. Retrieved December 19, 2008, from http://www.utexas.edu/safety/fire/safety/historic_fires.html.

Uranium Information Centre Ltd. 2001. Three Mile Island: 1979. March. Retrieved December 19, 2008, from http://www.uic.com.au/nip48.htm.

USCG Stormwatch. 2007. Coast Guard response to Hurricane Katrina. June 7. Retrieved December 19, 2008, from http://www.uscgstormwatch.com/go/doc/425/119926/.

USDA Forest Service. 2007. Mount St. Helens national volcanic monument. November 1. Retrieved December 19, 2008, from http://www.fs.fed.us/gpnf/mshnvm/education/teachers-corner/library/pre-eruption-0322.shtml.

U.S. Department of Commerce, National Oceanic and Atmospheric Administration. 2012. Eighteenth century Virginia hurricanes. Retrieved January 4, 2012, from http://www. hpc.ncep.noaa.gov/research/roth/va18hur.htm.

U.S. Department of Energy. 2005. Hurricane Katrina situation report #1. August 30. Retrieved December 19, 2008, from http://www.oe.netl.doe.gov/docs/katrina/ katrina_083005_1600.pdf.

U.S. Department of Health and Human Services. 2007. Hurricane Katrina. August 27. Retrieved December 19, 2008, from http://www.hhs.gov/disasters/emergency/ naturaldisasters/hurricanes/katrina/index.html.

U.S. Department of the Interior. 2007a. A roar like thunder. December 12. Retrieved December 19, 2008, from http://www.johnstownpa.com/History/hist19. html.

U.S. Department of the Interior. 2007b. Hurricane Katrina photographs: August 30, 2005. October 4. Retrieved December 19, 2008, from http://www.nwrc.usgs.gov/hurricane/ post-hurricane-katrina-photos.htm.

U.S. Department of the Interior. 2011. Historic earthquakes—Prince William Sound Alaska—1964 March 28 03:36 UTC—1964 March 27 05:36 p.m. local time— Magnitude 9.2. Retrieved February 1, 2012, from http://earthquake.usgs.gov/ earthquakes/states/events/1964_03_28.php.

U.S. Department of the Interior, National Parks Service. 2010. 1906 earthquake: Law enforcement. September 4. Retrieved January 4, 2012, from http://www.nps.gov/prsf/ historyculture/1906-earthquake-law-enforcement.htm.

U.S. Department of Justice. 1995. Occidental to pay $129 million in Love Canal settlement. Document 95638. December 21. Retrieved December 19, 2008, from http://www. usdoj.gov/opa/pr/Pre_96/December95/638.txt.html.

U.S. Government Accountability Office. 2006. Coast Guard: Observations on the preparation, response, and recovery. Missions related to Hurricane Katrina. July. Retrieved December 19, 2008, from http://www.gao.gov/new.items/d06903.pdf.

USGS. 2005. Mount Saint Helens—From the 1980 eruption to 2000. U.S. Geological Survey Fact Sheet 036-00, online version 1.0. Retrieved March 5, 2009, from http:// pubs.usgs.gov/fs/2000/fs036-00/.

USGS. 2006. The great 1906 San Francisco earthquake. November 6. Retrieved December 19, 2008, from http://earthquake.usgs.gov/regional/nca/1906/18april/index.php.

USGS. 2007. Historic earthquake. U.S. Department of the Interior. January 24. Retrieved December 19, 2008, from http://earthquake.usgs.gov/regional/states/ events/1964_03_28.php.

USGS. 2008. Historic earthquake. U.S. Department of the Interior. July 16. Retrieved January 13, 2009, from http://earthquake.usgs.gov/regional/world/events/1960_05_ 22.php.

USGS. 2009. Plate tectonics and people. Retrieved March 4, 2009, from http://pubs.usgs. gov/gip/dynamic/tectonics.html.

USGS. 2010. Mount St. Helens precursory activity April 12–25, 1980. Retrieved January 3, 2012, from http://vulcan.wr.usgs.gov/Volcanoes/MSH/May18/ MSHThisWeek/412425/412425.html#423.

USGS. 2012. Mount St. Helens precursory activity March 15–21, 1980. Retrieved January 3, 2012, from http://vulcan.wr.usgs.gov/Volcanoes/MSH/May18/ MSHThisWeek/31521/31521.html.

USGS Newsroom. 2004. 40th anniversary of Good Friday earthquake offers new opportunities for public and building safety partnership. U.S. Department of Interior, U.S. Geological Survey. March 26. Retrieved December 19, 2008, from http://www.usgs.gov/newsroom/article.asp?ID=106.

U.S. News Rank. 2012. 1906 San Francisco earthquake. News Rank. Retrieved January 4, 2012, from http://www.usnewsrank.com/1906-san-francisco-earthquake.html.

U.S. Nuclear Regulatory Commission. 2007. Fact sheet on the Three Mile Island accident. February 20. Retrieved December 19, 2008, from http://www.nrc.gov/reading-rm/doc-collections/fact-sheets/3mile-isle.html/.

U.S. Nuclear Regulatory Commission. 2011. Backgrounder on the Three Mile Island accident. Retrieved December, 2, 2011, from http://www.nrc.gov/reading-rm/doc-collections/fact-sheets/3mile-isle.html.

Vervaeck, Armand, and Daniell, James. 2011. The May 12, 2008 deadly Sichuan earthquake—A recap 3 years later. *Earthquake Report*, May 10. Retrieved May 31, 2012, from http://earthquake-report.com/2011/05/10/the-may-12-2008-deadly-sichuan-earthquake-a-recap-3-years-later/.

Victoria Internet Providers. 2007. Texas settlement region. December 2. Retrieved December 19, 2008, from http://www.texas-settlement.org/markers/goliad/.

Virtual Museum of the City of San Francisco. 2012. 1906 San Francisco earthquake exhibit. Retrieved January 4, 2012, from http://www.sfmuseum.org/1906.2/arson.html.

Wald, Matthew. 2008. Faulty design led to Minnesota bridge collapse, inquiry finds. *New York Times*, January 15. Retrieved January 14, 2009, from http://www.nytimes.com/2008/01/15/washington/15bridge.html.

Washington Post. 1997. The other great fire of 1871. LexisNexis. November 8. Retrieved December 19, 2008, from http://www.lexisnexis.com/us/lnacademic/results/docview/docview.do?docLinkInd=true&risb=21_T5398559146&format=GNBFI&sort=RELEVANCE&startDocNo=1&resultsUrlKey=29_T5398559150&cisb=22_T5398559149&treeMax=true&treeWidth=0&selRCNodeID=368&nodeStateId=411en_US,1,364&docsInCategory=6&csi=8075&docNo=3.

Washington Post. 1999. Three Mile Island. Retrieved December 19, 2008, from http://www.washingtonpost.com/wp-srv/national/longterm/tmi/gallery/photo1.htm.

Watkins, Thayer. 2012. The catastrophic dam failures in China in August 1975. Retrieved May 30, 2012, from http://www.sjsu.edu/faculty/watkins/aug1975.htm.

Watson, John F. 1812. Richmond theater fire, 1811. Record 1044058740A037A0. Philadelphia: American Antiquarian Society and Newsbank.

Weather Channel Interactive. 2007. 1900 Galveston hurricane. Part 2. Disaster waiting to happen. December 12. Retrieved December 19, 2008, from http://www.weather.com/newscenter/specialreports/sotc/storm4/page2.html (new link: The 1900 Storm).

Wicker, Tom. 1982. In the nation, a mighty mystery. *New York Times*. LexisNexis. August 22. Retrieved December 19, 2008, from http://www.lexisnexis.com/us/lnacademic/results/docview/docview.do?docLinkInd=true&risb=21_T5398545928&format=GNBFI&sort=RELEVANCE&startDocNo=1&resultsUrlKey=29_T5398545938&cisb=22_T5398545937&treeMax=true&treeWidth=0&selRCNodeID=38&nodeStateId=411en_US,1,37&docsInCategory=29&csi=6742&docNo=6.

Willow Bend Press. 2007. The Hartford Circus fire July 6, 1944. Retrieved January 12, 2009, from http://www.hartfordcircusfire.com/background.htm.

World Health Organization. 2012. Pocket emergency tool. Retrieved January 4, 2012, from http://www.wpro.who.int/nr/rdonlyres/e1c1dbff-82ea-45ff-bac7-9666480e28cc/0/who_oct1.pdf.

World Nuclear Association. 2012. Chernobyl accident 1986. World Nuclear Association. April. Retrieved May 30, 2012, from http://www.world-nuclear.org/info/chernobyl/inf07.html.

Xinhua. 2005. After 30 years, secrets, lessons of China's worst dams burst accident surface. The People's Daily Online. October 1. Retrieved May 31, 2012, from http://english.people.com.cn/200510/01/eng20051001_211892.html.

Zasky, Jason. 2008. Fire trap. The legacy of the Triangle Shirtwaist fire. *Failure Magazine*, September 24. Retrieved January 6, 2009, from http://www.failuremag.com/arch_history_triangle_fire.html.

Zeman, David. 1999. A ghost of the University of Texas: Tragic tower will reopen. *Detroit Free Press*. LexisNexis. September 1. Retrieved December 19, 2008, from http://www.lexisnexis.com/us/lnacademic/results/docview/docview.do?docLinkInd=true&risb=21_T5398518787&format=GNBFI&sort=RELEVANCE&startDocNo=1&resultsUrlKey=29_T5398518790&cisb=22_T5398518789&treeMax=true&treeWidth=0&selRCNodeID=75&nodeStateId=411en_US,1,75&docsInCategory=83&csi=222065&docNo=5.

Zhao, Xu. 2012. Interview with, May 30. Senior institutional research associate, the University of Texas at Dallas.

Zuesse, Eric. 1981. Love Canal. The truth seeps out. *Reason Magazine*, February. Retrieved December 19, 2008, from http://www.reason.com/news/show/29319.html.

Index